CRIMINAL JUSTICE GROUP TRAINING
A Facilitator's Handbook

by

MICHAEL E. O'NEILL
Consultant
San Jose, California

and

KAI R. MARTENSEN
Consultant
Sunnyvale, California

University Associates, Inc.
7596 Eads Avenue
La Jolla, California 92037

Copyright © 1975 by University Associates, Inc.
ISBN: 0-88390-100-5
Library of Congress Catalog Card Number 75-11040

The instructions, worksheets, forms, and instruments in the Structured Experiences section of this book may be freely reproduced for use in educational/training events. Special permission is not required for such uses. The publishers do, however, ask that the following statement appear on all reproductions:

> Reproduced from
> *Criminal Justice Group Training:*
> *A Facilitator's Handbook*
> by Michael E. O'Neill and Kai R. Martensen
> La Jolla, Ca.: University Associates, Inc., 1975

This permission statement, however, does *not* include (1) permission to reproduce these materials for sale or large-scale distribution; (2) permission to include them in other publications (prior written permission is required); or (3) permission to reproduce any material in this book other than that specified above. *The papers included in the Readings section of this book may not be reproduced without permission from the original sources.*

Printed in the United States of America

PREFACE

The intent of this handbook is to provide facilitators, trainers, and educators with the necessary materials and resources for use in effective criminal justice training.

The first portion of the book contains twenty structured experiences—designs for experience-based learning. We have endeavored to develop experiences that meet the particular needs of those involved in criminal justice administration. These materials, however, can easily be adapted to fit other purposes or participants.

The remainder of the handbook consists of selected readings and resources for further reading. The supplemental readings present material that is especially pertinent and valuable for training and organization development. These selections were made to show the variety and scope of the material, studies, and viewpoints current in the criminal justice field. The list of periodicals and the brief bibliography provide a wide range of available literature for further reading and investigation.

We wish to state our indebtedness to *A Handbook of Structured Experiences for Human Relations Training,* Volumes I-IV, edited by J. William Pfeiffer and John E. Jones.[1] These handbooks provided not only the inspiration but also, in many cases, the sources for the experiences in this book. Indeed, some individual experiences are direct variations of those in the Pfeiffer and Jones *Handbooks.* In such cases, we have attempted to cite exact references. We have also followed the format of the *Handbooks* in the Structured Experiences section.

Finally, our thanks go to Dorothy for her countless hours of typing and to Tanya, whose patience and understanding made this handbook possible.

Michael E. O'Neill
Kai R. Martensen

Sunnyvale, California
June, 1975

---

[1] La Jolla, Ca.: University Associates, 1969 & 1974; 1970 & 1974; 1971 & 1974; 1973.

TABLE OF CONTENTS

        page

Preface iii
Introduction 1

STRUCTURED EXPERIENCES

Things on Your Mind: A Group Starter 7
First Impressions: A Feedback Experience 9
Orientation: An Information-Dissemination Activity 11
Locker Room: A Rumor Exchange 15
Not Being Heard: A Role-Playing Experience in Listening
    Frustration 19
Active Listening: A Paraphrasing Activity 24
Constraints: A Group Problem-Solving Experience 29
Brainstorming: An Idea Generator for Group Problems 35
Security and Privacy: A Role-Development Activity 40
Goal Priorities: A Consensus-Seeking Activity 44
Police Actions: A Decision-Making Study 49
Developing Group Commitment: A Value-Clarification
    Activity 55
Criminal Justice Encounter: A Multiple Role Play 59
Ombudsman: A Multiple Role Play 67
Citation Release: An Evaluation Activity 74
Cut Your Budget: Intergroup Conflict 78
Multi-Organization Problem Analysis: A Problem-Solving
    Experience 83
The Organization Man: Insights into Motivation 87
Reveal: Positive and Adverse Feedback 91
Impressions: A Group Feedback Experience 93

SELECTED READINGS

Determining Training Needs, by James H. Auten 95
Human Relations Training: Laboratories and Team Policing,
    by Byron L. Boer and Bruce C. McIver 103
Sensitivity Training and the Police, by Donald Bimstein 112
Training Programs for Treatment Specialists in Corrections: A
    University-Based Model, by Albert R. Roberts 123
Is External Management Training Effective for Organizational
    Change?, by Yoram Zeira 132
Measuring the Qualities of Police Leadership,
    by Edward E. Peoples 143

Leaderless Group Discussion as an Assessment Tool for
    Supervisory and Command Promotions,
    by Preston Horstman 148
"Winning" and "Losing" at Work, by Michael Maccoby 153
Common Questions and Tentative Answers Regarding
    Organization Development, by Lyman K. Randall 175
Training: A Conceptual Model for Organizational Develop-
    ment, by Michael E. O'Neill and Frank R. Benaderet 187
Organization Development: An Action Plan for the Ontario
    Police Department, by Revis O. Robinson II 192
Stress and Tension—Teambuilding for the Professional Police
    Officer, by Edward S. Esbeck and George Halverson 204
Change Through Participation (And Vice Versa),
    by Hans Toch 217
Conflict Resolution in Criminal Justice, by Vincent O'Leary
    and Donald J. Newman 228

RESOURCES FOR FURTHER READING
Useful Periodicals for the Criminal Justice Practitioner:
    An Annotated List 253
A Brief Bibliography 259

APPENDICES
 I. National Advisory Commission Reports on Standards and
    Goals for Criminal Justice 267
II. Goal Setting and Guidelines for Evaluation 285

INTRODUCTION

This book addresses itself to students, instructors, and practitioners in the criminal justice field. These professionals often have a special need for effective human relations approaches in their work with others.

The structured experiences focus on individual behavior, constructive feedback, and psychological integration. To make the experiences more meaningful to the various disciplines involved in the administration of criminal justice, the authors have tailored these experiences around operational and managerial activities. The facilitator who uses these experiences should feel free to revise, develop, or adapt them to fit the needs of his particular training session.

CHOOSING A STRUCTURED EXPERIENCE

One requirement in the effective use of structured experiences is choosing an experience to relate to the special needs of the participants and the purposes of the training event. The following guidelines[1] should help the facilitator make an appropriate choice.

Goals. These should be limited in number and stated in language that participants can understand. A good goal is specific; it is performance oriented, to guide the person toward what he is going to do; it involves the individual in his goal objective; it is observable, so that other people can see the result; and, most important, it is realistic. For maximum effectiveness, a goal must be attainable.

Group Size. The facilitator's choice of experience is often guided by the size of the group with which he is working. The minimum and maximum numbers of participants, the optimum size of the group, and the number and size of subgroups as noted in the experience should be considered. If there are

---

[1] Adapted from J. W. Pfeiffer and J. E. Jones (Eds.), *The 1974 Annual Handbook for Group Facilitators,* La Jolla, Ca.: University Associates, 1974, pp. 3-4.

extra participants, they could be utilized in various ways; they could, for example, be designated as observers or be added to subgroups.

Time Required. Realistic expectations are given for each experience, based on actual trials. If the experience requires a long period of time, the facilitator may consider dividing it into more than one session.

Materials. A practical experience stresses the easy availability, utility, and uncomplicated preparation of materials. The specific forms, sheets of information, or worksheets needed and the quantities of each are noted. If appropriate, an observer sheet could be devised for the activity. Audio-visual aids (such as felt-tipped pens, newsprint, sound or film equipment, etc.), pencils and paper, and any other special materials need also to be considered.

Physical Setting. In choosing an experience, the facilitator needs to be aware of participants' particular needs as indicated by the type of activity: Must groups be private, quiet, isolated? Do participants sit around tables or lie on the floor? Do they need writing surfaces? Can the experience take place outdoors? Do rooms need to be specially designated or arranged for certain groups or subgroups? Easily movable furniture is usually desirable to aid in the flexibility of the group.

Process. For the convenience of the facilitator, this step-by-step procedure indicates what he does and says and what the participants do in the appropriate sequence. The beginning and end of each step are specified. A time estimate may be given for each step or phase.

Variations. These can often extend or vary a particular experience in such a way as to make it more useful and pertinent to the facilitator's needs. Adaptations may vary the activity's content, sequence, use of observers, time for each step, materials, size of groups, complexity of process, and use with intact groups.

References. If and when relevant, similar structured experiences, lecturette sources, or additional readings are indicated to give the facilitator a firmer background for the use of the experience.

Worksheets. These are designed and written so that they have sufficient room in which the participants may write; are simple and easy to reproduce; have clear instructions; and are necessary and meaningful to the activity. Wherever possible, each worksheet is complete on one page so as to simplify reproduction. In most cases, the worksheet contains its own instructions. If it does not, the facilitator should give the participants oral instructions.

Handouts. Especially useful for a discussion of the theory underlying a structured experience, handouts can be used in several ways by the facilitator—as background or special information, summaries, or suggestions for further use of the learnings attained in the experience. Unless necessary, participants should not be allowed to read handout materials while the activity is in process. However, if handouts are to be provided, participants should be told at the beginning of the experience so that they will not have to take notes on what the facilitator says.

ADEQUATE PROCESSING

Not only must the facilitator choose structured experiences with care, he must also be especially concerned with the need for adequate processing of any experience. In fact, the processing of the data generated by an activity is more significant than the activity itself.

The facilitator is responsible for seeing that the data are adequately talked through, sifted out, and integrated with the participants' learnings. Stress generated by unacknowledged feelings or lack of understanding must be resolved. This processing skill is perhaps the most important ability of the group facilitator. He should be able to help participants to develop generalizations from their specific experiences and to process and evaluate them.

Some useful strategies can be used to provide adequate processing: participants interviewing each other about what they learned; process observers reporting what they observed; lecturettes to inject theory; subgrouping; an empty-chair design; a group-on-group pattern in which one group observes another; and questionnaires and instruments to collect data.

Again we cannot stress too firmly the significance of fully processing learning experiences. The effectiveness of structured experiences depends heavily on how well this is done.

SEQUENCE OF MATERIAL

The experiences in this handbook are arranged in order of the increasing understanding, skill, and experience required by the facilitator to use the activities effectively and responsibly. The first structured experience, therefore, requires less background of the facilitator than does the last; in general, the earlier experiences generate less affect and less data than do the later ones.

Any facilitator, however, regardless of his background, can usefully employ these structured experiences, if he is committed to the growth of individuals in his group. He should choose appropriate activities based on two criteria: his own competence and the participants' needs.

In the Selected Readings section, five pieces on training have been included: from determining needs, through discussions of human relations for police, to treatments of external and internal training functions.

Two pieces on specific techniques follow: FIRO-B (which is useful both in the evaluation of programs and as a training device) and leaderless group discussion as a selection strategy.

Closing the Selected Readings section are seven articles on organization development: man in the corporate structure, an introduction to OD, the relation of training to OD, an OD plan for a police department, team building, an OD case study in criminal justice, and a discussion of approaches to conflict resolution.

HOW TO USE THIS BOOK

This handbook was planned to serve two basic purposes. First, it is a convenient source book for facilitators in the criminal justice training field. It offers not only practical structured experiences that the facilitator can use effectively in his work, but also resources especially valuable for background, additional information, and added support. *Criminal Justice Group Training* also functions as a book of readings for the group facilitator.

Second, the book can be used as a textbook or training manual for those teaching and training in the field of criminal justice work.

STRUCTURED EXPERIENCES

THINGS ON YOUR MIND: A GROUP STARTER

Goals
    I. To have participants discuss unresolved problems by sharing them with the group.
    II. To acquaint group members with each other in a non-threatening manner.

Group Size
    Unlimited.

Time Required
    Approximately twenty minutes.

Materials
    None.

Physical Setting
    A large room that allows the group to sit in a circle.

Process
    I. The facilitator addresses the group members, stressing the importance of freeing their minds of thoughts that might interfere with their concentration.
    II. The facilitator asks the group members to reflect for one minute on any unfinished business or unresolved problems they have, e.g., reports due, vacations, etc. He then asks each member to share with the group what is on his mind.

Variation

The structured experience can be based on any of the following: expectations of the meeting, thoughts left over from the last meeting, the best/worst things that might happen in the meeting, or what the participants are feeling or thinking at the moment.

Notes on the Use of "Things on Your Mind":

FIRST IMPRESSIONS: A FEEDBACK EXPERIENCE

Goals
    I. To study the impact of first impressions: their accuracy and effects.
   II. To acquaint members involved in a mixed criminal justice group with each other.

Group Size
    Ten to twelve participants.

Time Required
    Approximately forty-five minutes.

Materials
    Paper and a pencil for each participant.

Physical Setting
    A room large enough to accommodate a large circle of chairs.

Process
    I. The facilitator instructs the participants to give their first names and their agency affiliations.
   II. The participants are then directed to turn their chairs away from the circle so that they cannot see each other. They write down as many first names and agency affiliations as they can remember and note any comments.
  III. After five minutes, the facilitator instructs the participants to turn their chairs back toward the circle.
  IV. The facilitator reads aloud the first names, agency affiliations, and first-impression comments recorded by group

---

    Adapted from "First Names, First Impressions: A Feedback Experience," Pfeiffer and Jones, Volume II.

members. He asks each participant to react to comments about himself and his agency affiliation.

V. The facilitator leads a discussion on the accuracy of name and agency first impressions and the reactions of participants to this feedback.

Variations

See Pfeiffer and Jones, Volume II, p. 89.

Notes on the Use of "First Impressions":

ORIENTATION: AN INFORMATION-DISSEMINATION ACTIVITY

Goals
　I. To provide for dissemination of information from participant resources during a conference, workshop, or institute.
　II. To make participants aware of criminal justice disciplines (police, courts, corrections, etc.). If the conference is attended by one discipline (e.g., probation), then this can be divided by function (e.g., investigation, supervision, etc.) or by department (e.g., community; A, B, C, etc.).

Group Size
　Unlimited.

Time Required
　Approximately two hours.

Materials
　I. Several blank course cards, 5" × 8", for each participant.
　II. Pencils with erasers.
　III. A bulletin board or wall space for posting the course cards.
　IV. Newsprint and felt-tipped markers.
　V. A copy of the Orientation Sample Course-Description Cards for each participant (optional).

Physical Setting
　A large room for the entire group and several smaller rooms for subgroup meetings (dependent on the number of concurrent sessions).

Adapted from "Miniversity: Sharing Participants' Ideas," Pfeiffer and Jones, Volume II.

Process

I. The facilitator announces that participants will have the opportunity to contribute their special knowledge or experience to the group. This will take the form of half-hour courses offered to fellow participants. The facilitator stresses the need for all members of the criminal justice community to be aware of and knowledgeable about the various criminal justice disciplines. This activity offers an excellent opportunity to explain one's agency's goals, objectives, organization, facilities, procedures, or services.

II. The facilitator then illustrates how to make course cards and posts samples for participants. He may wish to distribute the Orientation Sample Course-Description Cards.

III. The facilitator distributes blank cards to the participants who wish to present a course.

IV. If the group is large, the facilitator chooses a screening committee to select the courses to be offered and to establish a course schedule.

V. He posts the offered courses on newsprint, using the suggested Format for Course Offerings. If necessary, courses may be repeated (offered at several times) so that the largest number of persons may attend a particular course.

Format for Course Offerings

	Location			
Time	Room 1	Room 2	Room 3	Room 4
0900-0930	Presentence Investigation	Processing a Citizen's Call		
0945-1000				
1030-1100				

VI. Courses now begin.

Variations

See Pfeiffer and Jones, Volume II, p. 9.

Notes on the Use of "Orientation":

14 *Criminal Justice Group Training*

ORIENTATION SAMPLE COURSE-DESCRIPTION CARDS

Title: Processing a Citizen's Call

Lt. Richard Lawful

Patrol Watch Commander

City of California Police Department

A description of how the CPD processes a citizen's complaint from the receipt of the initial call to prosecution: the receipt of the call in the communication center; the initial investigation by patrol; the follow-up investigation by detectives; the identification, apprehension, and case-preparation phase; the presentation of the case; the prosecution.

Title: Handling Presentence Investigation

Betty Davis

Supervisor

Arizona County Probation Department

A discussion of the authority, responsibilities, and procedures involved in conducting a social-background report (required in order that the judge can determine the sentence) on a defendant who has been found guilty.

LOCKER ROOM: A RUMOR EXCHANGE

Goal

To illustrate the distortions that occur as information is transmitted from the original source through several individuals to a final destination.

Group Size

Six participants plus an unlimited number of process observers.

Time Required

Thirty minutes.

Materials

I. A copy of the Locker Room Observation Form for each process observer.

II. Newsprint and felt-tipped markers.

III. Tape recorder (optional).

Physical Setting

A room large enough to accommodate all participants and an additional room or area where participants can be isolated.

Process

I. The facilitator selects six participants from the group. (Any individual who has been involved in a similar experience should not participate.)

II. The facilitator asks the first participant to remain with him while participants two, three, four, and five leave the room.

Adapted from "Rumor Clinic: A Communications Experiment," Pfeiffer and Jones, Volume II.

III. The facilitator then distributes the Locker Room Observation Form to the remainder of the participants, who will act as observers.

IV. If a tape recorder is being used, the recording session begins. The facilitator states that at the conclusion of the experience the recording will be played so that participants can hear their comments.

V. The facilitator reads the message once to the first participant.

VI. The facilitator asks the second participant to return to the room.

VII. The first participant repeats what he heard from the facilitator to the second participant. No help is to be given from any of the other participants or observers.

VIII. The third participant is asked to return, and the second participant repeats to him what he heard from the first participant. The process is repeated until all but the sixth participant has had the message transmitted to him.

IX. When the sixth participant returns to the room he becomes the supervisor. The fifth participant repeats the message to the supervisor, and he in turn writes the message on newsprint so that the entire group can read it.

X. The facilitator then writes the original message. This is compared with the supervisor's message.

XI. The observers report their recorded observations.

XII. The facilitator leads a short discussion with the entire group on the implication of the locker room experience, utilizing the tape recorder if it has been used. Participants are asked to discuss their reactions to the structured experience.

Variations

See Pfeiffer and Jones, Volume II, p. 13.

Notes on the Use of "Locker Room":

LOCKER ROOM OBSERVATION FORM

"Hey, I heard from Joe that the chief had an important meeting with the city manager and the City Council Finance Committee.

"The Patrolman's Association is going to call a special session at 8:15 tonight to discuss actions on the possible reduction of various promotional positions and certain work performance standards.

"The Association was asked to decide on the new 4-10 plan. The department recommends 7:00 a.m. to 5:00 p.m., 3:00 p.m. to 1:00 a.m., and 9:00 p.m. to 7:00 a.m. Most patrolmen favor a modified plan where only one overlap shift occurs from 6:00 p.m. to 2:00 a.m.

"There is a major reorganization planned to change the traffic-enforcement unit.

"Patrolmen will be required to write one or two citations per day."

Participant	Additions	Deletions	Distortions
1			
2			
3			
4			
5			
6 (Supervisor)			

NOT BEING HEARD: A ROLE-PLAYING EXPERIENCE IN LISTENING FRUSTRATION

Goals

  I. To understand and experience the frustration of not being listened to.
  II. To emphasize the importance of attentive listening.

Group Size

  Up to fifteen participants.

Time Required

  Approximately thirty minutes.

Materials

  I. A copy of the appropriate Not Being Heard Role-Description Sheet for role players.
  II. Newsprint and felt-tipped markers.

Physical Setting

  A room large enough to accommodate two groups.

Process

  I. The facilitator gives a brief lecturette on the goals of the activity.
  II. The facilitator then forms two subgroups of five to eight participants each. He asks for two volunteers from each group to assume the roles of police chief and of coordinator of planning, research, and training.
  III. Each role player is given the appropriate Not Being Heard Role-Description Sheet and is instructed to play

---

Adapted from "Not-Listening: A Dyadic Role-Play," Pfeiffer and Jones, Volume III.

19

the role of nonlistener toward each other. The role players are given a few minutes to study their roles. In each group, the seating arrangement should be as follows:

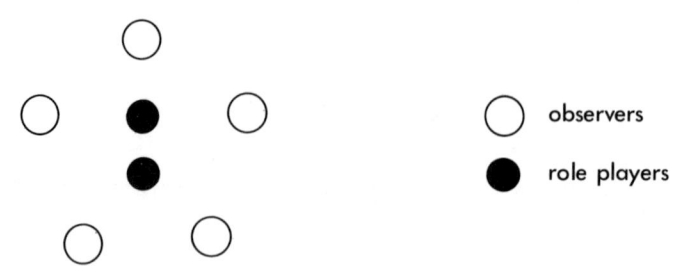

○ observers
● role players

IV. The facilitator instructs the observers to pay particular attention to the role players' behavior during the activity.
V. The two groups then begin the role playing at the same time.
VI. The facilitator checks that the role players are *not* listening to each other.
VII. After approximately ten minutes the role players should be experiencing maximum frustration and the facilitator stops the exercise.
VIII. The facilitator then leads a discussion of the activity. The observers offer their observations on how the frustration manifested itself.

Variations

See Pfeiffer and Jones, Volume III, p. 52.

Reference

Pfeiffer, J. W. Conditions which hinder effective communications. In J. W. Pfeiffer & J. E. Jones (Eds.), *The 1973 annual handbook for group facilitators*. La Jolla, Ca.: University Associates, 1973.

Notes on the Use of "Not Being Heard":

NOT BEING HEARD ROLE-DESCRIPTION SHEET #1:
Coordinator of Planning, Research, and Training

You have recently been hired by the police department of a large city. Your title is Coordinator of Planning, Research, and Training. You have a Master's Degree in criminology and have published several articles in your field. You see that the best chance of bringing the organization together as a team is to expand the training emphasis of the department and to commit the department to true "participative management."

You have decided that the only way to put your expanded training and participative management into practice is to represent the lower-echelon needs and desires in the staff meetings. The chief has found out about this and has called you into his office for a discussion. You know you are going to meet stiff opposition; however, you have expertise in management and are in a position to bring about needed changes. You are determined you will not be swayed by objections, as you are the only one who knows the "total" picture.

NOT BEING HEARD ROLE-DESCRIPTION SHEET #2:
Police Chief

You are the police chief of a large city. You have been in police work for over fifteen years and have worked your way from department to department until being promoted to chief. No one knows more than you about the *inner* workings of the organization. In fact, last year the city manager and his staff gave you a testimonial dinner to commend you on the fine job you are doing.

You have just received word that at the next staff meeting the new coordinator of planning, research, and training is going to try to sell his training and "participative management" program. While this plan may sound good, you know that the strength of the organization has been control. The key to this control is clever manipulation of employees. You are aware that if this new management program takes place, it will not only reduce control but limit your decision-making prerogatives.

You are determined that the coordinator will not implement his strategies. He probably means well, but he does not understand the "big city" picture. Besides, you have over fifteen years of experience and are more competent than anyone in setting the direction of the organization. It is clear that you will have to be decisive in making your point; he has to know who is the boss. Your prestige with your police commander rests on the outcome of this meeting.

ACTIVE LISTENING: A PARAPHRASING ACTIVITY

Goals

    I. To develop an understanding of the dynamics of being an active listener.

    II. To become aware of the barriers that inhibit effective listening in criminal justice groups.

Group Size

    A minimum of twelve participants.

Time Required

    Approximately one hour.

Materials

    I. A copy of the Active Listening Topics for Discussion Sheet for each participant.

    II. A copy of the Active Listening Observer Discussion Sheet for each observer.

Physical Setting

    A room large enough so that dyads may work without distracting other dyads.

Process

    I. The facilitator discusses with the group the goals of the activity.

    II. Four dyads are formed (two participants each).

    III. The remaining group members are assigned as observers to the four dyads.

    IV. The facilitator distributes the Active Listening Topics for Discussion Sheet to all participants and the Active Listening Observer Discussion Sheet to the observers only.

Adapted from "Listening Triads: Building Communications Skills," Pfeiffer and Jones, Volume I.

V. The facilitator gives the following instructions:
1. Each dyad will have a speaker and a listener. The first speaker chooses a topic from the Topics for Discussion Sheet.
2. The listener in the dyad must summarize in his own words what the first speaker discussed. He may not take notes.
3. The speaker has six minutes to discuss his chosen topic with the listener.
4. If the summary by the listener is incorrect, the speaker may interrupt and correct the misunderstanding.
5. The observers assigned to each dyad make certain that the listener does not omit, distort, or add to what the speaker has said.

VI. After the first topic is discussed, the speaker becomes the listener and the listener becomes the speaker. The above process is then repeated.

VII. When each dyad member has had an opportunity to be a speaker and a listener, the facilitator processes the activity with the total group. He conducts a discussion, soliciting comments about communication barriers and active listening from the members.

Variations

I. Dyads can generate their own topics.
II. Triads can be used with one person as the listener, one the speaker, and one the observer.
III. See Pfeiffer and Jones, Volume I, p. 32.

References

Structured Experiences 4, 21, 25, 52, 66, and 70. In J. W. Pfeiffer and J. E. Jones (Eds.), *A handbook of structured experiences for human relations training* (Vols. I, II, and III). La Jolla, Ca.: University Associates, 1969 & 1974; 1970 & 1974; 1971 & 1974.

Notes on the Use of "Active Listening":

ACTIVE LISTENING TOPICS FOR DISCUSSION SHEET

Each speaker selects one topic from the list below:

1. Probation Subsidy
2. Team Policing
3. Community-Based Corrections
4. Criminal Justice Training
5. Case Management for Prosecutors
6. Security and Privacy—Computer Systems
7. Crime-Oriented Planning
8. Police Response Time
9. Offender-Based Transactional Statistics
10. Plea Bargaining
11. Prisoner Rehabilitation
12. Juvenile Delinquency
13. Juvenile Diversion
14. Public Defender's Role
15. Education Requirements for Criminal Justice Personnel
16. Police Unions
17. Technology Change in Criminal Justice
18. Crime Prevention
19. Court Calendars

ACTIVE LISTENING OBSERVER DISCUSSION SHEET

	Barriers	Additions	Deletions	Comments
Speaker:_____ Listener:_____				
Speaker:_____ Listener:_____				

1. What difficulties did the individuals have in the roles of speaker and listener?

2. Were there barriers that consistently caused communication distortions? What were they? How did they affect communication?

3. Why is it important to paraphrase correctly?

4. What does this exercise tell you about communications that would be useful for your organization?

CONSTRAINTS: A GROUP PROBLEM-SOLVING EXPERIENCE

Goal

    To become familiar with various behaviors that constrain effective problem solving.

Group Size

    Fifteen to thirty participants divided into groups of no more than five individuals each.

Time Required

    Approximately one hour.

Materials

    I. Newsprint and felt-tipped markers for each group.

    II. A copy of the Constraints Group-Leader Instruction Sheet and of the appropriate Constraints Role-Description Sheet for each group leader.

    III. A copy of the Constraints Problem Worksheet I and of the Constraints Problem Worksheet II for each participant.

    IV. A copy of the Constraints Group-Observer Question Sheet for each group observer.

Physical Setting

    A room large enough to accommodate several groups without disrupting one another.

Process

    I. The facilitator gives a brief overview stating that because a number of problems facing organizations are typically given to committees to resolve, committee participants must be able to identify various behaviors of individuals in groups.

    This experience is effective used as a prelude to "Brainstorming: An Idea Generator for Group Problems," p. 35.

II. The facilitator selects three individuals as group leaders, giving each a Constraints Group-Leader Instruction Sheet, a Constraints Role-Description Sheet, and a Constraints Problem Worksheet I. The three group leaders then leave the room and are given five minutes to study their materials. The facilitator warns the leaders not to reveal their roles.

III. The facilitator then selects three to four participants to complete each of the three groups. Each group member is given Constraints Problem Worksheet I. The remaining participants are assigned as group process observers and receive the Constraints Problem Worksheet I and the Constraints Group-Observer Question Sheet.

IV. After five minutes, the group leaders return, take charge of their respective groups, and begin the meetings.

V. After fifteen minutes the groups' meetings are terminated.

VI. The process observers for group 1 are asked to report their observations and then the group leader reads his role. This process is repeated for groups 2 and 3.

VII. Steps II through VI are repeated with the same groups and leaders, using Constraints Problem Worksheet II.

Variations

I. A problem worksheet relevant to a local situation can be created.

II. Leaders, group members, or roles can be changed for step VII.

References

Structured Experiences 3, 4, and 53. In J. W. Pfeiffer and J. E. Jones (Eds.), *A handbook of structured experiences for human relations training* (Vols. II and III). La Jolla, Ca.: University Associates, 1970 & 1974; 1971 & 1974.

Notes on the Use of "Constraints":

CONSTRAINTS GROUP-LEADER INSTRUCTION SHEET

1. Read your part carefully.
2. Do not discuss your role with anyone in your group.
3. Place yourself in the role that you are given and play the role conscientiously.
4. Do not overact.
5. Be natural, but emphasize behavior aimed at fulfilling your role.

CONSTRAINTS ROLE-DESCRIPTION SHEET—#1

As group leader you want to assure that each suggested solution or idea is well developed, practical, reasonable, and a credit to you and your ability to work with the committee. To accomplish this you must make sure that each suggestion offered is thoroughly discussed and analyzed as to its merits and liabilities before going to another solution. If possible, you want to get a consensus on the various points of each solution.

CONSTRAINTS ROLE-DESCRIPTION SHEET—#2

As group leader, you feel this is a game of "Yes, but . . ." You really do not want a solution and intend to stall the others for as long as possible. The best method of avoiding suggestions is to point out that the solution was tried some time ago by another agency with poor results, that it is too costly, etc. Your purpose is to reject suggestions.

CONSTRAINTS ROLE-DESCRIPTION SHEET—#3

As group leader you have one specific idea you want the entire committee to agree to implement. You consider any other solution as weakening your idea; therefore you will try to minimize other ideas, except as they enhance or complement your proposed solution. You do not want the group to know you have already decided on a solution. You may choose any solution, but decide what it is to be before you join your committee.

CONSTRAINTS PROBLEM WORKSHEET I

There is substantial local government interest in expanding the use of the paraprofessional and volunteer staff in your department. This interest was generated by the National Advisory Commission on Criminal Justice Standards and Goals. Some of their ideas are:

1. Employ civilian personnel in supportive positions.
2. Employ reserve officers.
3. Recruit and employ ex-offenders.
4. Recruit and use volunteers.

Your committee has been asked to develop and present ideas on how to comply with these suggestions. Your department has very few continuing activities utilizing anyone other than career department professional employees.

CONSTRAINTS PROBLEM WORKSHEET II

There is substantial local government interest in diversion programs to reduce the number of individuals who are formally processed through the criminal justice system. This interest is based on cost, humanity, and more efficient administration of criminal justice. The National Advisory Commission on Criminal Justice Standards and Goals made a number of recommendations, including the following:

1. Divert offenders into youth services bureaus.
2. Formalize police use of discretion.
3. Formalize diversion procedures to insure equitable treatment.
4. Utilize alternatives to arrest and pretrial detention.
5. Divert drug addicts and alcoholics to treatment centers.
6. Screen certain accused persons out of the criminal justice system.
7. Utilize, as appropriate, diversion into noncriminal justice programs before trial.
8. Maximize use of citation or summons in lieu of arrest.
9. Authorize police to divert juveniles to other programs.
10. Establish staff procedures for recognizance release.

Your committee has been asked to develop and present ideas on how your department can comply with these suggestions. Presently, your department has little or no continuing diversion activity.

CONSTRAINTS GROUP-OBSERVER QUESTION SHEET

1. What was the leader's attitude during the meeting?
   Was it cooperative and helpful or uncooperative and restrictive?
2. What effect did his attitude have on the group?
3. How far did the group get in achieving its goal?
4. How could the group have accomplished more?

BRAINSTORMING: AN IDEA GENERATOR FOR GROUP PROBLEMS

Goals
　I. To produce numerous solutions or ideas for a situational problem by suspending criticism and evaluation.
　II. To develop creative problem-solving techniques.
　III. To develop the ability to discriminate between solutions and ideas.

Group Size
　Three groups of five individuals each.

Time Required
　Approximately one and one-half hours.

Materials
　I. Newsprint and felt-tipped markers for each group.
　II. A copy of one Brainstorming Problem Worksheet for each group.
　III. A copy of the Brainstorming Evaluation Criteria Worksheet for each group.

Physical Setting
　A room large enough to accommodate several groups and allow them to work without disrupting one another.

Process
　I. The facilitator presents a brief overview of the importance of creative problem solving in an organizational setting.

Adapted from "Brainstorming: A Problem-Solving Activity," Pfeiffer and Jones, Volume III. This experience is effectively preceded by "Constraints: A Group Problem-Solving Experience," p. 29.

II. The facilitator forms three subgroups of five individuals each and labels the groups 1, 2, and 3. One person in each group acts as recorder and documents every idea on newsprint.
III. The facilitator announces the rules:
1. There will be absolutely no criticism during the brainstorming phase of the exercise.
2. Wild and nontraditional ideas are encouraged, as they may provoke practical ideas.
3. As many ideas as possible are desirable.
IV. The facilitator distributes a Brainstorming Problem Worksheet to each group. He instructs the groups to concentrate on their problems and to generate as many ideas as possible. (Twenty-five minutes.)
V. At the end of the allotted time the facilitator informs the groups that the ban on criticism is over. He then distributes the Brainstorming Evaluation Criteria Worksheet to the groups and directs them to rank-order the ideas from the best to the worst. (Thirty minutes.)
VI. The facilitator asks each group to describe its selection process and to present its best ideas.
VII. The facilitator leads a general discussion on the merits of brainstorming as an approach to creative problem solving.

Variations

I. The groups may identify their own problems and then proceed through the activity.
II. Different problems may be generated by the facilitator depending on the composition of the criminal justice group.
III. The same problem may be given to all groups, thus creating a competitive situation.
IV. See Pfeiffer and Jones, Volume III, p. 15.

References

Structured Experiences 31 and 53. In J. W. Pfeiffer & J. E. Jones (Eds.), *A handbook of structured experiences for human relations training* (Vols. I and III). La Jolla, Ca.: University Associates, 1969 & 1974; 1971 & 1974.

Spier, M. S. Kurt Lewin's "Force-field analysis." In J. W. Pfeiffer & J. E. Jones (Eds.), *The 1973 annual handbook for group facilitators.* La Jolla, Ca.: University Associates, 1973.

Notes on the Use of "Brainstorming":

BRAINSTORMING PROBLEM WORKSHEET: GROUP I

You are faced with the problem of an increasing burglary rate. The rate has increased 20 percent since last year. The city has a population of approximately 60,000 and no minority problems. Most of the burglaries are occurring in the daytime between 9 a.m. and 4 p.m. Apartment dwellings and single-family residences seem to be the typical target.

BRAINSTORMING PROBLEM WORKSHEET: GROUP II

Your local criminal justice board has stated that it is very upset with the fact that it takes an average of 120 days to process felony offenders in your county. The board has stated that it wants you to explore ideas for solutions to reduce this processing time. It has directed you to look at the entire criminal justice spectrum:

- Police/Law Enforcement
- Prosecutor
- Lower Court
- Superior Court

BRAINSTORMING PROBLEM WORKSHEET: GROUP III

The board of supervisors has suggested that alternatives to arrest be explored by the criminal justice system in the county. The board has suggested that representatives from the criminal justice agencies jointly explore alternatives to arrest.

BRAINSTORMING EVALUATION CRITERIA WORKSHEET

Instructions: Each group is to evaluate its ideas by the following criteria. The value assigned to each criterion may be determined by the group. Feel free to add criteria that you feel are important.

Ideas	Manpower Required	Agency Capability	Costs	Social Feasibility	Political Feasibility	Ease of Operation	Time Required to Implement	Criminal Justice Agency Feasibility	Etc.
1.									
2.									
3.									
4.									
5.									
6.									
7.									
8.									
9.									
10.									

SECURITY AND PRIVACY: A ROLE-DEVELOPMENT ACTIVITY

Goals
  I. To develop group commitment and consensus.
  II. To become aware of role development in complex criminal justice systems.
  III. To observe the emergence of leadership in criminal justice groups.

Group Size
  Fifteen to twenty-five participants, divided into subgroups of six to eight each.

Time Required
  Approximately three hours.

Materials
  I. Newsprint and felt-tipped markers for each group.
  II. A copy of the Security and Privacy Role-Development Sheet for each group.
  III. A copy of the Security and Privacy Group-Observation Form for each observer.
  IV. Pencils for all participants.

Physical Setting
  A room large enough to permit groups to meet without interrupting each other.

Process
  I. The facilitator gives a brief lecturette on security and privacy issues in criminal justice information systems. He stresses the importance of role development and training in the security and privacy area. (See the summary of the reports of the National Advisory Commission on Criminal Justice Standards and Goals, Appendix I.)

II. The participants form subgroups. One observer is assigned to each group. The facilitator distributes the Security and Privacy Role-Development Sheet to each group and has the members draw the role-development matrix on newsprint. He then distributes the Security and Privacy Group-Observation Form to the observers.

III. The groups are instructed by the facilitator to identify the roles of criminal justice personnel based on the action items.

IV. The subgroups re-form into one large group and process the groups' results. The discussion centers on the observers' comments and the implications to their agencies.

V. The facilitator leads a discussion of the total experience.

Variation

The facilitator may adapt the Role-Development Sheet to any number of similar policy and procedural problems facing criminal justice agencies.

Notes on the Use of "Security and Privacy":

SECURITY AND PRIVACY ROLE-DEVELOPMENT SHEET

Group #_____

Instructions: Each group discusses the policies and procedures for which administrators (management), supervisors, and terminal operators should be responsible in a criminal justice information system. Each role is identified with an action. The group comes to a consensus on each role's responsibility and the actions necessary to accomplish it.

Actions: As group consensus is reached, the appropriate letter(s) is placed in each matrix box.

  (A) Input: sharing information and giving advice
  (B) Review: critiquing ideas and programs
  (C) Approval: giving permission and regulating
  (D) Implementation: carrying out plans and decisions

Policies and Procedures

Role	Privacy Policy	Privacy Procedures	Identification of Training Needs	Conduction of Training at Each Role Level	Security Policy	Security Procedures
Administrators (Management)						
Supervisors						
Terminal Operators						

SECURITY AND PRIVACY GROUP-OBSERVATION FORM

1. Which role(s) did you observe in the group as it worked on the role development?

2. How did the group accomplish the activity? How did leadership evolve?

3. How was consensus decision making resolved? Who influenced the decision process most? least?

4. Were the members of the group able to divorce themselves from their own *agency* biases?

5. General comments concerning:
    a) group commitment and consensus;

    b) role development;

    c) leadership.

GOAL PRIORITIES: A CONSENSUS-SEEKING ACTIVITY

Goals
  I. To assist the group to assess its values.
  II. To focus on the group decision-making process.
  III. To discover evolving leadership in the group.

Group Size
   A minimum of three groups and a maximum of five groups, each composed of three to five participants.

Time Required
   Approximately one and one-half hours.

Materials
  I. A copy of the summary of the reports of the National Advisory Commission on Criminal Justice Standards and Goals for each participant. (See Appendix I.)
  II. A copy of the Goal Priorities Assessment Sheet for each participant.
  III. A copy of the Goal Priorities Observer Form for each observer.
  IV. Newsprint and a felt-tipped marker.
  V. Pencils for all participants.

Physical Setting
   A large room with adjacent areas for small groups to meet.

Process
  I. The facilitator distributes to each participant a copy of the standards and goals compiled by the National Advisory Commission on Criminal Justice Standards and Goals. He gives a brief overview of the report.

II. The facilitator then distributes the Goal Priorities Assessment Sheet and has each participant establish priorities for the goals. (Fifteen minutes.)
III. The participants then form small subgroups to establish priorities for the goals based on group consensus. One member of each subgroup may be the process observer; he receives a copy of the Goal Priorities Observer Form. (Thirty minutes.)
IV. The facilitator asks each subgroup to reveal its goal priorities; these are listed on newsprint by the facilitator.
V. The total group discusses members' agreements and disagreements with the listed priorities.

Variations

See Pfeiffer and Jones, Volume IV, p. 54.

References

Jones, J. E. Synergy and consensus-seeking. In J. E. Jones & J. W. Pfeiffer (Eds.), *The 1973 annual handbook for group facilitators.* La Jolla, Ca.: University Associates, 1973.

Structured Experiences 11, 15, 30, 64, 69, and 115. In J.W. Pfeiffer & J. E. Jones (Eds.), *A handbook of structured experiences for human relations training* (Vols. I, II, III, and IV). La Jolla, Ca.: University Associates, 1969 & 1974; 1970 & 1974; 1971 & 1974; 1973.

Structured Experience 77. In J. W. Pfeiffer & J. E. Jones (Eds.), *The 1972 annual handbook for group facilitators.* La Jolla, Ca.: University Associates, 1972.

Notes on the Use of "Goal Priorities":

GOAL PRIORITIES ASSESSMENT SHEET

Instructions: Rank the following police goals in order of importance. Place a "1" in front of the most important, a "7" in front of the least important.

Ranking (Priority)

Individual	Group	Goal
_____	_____	To develop fully the potential of the criminal justice system to apprehend offenders.
_____	_____	To establish teamwork between police and citizens.
_____	_____	To establish teamwork among members of the criminal justice system.
_____	_____	To clearly determine and act on the local crime problem.
_____	_____	To make the most of human resources.
_____	_____	To make the most of technological resources.
_____	_____	To develop fully the police response to special community needs.

GOAL PRIORITIES OBSERVER FORM

1. What value differences were identifiable within the group?

2. How were the differences resolved?

3. Who readily accepted the consensus on priorities? Who did not?

4. How were decisions reached by the group?

5. What *facilitating* leadership behaviors emerged in the discussion?

6. What *inhibiting* leadership behaviors were observed?

POLICE ACTIONS: A DECISION-MAKING STUDY

Goals
I. To compare the decisions made by individuals with the decisions made by groups.
II. To generate data to discuss decision-making patterns in task groups.

Group Size
Any number of groups consisting of three to six participants each. Several groups may be directed simultaneously in the same room.

Time Required
Approximately one and one-half hours.

Materials
I. A pencil for each participant.
II. A copy of the Police Actions Ranking Worksheet for each participant.
III. A copy of the Police Actions Observer Sheet for each observer.
IV. A copy of the Police Actions Ranking Key for each participant (optional).

Physical Setting
A room large enough that groups may work without disrupting one another.

Process
I. The facilitator gives participants copies of the Police Actions Ranking Worksheet and tells them that they have ten minutes to complete it. They must work *independently* during this phase.

II. Each group then makes a ranking, using the method of group consensus. Each ranking must be agreed on by each member before it becomes a part of the group's decision. Members should try to make each ranking one with which all members agree—at least partially. There are two ground rules in this phase:
1. NO "averaging";
2. NO "majority rule" votes.

An observer should be assigned to each group to view the deliberations and complete the Police Actions Observer Sheet.

III. After thirty minutes of group work (or when the groups have finished), the facilitator announces the "correct" ranking (or distributes copies of the Police Actions Ranking Key). Individuals score their worksheets by calculating the differences between their rankings and the key rankings. All differences are made positive and summed. Low scores are better than high ones. Each group is also scored.

IV. The group now computes the average score of the individual members, compares this with the group score, and discusses the implications of the experience. Each observer discusses his findings using the Observer Sheet. The general discussion might be focused on leadership, compromise, decision-making strategies, the content of the exercise, roles that members played, or other aspects of group life.

References

Jones, J. E. Synergy and consensus-seeking. In J. E. Jones & J. W. Pfeiffer (Eds.), *The 1973 annual handbook for group facilitators*. La Jolla, Ca.: University Associates, 1973.

Structured Experiences 11, 15, 30, 64, 69, and 115. In J. W. Pfeiffer & J. E. Jones (Eds.), *A handbook of structured experiences for human relations training* (Vols. I, II, III, and IV). La Jolla, Ca.: University Associates, 1969 & 1974; 1970 & 1974; 1971 & 1974; 1973.

Structured Experience 77. In J. W. Pfeiffer & J. E. Jones (Eds.), *The 1972 annual handbook for group facilitators*. La Jolla, Ca.: University Associates, 1972.

Notes on the Use of "Police Actions":

POLICE ACTIONS RANKING WORKSHEET

Instructions: Rank the following police actions from 1 to 19 according to their desirability and probability of occurrence. Place a "1" in front of the police action that you feel to be *most desirable* and a "19" in front of the police action that you feel to be *least desirable*.

_____Allowing the accused to communicate

_____Being aware of racial discrimination problems

_____Communicating with citizen groups

_____Deterring pickpockets and purse snatchers in crowds

_____Establishing a friendly, helpful image

_____Explaining actions to the accused

_____Instilling respect rather than fear

_____Listening to a story before issuing a citation

_____Maintaining discipline in confrontations

_____Observing traffic regulations except in emergencies

_____Preventing the occurrence of crimes

_____Recognizing and handling emotional disorders

_____Respecting dignity when booking

_____Stimulating citizen participation

_____Strengthening the family

_____Treating all vehicle violators equally

_____Treating requests for service seriously

_____Using minimum force in arrests

_____Viewing community relations as part of the job

POLICE ACTIONS OBSERVER SHEET

1. Review how the group assumed its task and carried it out to achieve a consensus.

2. How was leadership established? Did it change frequently from one individual to another?

3. Did you identify any win-lose situations? What was the outcome?

4. How was consensus achieved?

5. How often was there a break in communications? How did this condition manifest itself?

6. What roles did various group participants assume or project?

POLICE ACTIONS RANKING KEY*

1. Preventing the occurrence of crimes
2. Observing traffic regulations except in emergencies
3. Explaining actions to the accused
4. Allowing the accused to communicate
5. Stimulating citizen participation
6. Communicating with citizen groups
7. Being aware of racial discrimination problems
8. Treating requests for service seriously
9. Establishing a friendly, helpful image
10. Maintaining discipline in confrontations
11. Using minimum force in arrests
12. Instilling respect rather than fear
13. Strengthening the family
14. Respecting dignity when booking
15. Deterring pickpockets and purse snatchers in crowds
16. Viewing community relations as part of the job
17. Recognizing and handling emotional disorders
18. Listening to a story before issuing a citation
19. Treating all vehicle violators equally

---

*Based on "Public Opinion of Criminal Justice in California," a survey conducted by Project STAR (Systems and Training Analysis of Requirements) and sponsored by California Department of Justice, Commission of Peace Officer Standards and Training. Marina Del Rey, Ca.: American Justice Institute, April 15, 1972, pp. 46-57.

DEVELOPING GROUP COMMITMENT: A VALUE-CLARIFICATION ACTIVITY

Goals
- I. To aid a group and/or organization in studying the degree to which members agree on certain values.
- II. To focus on the decision-making norms of a group.
- III. To discover the "natural leadership" functioning in a group.

Group Size

An unlimited number of groups of five to seven members each.

Time Required

Approximately one hour.

Materials

A copy of the Developing Group Commitment Functions of Police Unions Sheet for each participant.

Process
- I. The facilitator discusses the goals of the structured experience and tells the group members that they will engage in an activity to accomplish these goals. He then distributes copies of the Developing Group Commitment Functions of Police Unions Sheet. First each individual works independently; then the group works together. The facilitator functions as a timekeeper during this phase. One member may function as process observer for the group.
- II. After the allotted time, the group discusses the process in which it engaged. If a process observer was used, he gives his report.

From Paul M. Whisenand and R. Fred Ferguson, *The managing of police organizations*, © 1973, pp. 251-252. Reprinted by permission of Prentice-Hall, Inc., Englewood Cliffs, New Jersey 07632.

Variations

I. The ranking sheet is easily revised to fit groups other than police unions. The content may be the goals of the organization or group, characteristics of an ideal leader, desirable characteristics of teachers (principals, ministers, counselors, supervisors, employers, etc.), or any other relevant list. One suggestion might be to conduct a census of the problems in the organization or group and to use that list as the items to be ranked.

II. When several groups in the same organization (class, institution, etc.) engage in this experience simultaneously, it is often helpful to summarize the rankings for the several groups on newsprint and to discuss the agreements and disagreements among the groups.

Notes on the Use of "Developing Group Commitment":

DEVELOPING GROUP COMMITMENT
FUNCTIONS OF POLICE UNIONS SHEET

Instructions: Rank the following functions of police unions according to the importance you attach to them. Place a "1" in front of the function that you think is most important, a "2" in front of the function that you think is second most important, etc. You have seven minutes for this task.

After the members of your group have finished working individually, arrive at a ranking *as a group.* The group has twenty-five minutes for this task. *Do not* choose a formal leader.

Individual Group

_____ _____ 1. Police unions have a cohesive or unifying effect on the police department.

_____ _____ 2. Police unions should agitate for improved working conditions.

_____ _____ 3. Police unions develop professional and social relationships that tend to improve the efficiency of the organization.

_____ _____ 4. Police unions provide a sense of belonging to the department.

_____ _____ 5. The police union seeks to protect its members in the face of authoritarian management.

_____ _____ 6. The union is an organization within an organization, a situation that stimulates one to personal growth.

_____ _____ 7. Participation in union activities is similar to training for leadership within the police organization.

_____ _____ 8. Supervisors should not belong to police unions.

_____ _____ 9. Binding arbitration should be fostered between unions and police management.

_____ _____ 10. Management should maintain constant communication with the union on matters of mutual interest.

CRIMINAL JUSTICE ENCOUNTER: A MULTIPLE ROLE PLAY

Goals

To learn to identify various characteristics exhibited by individuals during a meeting.

Group Size

Ten or more participants.

Time Required

Approximately one hour.

Materials

I. A copy of the Criminal Justice Encounter Role-Player Instruction Sheet, a copy of the Criminal Justice Encounter Problem Sheet, and a copy of the appropriate Criminal Justice Encounter Role-Description Sheet for each role player.

II. A copy of the Criminal Justice Encounter Problem Sheet and a copy of the Criminal Justice Encounter Role-Player-Observer Question Sheet for each role-player observer.

III. A copy of the Criminal Justice Encounter Problem Sheet and a copy of the Criminal Justice Encounter Group-Observer Question Sheet for each group observer.

Physical Setting

A room large enough so that role players may study their roles without interference from observers. Observers are seated so that they can easily see their assigned role players. Other participants are seated around the role players.

Adapted from "Committee Meeting: Demonstrating Hidden Agendas," Pfeiffer and Jones, Volume I.

Process

I. The facilitator chooses five people as role players and distributes the Criminal Justice Encounter Role-Player Instruction Sheet, the Criminal Justice Encounter Problem Sheet, and a Criminal Justice Encounter Role-Description Sheet to each player. These five people leave the room and are given five minutes to study their material. The facilitator warns the role players not to reveal their roles.

II. Then the facilitator chooses five more participants to be observers of the role players. Each observer is assigned to observe a specific role player. The facilitator distributes the Criminal Justice Encounter Problem Sheet and the Criminal Justice Encounter Role-Player-Observer Question Sheet to each observer. The remaining participants are assigned as group process observers and receive the Criminal Justice Encounter Problem Sheet and the Criminal Justice Encounter Group-Observer Question Sheet.

III. After five minutes the role players return, take their places around the conference table, and state their role identities. The role players are told that the other participants are observers.

IV. The role players begin the meeting under the chairmanship of the assistant personnel director.

V. After fifteen minutes the role playing is terminated, even if the group has not completed its agenda. The group process observers are asked to report their observations.

VI. The role-player observers report their observations.

VII. The role players read their roles to the group.

VIII. The facilitator leads a discussion of the activity.

Variations

See Pfeiffer and Jones, Volume I, p. 38.

References

Berne, E. *Games people play.* New York: Ballantine Books, 1964.

Structured Experience 9. In J. W. Pfeiffer & J. E. Jones (Eds.), *A handbook of structured experiences for human relations training* (Vol. I). La Jolla, Ca.: University Associates, 1969 & 1974.

Notes on the Use of "Criminal Justice Encounter":

CRIMINAL JUSTICE ENCOUNTER ROLE-PLAYER INSTRUCTION SHEET

1. Do not look at each other's roles.
2. Read your part carefully.
3. Place yourself in the role that you are given and play the role conscientiously.
4. Do not overact.
5. Be natural, but emphasize behavior aimed at fulfilling your role.

CRIMINAL JUSTICE ENCOUNTER PROBLEM SHEET

Participants

1. assistant personnel director (who called the meeting)
2. commanding officer of traffic enforcement
3. patrol commander
4. chief of investigations
5. patrolman

Problem

You are at a meeting of a committee, selected by the chief of police, to work out a policy on preventing, investigating, and acting on vehicle accidents involving on-duty department employees. The City Council has learned that the city's insurance carrier is going to raise its premium because the city does not have a program to reduce and prevent such vehicle accidents. At present there is no departmental policy or procedure except to have the traffic supervisor on duty investigate the accident and submit the report. No citation is given and no hearing is held regarding the accident.

The chairman of the committee, who is the assistant personnel director, has specified that the committee is to develop an accident-prevention policy for police department employees. You are to establish the method of the investigation, the procedure for determining the cause of the accident, and the guidelines for disciplinary action.

CRIMINAL JUSTICE ENCOUNTER ROLE-DESCRIPTION SHEET—#1

You are the assistant personnel director. You also serve as the city's safety officer. The police department's accident rate is the highest of all city departments. You have had experience negotiating with various employee groups during salary negotiations and have been able to get employees to assume a more realistic attitude.

CRIMINAL JUSTICE ENCOUNTER ROLE-DESCRIPTION SHEET—#2

You are the commanding officer of the traffic enforcement unit, comprised of motorcycles and radar units. Your men see you as a strict disciplinarian and demanding task master. You truly believe that the best accident-prevention program is strict enforcement.

You have progressed through the various ranks in the traffic department, including six years on a motorcycle and a period as drill-team captain. You have had your share of accidents, including one that occurred when you were chasing a speeder and a car failed to heed your light and siren. That time you were in the hospital for several weeks.

CRIMINAL JUSTICE ENCOUNTER ROLE-DESCRIPTION SHEET—#3

You are the patrol commander, affectionately known as the "old man." You know most of your men by their first names. You are very protective of your men, believing that patrol employees usually get the short end of all benefits and are always made the scapegoat when it comes to problems such as police/community relations, shooting suspects, etc. You have supported most new programs as long as they benefit the patrol division and do not make your job more difficult.

CRIMINAL JUSTICE ENCOUNTER ROLE-DESCRIPTION SHEET—#4

You have been the chief of investigations for several years. You were on the force when you knew almost everyone in the community and people treated the police with respect. Now, you are inwardly appalled at being called "pig" and other seemingly personal insults. You believe the police should be treated with more dignity and be given more freedom than they now enjoy.

CRIMINAL JUSTICE ENCOUNTER ROLE-DESCRIPTION SHEET—#5

You are a patrolman and president of the Patrolmen's Association. You have been assigned to the youth bureau for the last three years. You believe that most new programs result from the desire to get Federal funds so that the city doesn't have to spend its money or that they are a form of harassment directed toward the rank-and-file patrolman.

CRIMINAL JUSTICE ENCOUNTER ROLE-PLAYER-OBSERVER QUESTION SHEET

1. What was the role player's attitude at the initial stages of the meeting—tough, righteous, indulgent, helpful?
2. Did this attitude change during the course of the meeting?
3. What effect did his participation have on the group?

CRIMINAL JUSTICE ENCOUNTER GROUP-OBSERVER QUESTION SHEET

1. Group Atmosphere
    a. Was the general atmosphere of the group cooperative or competitive, friendly or hostile?

    b. Did the atmosphere vary as the meeting progressed?

2. Player Participation
    a. Who participated most? least?

    b. What participation helped the meeting? What hindered the meeting?

    c. What effect did player participation have on the group?

3. Accomplishment
    a. How far did the group get in achieving its goal?

    b. How could it have gotten farther?

OMBUDSMAN: A MULTIPLE ROLE PLAY

Goals
I. To explore the dynamics of different roles.
II. To develop skill at resolving criminal justice conflicts in a negotiating atmosphere.
III. To provide participants with feedback and analysis.

Group Size
A minimum of eight participants.

Time Required
Approximately one hour.

Materials
I. A copy of the Ombudsman Event Data Sheet for each participant.
II. A copy of the appropriate Ombudsman Role-Description Sheet for each selected role player.
III. A copy of the Ombudsman Individual Observation Guide for each observer.

Physical Setting
A room that will accommodate a circle of eight or more chairs.

Process
I. The facilitator discusses role playing as a method of resolving conflict.
II. Four individuals are selected to assume the described roles.
III. The facilitator distributes a copy of the Ombudsman Event Data Sheet and of the appropriate Ombudsman Role-Description Sheet to the selected role players.

IV. The remaining participants are then assigned the observer roles—one observer for each role player. The observers form a circle around the four role players (see Figure 1).

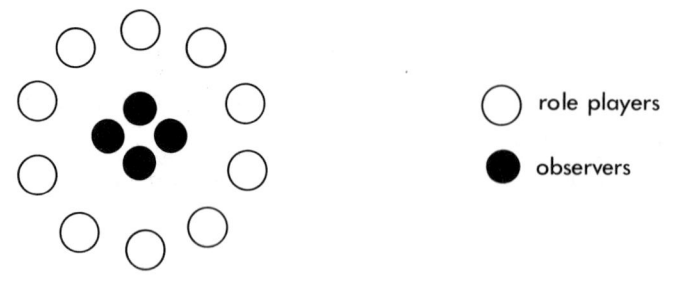

Figure 1

V. Each observer then receives the Ombudsman Role-Description Sheet for his assigned role player, the Ombudsman Event Data Sheet, and the Ombudsman Individual Observation Guide.
VI. The role players are given thirty minutes to assume their roles and resolve the problem.
VII. The facilitator stops the exercise and processes the learning experience, relying on input from the role players and from the observers.

Variations

I. Actual situations can be used.
II. Role reversals: persons can be assigned to roles other than those they ordinarily have.
III. The process can be interrupted intermittently for role players to be "coached" by observer groups.

Notes on the Use of "Ombudsman":

OMBUDSMAN EVENT DATA SHEET

The following is a chronological summary of events that led to the present problem of hiring an ombudsman.

6/1 The Citizen's Action Committee lodged general complaints against the county Sheriff and Probation Departments. The complaints focused on the fact that the citizens did not feel their grievances were being handled properly by those agencies.

6/3 The Employees' Association of the Sheriff and Probation Departments announced, via the press, that their internal grievances were not being resolved properly.

6/10 The county Human Relations Committee and the county administrator have recommended the recruitment of an individual for the position of ombudsman. The new ombudsman is to hear citizens' and employees' complaints regarding the two concerned agencies and to mediate and negotiate with the proper individuals in order to establish constructive ways to improve the situation.

6/12 Three county employees and one member of the county Human Relations Committee have been assigned to define and clarify the following concerning the ombudsman:
1. recruitment procedures for the new position;
2. qualifications for the new position;
3. organizational placement of the ombudsman.

OMBUDSMAN ROLE-DESCRIPTION SHEET #1

County Employee—Mr. Johnson

Mr. Johnson is a middle-aged career undersheriff with twenty-one years of experience. He has little formal education and was promoted through the ranks. Many of the men view him as an informal leader and frequently ask him for advice. He is opposed to establishing the position of ombudsman as it would endanger his position with the men.

OMBUDSMAN ROLE-DESCRIPTION SHEET #2

County Employee—Mr. Thomas

Mr. Thomas, staff development officer for the Probation Department, came to the department seven years ago after receiving his master's degree in criminology. Prior to that, he had been the manager of a county welfare department. He is very supportive of the new position and thinks the ombudsman should reside with the Probation Department.

OMBUDSMAN ROLE-DESCRIPTION SHEET #3

County Employee—Mr. Williams

Mr. Williams is a young administrator with a B.S. degree. He is assistant to the county administrator and takes the position that the Sheriff and Probation Departments should make their own decisions. He has some definite ideas on the qualifications for the position, e.g., that the ombudsman should have a master's degree and three years of experience, including one year in human relations training.

OMBUDSMAN ROLE-DESCRIPTION SHEET #4

Committee Member—Mr. Smith

Mr. Smith, a member of the Human Relations Committee, is a recent appointment to the committee. He has served for six months. He feels that the ombudsman should be a minority person with layman experience in human relations and that he should be placed under the control of the Human Relations Committee.

OMBUDSMAN INDIVIDUAL OBSERVATION GUIDE

1. Did you observe that the role player was restrained in playing his role?

2. To what degree did the role player cooperate to resolve the problem?

   Positive factors:

   Inhibiting factors:

3. What personal beliefs did you infer from the role player's behavior?

4. How effective was the role player in listening to the others?

5. What were the factors that had the most influence on controlling the group?

CITATION RELEASE: AN EVALUATION ACTIVITY

Goals

   I. To make individuals aware of the evaluation process in criminal justice.

   II. To provide individuals with evaluation skills.

   III. To explore intergroup competition.

Group Size

A minimum of eight participants divided into groups of four.

Time Required

Approximately one hour.

Materials

   I. "Goal Setting and Guidelines for Evaluation." (See Appendix II.)

   II. A copy of the Citation Release Information Sheet for each participant.

   III. A copy of the Citation Release Form for each participant.

   IV. Newsprint and felt-tipped markers for each group.

Physical Setting

A room large enough to accommodate several groups.

Process

   I. The facilitator states the goals of the experience. Then he gives a lecturette on goal setting and the guidelines for evaluation. (See "Goal Setting and Guidelines for Evaluation," Appendix II.)

   II. The facilitator has the participants form groups of four members each, and he distributes to each member a copy of the Citation Release Information Sheet and of the Citation Release Form. Time is allowed for participants to read the material carefully.

III. The facilitator then instructs the groups to develop the objectives and evaluation methodology for the activity.

IV. Each group documents its objectives and evaluation methodology on newsprint.

V. The facilitator processes the results and leads a general discussion on the importance of the evaluation process.

Variations

I. The exercise can be modified to suit any particular criminal justice group.

II. All groups but one can present their evaluation plans, while the remaining group role plays the funding agency and votes on funding approval.

Notes on the Use of "Citation Release":

CITATION RELEASE INFORMATION SHEET

(Based on the model in "Goal Setting and Guidelines for Evaluation")

The real test of an evaluation plan comes in its actual application. The question posed is whether a viable evaluation plan can be developed through the use of the evaluation model presented. Assume that your group concurs with the Task Force on Police that there is a "great need to divert offenders from the criminal justice system." The *burden* and *cost* of arresting and processing all felons and misdemeanants are not justified and alternatives must be explored.

Over a period of several months—by process of staff study, review of the literature, consultation with experts, etc.—a new citation release program to be used by the police agency has evolved. The new procedure is that the police agency will use a citation release program in lieu of arrest for certain misdemeanor and felony offenses. The offenses are theft, drunk cases, shoplifting, and certain cases of burglary and narcotics.

A Citation Release Form has been developed that enables officers to determine the offender's applicability to citation in lieu of arrest and booking.

Assume further that your group is agreed as to the format and design, content, and internal arrangement of the form. The D.A., courts, and probation departments are all in agreement, and all logistical, personnel, and operational requirements have been met. In essence "all systems are go," with one exception. A plan for evaluating the new citation system has not been developed. You have decided to delay the test of the program until a plan of evaluation has been prepared. Your task today is to devise this plan. You should concentrate on objectives and evaluation methodology.

CITATION RELEASE FORM

Local or State ID # _____

Name _____ FBI # _____

Address _____ Date _____

_____

Offense _____

_____

_____

Check the Appropriate Square	Yes	No
1. The offender has a prior criminal record (convictions only). 　　If so, how many: 　　　Felonies　　_____ 　　　Misdemeanors　_____	☐	☐
2. The offender is employed or has been going to school for the past six months.	☐	☐
3. He is married.	☐	☐
4. He has dependents living with him.	☐	☐
5. The offense committed involved violence.	☐	☐
6. The offender has lived at his current address for more than two years.	☐	☐

A score of four or more *no* marks makes the offender ineligible for a citation release. More than two felony convictions or four misdemeanor convictions also make the offender ineligible for release.

CUT YOUR BUDGET: INTERGROUP CONFLICT

Goals

    I. To explore criminal justice group behavior based on organization positioning.

   II. To study intergroup competition relative to the functions of the criminal justice system.

  III. To identify win-lose situations relative to the various criminal justice functions.

  IV. To study individual leadership styles.

   V. To study the communication processes of groups.

Group Size

    A minimum of fifteen participants, a maximum of thirty participants.

Time Required

    Approximately two and one-half hours.

Materials

    I. A conference table for five participants.

   II. Newsprint, felt-tipped markers, and five easels for the newsprint.

  III. Masking tape or scotch tape.

  IV. A copy of the Cut Your Budget Criminal Justice Process Guide for each participant (optional).

   V. A copy of the Cut Your Budget Observer Sheet for each group member.

Physical Setting

    A conference room sufficiently large to permit subgroups to meet without disturbing one another.

Process

I. The facilitator gives a brief lecture on the criminal justice system, identifying the various programs for each of the criminal justice processes (law enforcement, prosecution, defense counsel, judicial, and probation/parole) and indicating the dollar amount and/or percentage for each program as it relates to the entire criminal justice system. He may want to give the Cut Your Budget Criminal Justice Process Guide to each participant.

II. The facilitator then asks the participants to form five subgroups, each representing one of the criminal justice processes.

III. Each group selects a chairman and a recorder.

IV. The facilitator presents the following problem: "The Board of Supervisors adopted an austerity program requiring the criminal justice system to reduce its expenditures by 10 percent." He explains that each group must determine: (a) where in the criminal justice system the 10 percent reduction takes place and why; and (b) if the group (agency) must absorb the 10 percent reduction and, if so, which program(s) should be curtailed.

V. After all groups have completed their assignment, the participants regroup. The facilitator asks the group chairmen to meet at the conference table, bringing their materials with them. The facilitator explains that, as chairmen, they should consider themselves as having the authority and responsibility for their specific criminal justice process; they have been called together by the administrator of the board in order to arrive at a consensus on how to effect the 10 percent reduction; they must provide the administrator with a specific recommendation.

VI. The facilitator distributes the Cut Your Budget Observer Sheet to all participants except the chairmen. The chairmen are not to read the Observer Sheet until after the activity is completed.

VII. The facilitator asks for responses from the observers and for critiques of the activity.

Variations

I. There can be several rounds of negotiations among the chairmen.

II. There can be messengers across groups, to permit "horse-trading" and "deals."

III. The experience can be altered in an opposite direction: in the case of a windfall, who gets the extra money?

Notes on the Use of "Cut Your Budget":

CUT YOUR BUDGET CRIMINAL JUSTICE PROCESS GUIDE

Law Enforcement (Sheriff/Police)
>Crime prevention/suppression
Investigation/apprehension
Serving civil process
Custody prior to final disposition
Sentenced/local incarceration

Prosecution
>Initiation of prosecution
Proceedings prior to trial
Trial proceedings
Post-trial proceedings (Habeas Corpus)

Judicial
>Inferior Court (misdemeanor) proceedings
Superior Court (felonies) proceedings prior to trial
Superior Court (felonies) trial proceedings
Post-trial proceedings (commitments, appeals, etc.)
Juvenile/Family Court

Defense Counsel
>Investigation
Proceedings prior to trial
Trial proceedings
Post-trial proceedings

Probation/Parole
>Investigation
Supervision
Juvenile judicial process
Juvenile institutional corrections
Community treatment
Unadjudicated juvenile custody/corrections

CUT YOUR BUDGET OBSERVER SHEET

1. How well did your chairman represent your agency's interest? How well did he use the developed material?

2. Which agency appeared to have the most power? Why?

3. Which agencies appeared to be competing against one another? Which agencies appeared to be cooperating?

4. How often was there a lack of communication? How did this condition manifest itself?

5. Did you identify any win-lose situations? What was the outcome?

6. Which agency took the leadership role? Did the agency maintain this role or relinquish it? How?

7. Which agency was able to better its initial position? How? Which agency lost ground? Why?

MULTI-ORGANIZATION PROBLEM ANALYSIS: A PROBLEM-SOLVING EXPERIENCE

Goals

   I. To develop problem-solving skills.

   II. To explore group decision making.

Group Size

   Thirty participants is an ideal size, but other numbers can be used.

Time Required

   Approximately two and one-half hours.

Materials

   I. Newsprint and felt-tipped markers for each group.

   II. A copy of the Multi-Organization Problem Analysis Worksheet for each participant.

Physical Setting

   A large room with tables.

Process

   I. The facilitator forms participants into six groups and distributes the Multi-Organization Problem Analysis Worksheet to each participant.

   II. He announces that each group has forty minutes to define an organization problem and complete Part I of the Multi-Organization Problem Analysis Worksheet.

   III. When the groups have completed Part I of the worksheet, the facilitator presents a brief lecturette on the importance of identifying and isolating opposing forces that inhibit the problem-solving process. He stresses the

---

Adapted from "Force-Field Analysis: Individual Problem-Solving," Pfeiffer and Jones, Volume II.

necessity of considering these inhibiting forces in establishing a planned strategy change.

IV. The facilitator informs the groups that they have forty minutes to complete Part II of the worksheet by detailing a planned strategy for decreasing two or more of the forces in opposition to change. The problem and strategies are documented on newsprint for each group.

V. The facilitator asks group members to reveal their problem and their strategies for decreasing two or more of the opposing forces. The results are processed, and the facilitator evokes a general discussion on the use of the multi-organization problem-solving technique.

Variations

I. The activity can be used effectively in analyzing a criminal justice agency's problems.

II. The facilitator may have participants develop an implementation plan and schedule that would include organization and staffing requirements, responsibilities, budget, and time allowed for accomplishment.

Reference

Spier, M. S. Kurt Lewin's "Force-field analysis." In J. E. Jones & J. W. Pfeiffer (Eds.), *The 1973 annual handbook for group facilitators.* La Jolla, Ca.: University Associates, 1973.

Notes on the Use of "Multi-Organization Problem Analysis":

MULTI-ORGANIZATION PROBLEM ANALYSIS WORKSHEET

Part I. Problem Characteristics

Identify an organization problem that crosses the criminal justice agency boundaries. Respond to each item in order for other participants to be able to understand the problem.

A. The organization problem facing my agency is:

B. The criminal justice agencies relate to the problem in the following way:

Agency   *Relation to Problem*

1.
2.
3.
4.

C. List and explain the conditions relevant to the problem.

D. List the forces opposing change in the identified problem. Rank the opposing forces from a scale of 1 to 7, 1 indicating the force that is *most critical* and 7 indicating the force that is *least critical* in effecting change.

_____ a. _____

_____ b. _____

_____ c. _____

_____ d. _____

_____ e. _____

_____ f. _____

_____ g. _____

Part II. Strategy for Changing Opposing Forces

Detail a *strategy* for decreasing two or more of the opposing forces from the list in item D.

THE ORGANIZATION MAN: INSIGHTS INTO MOTIVATION

Goals
  I. To understand the motivators that enable individuals to work in an organization.
  II. To develop skills at diagnosing individual motivational needs.
  III. To understand one's motivators in the organization.

Group Size
  Unlimited.

Time Required
  Approximately thirty-five minutes.

Materials
  I. A copy of The Organization Man Diagnosis Questionnaire for each participant.
  II. A copy of The Organization Man Scoring Sheet for each participant.
  III. Newsprint and felt-tipped markers.

Physical Setting
  A large room to accommodate participants in a semicircle or a horseshoe arrangement.

Process
  I. The facilitator gives a brief overview of the goals.
  II. He then distributes The Organization Man Diagnosis Questionnaire to all participants and gives them fifteen minutes to complete it.
  III. The facilitator passes out The Organization Man Scoring Sheet to participants and instructs them how to score their answers. He posts the results on newsprint and generates a discussion on motivation and categorizing organizational typologies relative to character types.

Variations

I. People can predict their scores after a discussion of the types, prior to step III.

II. The four "types" can be role played with a realistic problem.

III. The instrument can be used as a feedback device for the participants. They can describe each other or solicit reactions from other group members.

Reference

Maccoby, M. "Winning" and "losing" at work. *IEEE Spectrum,* July 1973, pp. 39-48. Reprinted in the Selected Readings section of this book, p. 153.

Notes on the Use of "The Organization Man":

THE ORGANIZATION MAN DIAGNOSIS QUESTIONNAIRE

Instructions: Place an X over the number that best represents your perceptions of yourself and the organization.

1. The organization gives me freedom to develop the quality of my work.

   Strongly Disagree   0   1   2   3   4   Strongly Agree

2. My position affords me the opportunity to play an important part in creating services of the highest quality.

   Strongly Disagree   0   1   2   3   4   Strongly Agree

3. I feel that in the organization I must dominate or be dominated by someone else.

   Strongly Disagree   0   1   2   3   4   Strongly Agree

4. My greatest ambition is to crush an opponent who disagrees with my viewpoint.

   Strongly Disagree   0   1   2   3   4   Strongly Agree

5. I feel that situations in the organization are a win-lose proposition: triumph or humiliation.

   Strongly Disagree   0   1   2   3   4   Strongly Agree

6. Competition is the price for success.

   Strongly Disagree   0   1   2   3   4   Strongly Agree

7. The biggest competition I face is between myself and the material with which I work.

   Strongly Disagree   0   1   2   3   4   Strongly Agree

8. The thing I fear most in the organization is failure.

Strongly   _____   Strongly
Disagree   0   1   2   3   4   Agree

9. The organization requires me to get rid of the "dead wood."

Strongly   _____   Strongly
Disagree   0   1   2   3   4   Agree

10. Survival of the fittest is the name of the game in the organization.

Strongly   _____   Strongly
Disagree   0   1   2   3   4   Agree

THE ORGANIZATION MAN SCORING SHEET

1. Invert the scoring for questions #3, #4, #5, and #10.
2. Add the total of your score and place an X on the scale below.
3. The following characteristics of an individual can then be determined.

   10—Organization Deviate (cut-throat)
   20—Civil Servant (gamesman)
   30—Climber
   40—Organization Man

```
0          10          20          30          40
```

REVEAL: POSITIVE AND ADVERSE FEEDBACK

Goals
 I. To enable participants to see how others view their personal strengths and weaknesses.
 II. To develop feedback skills and to demonstrate the importance of giving adverse and positive feedback.
 III. To develop an individual's awareness of how others perceive him.

Group Size
 A minimum of five participants, a maximum of fifteen participants.

Time Required
 Approximately fifteen minutes for each participant.

Materials
 Several 3" × 5" cards for each participant.

Physical Setting
 Participants are seated in a circle.

Process
 I. The facilitator briefly discusses the goals of the activity.
 II. The facilitator then asks each participant to identify three to five positive and negative strengths that he sees in himself. These should consist of a list of descriptive adjectives—not sentences.
 III. Participants write their last name in the left-hand corner of several 3" × 5" cards (enough for every participant in the group). Then each participant selects positive and negative adjectives that describe each of the other participants. These descriptive adjectives are listed for each individual on his respective card.

IV. The cards are collected; the facilitator arranges the cards by name and returns them to the named individuals.
  V. The facilitator asks the participants to review the positive and adverse feedback given about them by the other participants and to compare this feedback with their perceptions about themselves.
  VI. He then leads a general discussion of the activity, focusing on the goals of the structured experience.

Variations

  I. Each participant can predict what he is going to hear.
  II. Feedback can be given orally.
  III. Cards can be made nonanonymous.
  IV. One feedback card (5" × 8") for each participant can be used, to be passed around and written on by all others, including "me-too" comments.

Notes on the Use of "Reveal":

IMPRESSIONS: A GROUP FEEDBACK EXPERIENCE

Goals
- I. To observe how groups interact with and stereotype each other.
- II. To improve relationships between groups.

Group Size
Three groups of no more than four participants each.

Time Required
Approximately two and one-half hours.

Materials
Newsprint, masking tape, and felt-tipped markers for each group.

Physical Setting
One room large enough to accommodate the total group. Three nearby rooms, one for each subgroup.

Process
- I. The facilitator discusses the goals of the meeting. Based on the following criminal justice agency affiliations, three groups are selected.
  - Law Enforcement
  - Courts-Prosecutors
  - Corrections-Probation
- II. The facilitator instructs the subgroups to meet for one hour and discuss (1) how they view the other two groups, and (2) how they think the other two groups view them. Their ideas are listed on newsprint.

Adapted from "Intergroup Meeting: An Image Exchange," Pfeiffer and Jones, Volume III.

III. The subgroups reconvene as a total group. A spokesman for each subgroup posts his group's list and explains it. The participants are not to respond to the feedback, but are merely to *listen* and to try to understand the *perceptions* of the others. (Thirty minutes.)

IV. Each of the three subgroups meets separately again to respond to the feedback and to discuss how to process it. (Thirty minutes.)

V. The subgroups re-assemble and share their reactions to the feedback they received. The groups should discuss how they can make commitments to be followed after the session is completed.

Variations

I. The participants can be divided into different criminal justice groups or the number of groups can be expanded.

II. The exercise can be used with only one criminal justice agency. Groups would then be divided by function, i.e., investigation, patrol, and community relations.

III. The experience can cover an extended period of time with group members being responsible for developing implementation strategies to improve group relationships.

Notes on the Use of "Impressions":

SELECTED READINGS

A "how to" approach for determining training needs.

Determining Training Needs

JAMES H. AUTEN

While the legitimacy of the training function is a well recognized responsibility of the organization by most police administrators, an untold number of law enforcement organizations still tend to view the training function as a "necessary evil." To quote The President's Commission on Law Enforcement and Administration of Justice: "While considerable progress has been made in recent years in the development of training programs for police officers, the total training effort in this country, when related to the complexity of the law enforcement task, is grossly inadequate.... While current police training programs are better than what has existed in the past, they nevertheless continue to be a somewhat fragmented, sporadic, and rather inadequate response to the training needs of the field in a day when police are confronted with some of the most perplexing social and behavioral problems we have ever known."[1]

Training within these organizations is usually conducted at minimum levels with little regard for the actual needs of the individuals or the organization. Any training, whether it be conducted within the organization or outside the organization, must be based upon actual identified training needs of the organization's members at all levels.

This responsibility for determining the training needs of a police organization ultimately rests with its administrative head since he must

---

From "Determining Training Needs," by James H. Auten, from POLICE courtesy of Charles C Thomas, Springfield, Illinois.

[1] The President's Commission on Law Enforcement and Administration of Justice: *Task Force Report: The Police*, pp. 36–37.

answer for the actions of his subordinates and the level of performance they achieve. While the ultimate responsibility rests with the administrative head, the identification of the training needs within the organization requires the complete cooperation of all its members. Members of the organization should understand the importance of the need-determination process, how it relates to the overall effectiveness of the training programs, and the methods to be employed to actually determine the training needs of the organization.

The training needs of the organization are usually discussed in four dimensions. The first of these dimensions relates to a general departmental need. This type of training need would either involve the entire department or a large segment of the department. An example of a training need of this type would be the need for improved intradepartmental communications. A need of this type would involve a significant number of organizational personnel who would have to be trained in the desired procedures.

The second dimension relates to the general training needs of a specific group or segment within the organization. A training need of this type would involve a specific element of the organization, for example, the traffic division which needs to improve a general operating procedure such as its reporting methods. A need of this type would require involvement of personnel within the element, but would not burden other organizational personnel who would not be affected by the reporting procedures.

The next dimension involves the identification of the special training needs of a specific group within the organization. As an example, it may be apparent that the supervisory staff of the patrol division has a need for additional training in completing the daily activity summary.

Finally, the scope and depth of the training need of the specific group within the organization must be recognized. In this respect it is not sufficient to merely state that the supervisory staff of the patrol division needs additional training in completing the daily activity summary, but also to indicate how much training is required to elevate their performance to a satisfactory level.

In general terms, the actual process utilized to identify training needs within the organization is based upon an analysis or examination of the organizational problems and conditions. In addition, this analysis or examination should encompass each employee's performance, problems, and potential. This process of analysis or examination may be accomplished by utilizing the following techniques: (1) questioning; (2) observing, and (3) studying. In a majority of cases a combination of these techniques will be the most effective method of obtaining the desired information. This entire process of analysis or examination must be a cooperative effort of operational level personnel, supervisors, management, and training staff.

The initial technique of analysis by questioning should be applied to all three general levels of the police organization—operational, supervisory, and management. The questioning at each level of the organization will, of necessity, take various forms, since their orientation concerning the organization will vary. Examples of the types of questions which should be asked of those at the management level are:

(1) Regarding the general operations of the organization, what aspects of the operation need the most improvement?
(2) In your opinion how should these improvements in the general operation of the organization be accomplished?
(3) Concerning the staff level personnel within the organization, what tasks or functions should they be better able to perform than they can now?
(4) Why should members of the staff be able to perform these tasks in an improved manner?
(5) What steps should be taken to improve the performance of those employed in staff positions?
(6) How do these weaknesses within staff level personnel affect the overall operation of the organization?
(7) What is the nature, in terms of abilities and numbers, of your need for replacement personnel, both for the present and in the near future, especially in key administrative, technical, and supervisory positions?
(8) How will this need for replacement personnel affect, and be affected by, anticipated program trends and plans for expansion or contraction of the organization?
(9) How do you plan to meet these needs for replacement personnel?

This list of questions is not all-inclusive, but does indicate the general nature of the questions which should be asked of management level employees. Questions of this type tend to focus attention on immediate, already recognized training needs. Training needs which are perhaps less obvious to those at the management level can be identified by a less direct approach involving more of a discussion of the organization in total, rather than by the direct questioning approach.

Generally speaking, the best source of organizational training needs will be the first-line supervisor. Questioning at the first-line supervisory level, if properly conducted, will be most beneficial, since the first-line supervisor has a daily working relationship with the other two general levels of the organization. It is important to understand that those needs identified by the first-line supervisor will generally relate to the operational level activities. Symptoms indicating training needs at the supervisory and management levels may come to the attention of the first-line supervisor, but generally, the actual needs will not be identified. Examples of the types of questions which should be directed to the first-line supervisor are as follows:

(1) In what specific areas would you like to see your subordinates most improve their level of performance?
(2) What are the causes for the needed improvement in these areas?
(3) What steps should be taken to improve the performance of your subordinates in these areas?
(4) How do the problems facing your subordinates affect the overall programs of the organization?
(5) In what areas would you like your subordinates to develop a proficiency which does not now exist?
(6) What positive actions have you taken to assist your subordinates in improving their level of performance?
(7) In order to raise your subordinates' performance to a satisfactory level, what type of assistance do you need, and from whom do you need it?
(8) To what extent do you agree with your subordinates' assessment of the problems facing the organization?
(9) Concerning your working relationships with management level personnel, what are your feelings as to how they may specifically be improved?
(10) Regarding the general operations of the organization, what aspects of the operation need the most improvement?
(11) In your opinion, how should these improvements in the general operation of the organization be accomplished?

As with the examples of the questions to be asked at the management level, these questions represent less than an all-inclusive list, but they do indicate the general nature of the questions which should be directed to the first-line supervisor. The nature of the training needs can be further refined utilizing the discussion approach rather than by being restricted entirely to the direct question approach.

The next level of questioning takes place at the operational level, and if conducted properly, can be most beneficial, since the operational level employees are directly involved in implementing the organizational programs. Generally speaking, when questioning those at the operational level it is advisable not to ask them what type of training they think they need. Operational level personnel will tend to respond with the types of training they personally would like to have, rather than those which they actually need. Examples of the types of questions to be asked of those at the operational level are:

(1) How do you feel about your job with the organization?
(2) What do you like the most about your job?

(3) What do you like least about your job?
(4) What part(s) of your job gives you the greatest difficulty?
(5) What is the effect of this difficulty upon you personally?
(6) How, do you feel, does this difficulty affect your supervisor?
(7) How, do you feel, does this difficulty affect overall departmental programs?
(8) What aspects of your performance would you most like to improve?
(9) If you are experiencing difficulty in performing certain aspects of your job, why are you experiencing difficulty?
(10) What are you personally doing to try to improve your level of performance?
(11) Do you need additional help from others to improve your level of performance?
(12) Does your supervisor prove to be helpful in improving your level of performance?
(13) What kind of help, and from whom do you need help, to improve your level of performance?

Once again this is not an all-inclusive list of questions, and modifications should be made to fit the individual circumstances.

The second phase of the analysis or examination should be directed to looking at the department in its operation. In other words, the second phase involves a critical analysis or examination of the organization in its day-to-day operations. This observation of the organization should encompass the following areas:

(1) *Morale factors*—Does personal friction exist between all three levels of the organization? Does personal friction exist between those personnel comprising each of three levels? Does "buck passing," the failure to accept responsibility, exist among those who should be accepting the responsibility? Do complaints, either unfounded or based on fact, generate from those involved in supervisory-subordinate relationships? Is there evidence of inattention to work by members of the organization? Are there cases where leadership roles have been assumed by those not in appointed positions of leadership? Are supervisors ineffective in providing their subordinates with some sense of worth, belonging and security? Are there indications of a lack of supervisory support for subordinates? Is there a lack of authoritative leadership among those so delegated? Generally speaking, does there seem to be an absence of a sense of purpose and accomplishment among those in the organization?

(2) *Job knowledge*—What is the level of performance in the technical, administrative and supervisory phases of the operation? Are employees performing at levels lower than is expected, and as a result, causing subordinates to "carry the load"?

(3) *Communication failures*—Are written and oral instructions misunderstood? Is there a failure in the flow of information, either across or up and down, within the organization? Are accepted lines of com-

munication being ignored or bypassed for informal lines? Is there an ability on the part of those required to do so, to express themselves either orally or in writing?
  (4) *Supervision*—Are work assignments being made in accordance with abilities and the overall aims of the organization? Are supervisors planning and scheduling work in accordance with accepted techniques? Are supervisors instructing subordinates properly? Are grievances, both real and imagined, being handled at the supervisory level when appropriate? Is there a lack of job pride on the part of supervisors and/or their subordinates? Does the supervisor and/or his subordinates display a lack of interest in the job? Does the supervisor fail to motivate and recognize his subordinates?
  (5) *Job application*—Are employees applying the job knowledge and skills they possess to the performance of the job? Is there a desire to better one's performance through self-improvement?

The third and last phase of the analysis or examination concerns itself with studying the organizational elements and their operation. This aspect of the analysis differs from the second phase in that the individual elements are examined rather than the organization as a whole. In addition, this phase differs from the second phase in that the objective is to study the elements rather than just observing them. The existing elements within the organization will govern where this study phase of the analysis should occur:
  (1) *Organizational plans*—Are there any projected changes in the mission, structure, personnel, or procedures? What organizational plans exist concerning the training function?
  (2) *Employee records*—Has the organization been experiencing a higher than normal turnover rate? Is the rate of absenteeism higher than normal? Are employees becoming involved in accidents at an abnormal rate? Are grievances being presented at an abnormal rate and generally not based on fact? Do merit ratings reflect the true status of personnel? What is the composition of the supervisory staff?
  (3) *Official inspection records*—Study both those done by the organization and those completed by outside agencies.
  (4) *Work and work flow*—Do bottlenecks exist in the work flow? Is work production more or less consistent, or do peaks and valleys appear? Do records indicate high costs, waste, and excessive errors?
  (5) *Supervisory selection policy*—Are the requirements for positions such that the most qualified are selected? What is the experience and training background of the present supervisory staff?
  (6) *Records*—Does the daily activity report (if used) provide the necessary information? Are other records providing the information they were designed to provide?

These represent only brief examples of the methods which may be utilized in conducting an analysis or examination of the organization and its employees. None of these methods of analysis or examination will prove to be totally effective by themselves, and they will, of necessity, require modification in application to various organizations. In most cases, combinations of the methods cited will be the most effective in obtaining the desired information.

At this point, nothing has been mentioned concerning the actual implementation of the methods. The first of these modes of implementation is the interview. One of the distinct advantages of the interview in the need-determination process is that it reveals the facts, as well as the feelings, causes, and possible solutions relating to certain problems. The interview, if conducted properly, affords a maximum opportunity for the free exchange of ideas relating to possible solutions to problem areas.

The interview is limited in that it can make the interviewee feel that he is "on the spot" and therefore somewhat reluctant to be open and candid. In addition, the interview can be quite time consuming, thereby limiting the number of participants. Finally, the results of the interview can be difficult to quantify due to the very nature of the interview situation.

The questions to be used in the interview should be pretested to ensure that the information sought will be obtained. Make certain that the interviewer can and does listen, and that he does not sit in judgment of the responses. The interview situation should not be used to interpret, sell, or educate, but rather to gain information.

Another method which may be employed in the need-determination process is the questionnaire. One of the obvious advantages of the questionnaire is that it can be used to reach a large number of people at a relatively low cost. In addition, the questionnaire affords the recipient the opportunity for expression without fear or embarrassment, and the resulting data can easily be summarized and reported. One of the severe limitations concerning the questionnaire is that there is little provision for free expression of ideas unless the questions are open-ended. Also, time must be taken in the questionnaire construction phase to ensure that the probes will be effective in providing the desired results. Finally, the questionnaire is limited in that it generally will reveal the symptoms of the problem rather than identifying causes and possible solutions.

As with the interview, pretest and revise the questions prior to administering the questionnaire. Remember, if you do utilize the questionnaire in the need-determination process, be prepared to report the results, both favorable and unfavorable, and be prepared to take action concerning the unfavorable aspects.

The final method which may be utilized as part of the need-determination process is the job analysis and performance review. This method can provide you with specific and precise information about job performance since it is directly applied to actual jobs and performance of them. Through job analysis the job is broken into segments manageable both for training and appraisal purposes. This method of need-determination is limited in that it is extremely time consuming and difficult for those not adequately trained in job analysis techniques. Another limitation of this technique is that it generally will only reveal the training needs of individuals and not those based upon the needs of the entire organization. The exception to this, of course, is when a significant number of common training needs are revealed in a large portion of job analyses.

When preparing to conduct a job analysis and performance review make certain that your job analysis is based upon a current job description which reflects the current performance. In addition, you should be prepared to review with the employee your analysis of the job and appraisal of his performance. Job analysis and job or performance review, then, is nothing more than breaking the job into measurable elements and then measuring the individual's performance of the various elements against an acceptable level.

As with the methods of analysis, these methods of implementation are usually most effective when used in combination. Each method is limited in its application to a given situation, and as is the case concerning the methods of analysis, each will require modification to be properly applied to various situations.

The application of the need-determination process is essential before any training program can be devised, since meaningful training must be based upon actual identified needs within the organization. The need-determination process must involve all levels of the organization so that priorities may be fixed among the needs, and so that the training programs may be integrated into a meaningful whole. Effective training programs should complement each other and be part of the established activities of the organization.

ABOUT THE AUTHOR: *James Auten received his Bachelors degree from Michigan State University with a major area of study in police administration. He is currently working toward a Masters degree at the University of Illinois.*

Mr. Auten served with the Michigan State University Department of Public Safety for eight years, attaining the rank of Sergeant. During that time he was directly involved in the development and implementation of departmental training programs dealing with recruit level, in-service, and advanced level training. He currently holds the rank of Instructor with the University of Illinois Police Training Institute, and instructs primarily in the basic law enforcement programs.

"There are great benefits for policing to be derived from human relations laboratories..."

Human Relations Training: Laboratories and Team Policing

BYRON L. BOER
BRUCE C. McIVER

Human relations training has been slow in reaching police departments. When it has occurred, this kind of training has tended to be of the "sound and fury" variety—for instance, interchange role plays with ghetto youths, or formless and vague "community dialogue" sessions. Human relations training of this type, though it may have some short-term effects in that it tends to boil long submerged emotions to the surface, generates a lot more heat than light. Emotions are raised, but there is rarely an inkling about what to do with them. In many cases this kind of training raises anxieties to such a level that not only is there a tremendous fall-off effect because it is hard to sustain unfocused emotion, but there is also a "walking on eggs" effect created in the participant who must now go back to the street "sensitized" but with nothing in which to wrap his new sensitivity—no techniques, no plan. The discomfort is often articulated as "okay, now you ought to go out there and train all those people", or in some cases, "okay, now you ought to train all the bosses on this job".

Statements such as these are indicative of the difficulty that human relations laboratory training has had in translating itself into on-the-job policing. There are no easy answers to this problem. At least part of the problem lies in the fact that rarely in these "sound and fury" sessions is there anything to translate. They tend to be "pseudo-labs" in which the chrome of, for instance, psychodrama obscures the pointlessness that it encloses. If the only point of these laboratory experiences is for the police officers to have an "intensive experience", then they seem to be not only unworthy of the effort but also positively detrimental.

Reprinted by permission of the *Journal of Police Science and Administration*, Copyright © 1973 by Northwestern University School of Law, Volume I, Number 2.

A real training laboratory—one with a clear direction and behaviorally stated goals—is not so sorely afflicted with the translation problem. Real laboratories do not simply raise emotions and leave them dangling; they attempt to relate them to behavioral changes on the job.

One of the handiest ways of conceiving an effective, efficient laboratory is to think of it as laboratory training in which one creates situations similar to or analogous to real life situations. These situations are slowed down in the laboratory so that the dynamics and details can be examined rigorously and analytically, and all the irrelevant variables separated so as not to cloud the base dynamic of the situation; in other words, the experience is reduced to its essentials and examined in its purest attainable form.

As a rule of thumb against which to check laboratory training, one could well ask:
- Is this experience analogous to real life?
- Is it slowed down so that the pertinent dynamics are apparent?
- Are the nonessential variables separated?

If the answer to any of these questions is "no", then chances are the laboratory training will not be useful.

There is no guarantee that even viable human relations laboratories actually are job related or translatable into on-the-job policing. Unfortunately, a lot more is known about what does not work than what does. Two points, however, are beginning to emerge from the obscurity surrounding this problem, which can be stated as principles of human relations laboratories: 1) there are great benefits for policing to be derived from the human relations laboratories and 2) those benefits can become available to the policing effort *if the translation of those benefits into policing is imbedded into the training design.* The problem of translation is brought up in a laboratory context, subjected to a rigorous problem-solving format, and treated as a human relations problem. In other words, an integral component of any human relations training design must be a problem solving effort in which *the participants* themselves, not the trainers, translate the training into on-the-job effects. Simply saying, "one must be more sensitive to interaction with people, both civilian and bosses" does not work. Asking "how this laboratory training can be applied to problems on the job" can and will work, if the question is asked right, and a sequence of suggested steps is used in answering the questions presented.

Laboratory training in policing is still in its infancy, but some idea of how men are using that experience on the job is beginning to emerge. Laboratory training seems to get translated into work situations in two basic ways, and it may be helpful to think of these as "levels". Level one is the hard edged use of techniques, which means the direct translation of a technique displayed in the laboratory to some aspect of the work environment. Level two is the meta-learning or functional awareness level where values that are focused on and reinforced in the laboratory become part of the participant's work ethic.

Level One: Hard-edge Use of Techniques. In a number of laboratory training intensives conducted in New York City, particular attention was given to consensus decision making, the dynamics of group decisions, the efficacy of group decisions, how resources are used for making decisions under uncertainty conditions, and so on. The specific activities used were of the kind that could be scored on effectiveness. An attempt was made to generate in the laboratory a style of decision making appropriate to the people who would be making similar decisions in the field. For instance, the "NASA Experiment", "Energy International" and "Twelve Angry Men" approaches were used. These approaches are exercises done in small groups with set data and set situations that examine the process of collaborative or consensus decision making.

Toward the end of the laboratory training, the question of how to apply the laboratory training to the job situation was asked. The answer, somewhat surprising to the trainers, was a quite literal translation of the techniques of consensus decision making into a police context. If one wants to generate a description of a perpetrator, then, by laboratory experience, it is necessary to bring the witnesses together in a consensus making group rather than to separate them.

The participants designed an experiment by which the laboratory group could try out its new hypothesis. Early returns suggest that most of the time the group's description is, by score, half again as adequate as any single description and nearly twice as good as the average description. Although there are rules and procedures, as well as legal questions that must be considered in the actual application of the training in the field, in the laboratory an old sacred cow ("always separate your witnesses") was slaughtered *by the participants.*

This is a rather startling example of the hard-edge use of techniques. At this point, however, it should be emphasized that, as persuasive as this demonstration is, and no matter how much "chrome" is used, it is by far the least important of the two levels. It is rare that laboratory training can be translated directly into action. Because the other level, the meta-learning, is more difficult to perceive and talk about, the trainee tends to use the "chrome" and the hard-edge of level one. When the hard edges are not there, the evaluator (usually not a participant) tends to assume that the laboratory had no effect. This is an accusation that laboratory trainers have had to defend since the inception of laboratory training.

Level Two: The Meta-learning, or Functional Awareness. The translation of this kind of learning into the job context is, obviously, much more difficult to assess. However, some examples can illustrate how it works. An investigating officer decides, during the course of his investigation of an armed robbery, to bring the witnesses together in order to arrive at a consensus description of the perpetrator. (Ignore, for a moment, the legal problems of this procedure.) Here the investigating officer has not only made use of a concrete laboratory technique, but has also *recognized his choices* in the situation at hand. Recognition of choices is one of the most important distinctions between the military and professional models of behavior. The recognition that he has choices, that options of behavior are open to him, and that he is obligated not only to take those options seriously, but analytically as well, is called meta-learning, or, if you like, functional awareness. The investigator has the option of choosing the standard operating procedure of separating the witnesses, the new consensus technique learned in the laboratory, or any other mode of behavior that seems appropriate. The important thing is that he thinks analytically about his options. One understands, of course, that policing has always presented the officer with choices, that choosing among options is in the very nature of the incredibly complex job. But policing rules and procedures have steadfastly denied this fact—just by being rules and procedures. Consequently, police officers are not trained to make choices in any systematic, analytical way. Rather, they are trained to pretend choices *do not even exist!* When a police officer recognizes his options and recognizes that he must take his selection seriously, then, in some quasi-conscious way, he has made a role choice as well. Without quite verbalizing it he has elected to define himself in the professional role rather than the military role. In so doing, he has taken on a role very similar to the professional role of group leader. He has, in other words, approached the situation as if it were a laboratory situation.

But meta-learnings are not always so easy to analyze as this hypothetical case. These kinds of learning work themselves out situationally on the job in nuances too delicate to pin down or in development patterns that are too difficult to see at a glance. The professional model is "in the air" in the laboratory; it is part of the ethos, the milieu that a laboratory attempts to generate, and the idea is to keep it "in the air" when on the job.

This kind of learning cannot be planned. Laboratories are set up on the assumption that men *are* professional officers rather than military drones, and a professional model is the presupposition from which all movement in the laboratory begins. On the job, this meta-learning or professional model may work itself out as a dynamic by the recognition of choices and allows for the possibility (not the certainty) of more adequate decisions. It may work itself out as an unfreezing of role expectations or as an acceptance of an analytical cast that allows an attempt to slow down the action of, for example, family dispute, thus separating the independent variables in order to look at the generalizable dynamics. In New York, the Family Crisis Unit, operating under an analytical laboratory assumption concerning family crisis, developed a very concrete set of action steps to use in a dispute. The result was a drastic reduction of the frequency of injuries to police officers investigating family disputes. Here is a case in which the meta-learning generated hard-edge techniques.

Warren Bennis of the National Training Labs has worked out four "meta-goals" or meta-learnings of laboratory training.[1]

- Expanded consciousness and recognition of choices
- A "spirit of inquiry"
- Authenticity in interpersonal relations
- A collaborative conception of the authority relationship

The latter goal, the "collaborative conception of authority" deserves to be further explained. Bennis states:[2]

> ... most important is the realization that the teaching-learning process of laboratory training is a prototype of the collaborative conception of authority. Putting it differently, we can say that learning is accomplished through the requirements of the situation and a joint collaborative venture between the trainer and the participants.

Translating Bennis' formulation directly into the policing context, one could say "... work is accomplished through the requirements of the situation and a joint collaborative venture between the 'boss' and the police officer (or the lieutenant and sergeant and so on through the chain of command)".

When one starts talking about "joint collaborative ventures" and collaborative authority to police officers, they tend to become uneasy. The military model has been *the* model of authority in policing for so long that any suggestion that it may not always be appropriate is met with suspicion. Lately there has been a lot of fresh thinking on the matter in such progressive departments as New York; Cincinnati; Holyoke, Massachusetts; and Syracuse; and language like "team policing," "beat command," and the like have been used. One thing that all of these programs have in common is that they adhere—implicitly

---

[1] Bennis, "Goals and Meta-Goals of Laboratory Training," in Golembiewski and Blumberg (ed.), *Sensitivity Training and the Laboratory Approach* (1970).

[2] *Ibid.*, p. 23.

or explicitly to a collaborative conception of authority. The training laboratory is the prototype of the collaborative conception of authority, and the coming together of team policing and the training laboratory under the umbrella of collaborative authority has tremendous implications for the future of both team policing *and* training laboratories. The two are too congenial not to operate side by side. Some of the parallels are:

- Both coalesce around goals (the requirements of the situation for the police team, the requirements of behavioral objectives for the laboratory.
- Both use "collaboration" as a model.
- Both deny the paramilitary model of command as the most efficient.
- Both deny unilateral decision making as the most efficient.
- Both affirm consensus as the most efficacious model of decision making.
- Both espouse some sort of concept of "openness" and honesty as a component of desirable group or team behavior.
- The team policing concept stresses the importance of seeing the team leader as trainer, while the training group sees the trainer as leader. Leader and trainer are virtually indistinguishable roles in both the training group and the police team.

The point is that it is becoming more and more apparent that the best way to train effective police teams and effective team leaders is to get them first into a training laboratory, and then get them to plan the construction of their teams—collaboratively.

Police departments tend to be large, complex organizations, especially in the cities, and the collaborative model of authority pioneered by police teams and laboratory methods has a whole spectrum of other applications. So versatile is this model that it finds ready application in such diverse branches of policing as anti-crime units, investigation teams, and emergency service squads. The model seems particularly useful to police academy training staffs. In short, collaborative authority would seem appropriate anywhere within the aegis of the policing function where the task at hand, the requirements of the situation, are complex and not susceptible to programmed action and rote learning, and where the number of men involved in that situation is limited to a workable group size.

The transition from the old authoritarian model of authority toward a collaborative model tends to be long, painful, and subject to awkwardness and recidivism. Because of the similarities and because of the quick, intense learning afforded in laboratories, a laboratory experience can speed the process of transition and relieve some of the growing pains. Further, the laboratory can be the scene where a team works out the kind of decision-making model appropriate to its function, and the laboratory can ease the opening of the communications systems necessary to provide the lateral and vertical feedback within the team.

Also from the New York experience, a two-fold expectation from these teams was deduced: one, with a stable geographical assignment, the men in these teams are expected to move toward a better working relationship with the members of the community in those team areas; and two, with an organization stabilized around a single sergeant and a regular group of peers, the team is expected to generate a more efficient working ethos. Whether these expectations will be met remains to be seen, and it is becoming apparent that the question hinges on how well the teams put laboratory training to work to meet these expectations.

At any rate, there is a tendency toward a greater degree of intimacy between the police officer and the community and between the police officer and the supervisor. This greater degree of intimacy brings problems as well as benefits to the men involved, who are, generally speaking, unskilled in the behaviors appropriate to the situation. Inappropriate behaviors are often simply a function of misunderstood motives or an unclear perception of the dynamics involved in a social transaction. In team policing, these transactions run the gamut from family dispute investigations, through riot situations; and these transactions frutifully can be explored in the human relations laboratory.

If it is true that neighborhood police teams bring a more collaborative law enforcement effort between the community and the police officer, then it would seem that the police officer's relationship with the community would be analogous to his sergeant's relationship with him. And the sergeant's relationship with the police officer is analogous to the trainer's relationship with the training group. It would not be stretching the point, it is believed, to conceive that one of the goals of laboratory training is to make a team police officer capable of a modicum of behavior appropriate to the trainer's professional behavior.

Therefore, although a very strong case can be made for laboratory training—particularly for team policing—there remains much apprehension about it at all ranks. The easiest of these objections to deal with are the purely pragmatic considerations. Early experience in the New York City project indicates the difficulty of integrating laboratory training into the on-going police team operations. Work charts and scheduling problems are the largest hindering factors, along with the chronic manpower shortage. This means that training must be telescoped so that training and normal coverage occur concurrently. One way to accomplish this telescoping is to make arrangements so that the data used in the laboratory is generated in the field. The greatest asset here is a sympathetic planning officer who can be responsible for rotating men on a consistent basis and at the same time deploy his remaining men so that coverage is adequate. Though scheduling and shortage problems can be met with a modicum of success, there remains a great need for the development of a methodology by which the laboratory can telescope even more into its alloted time. One wants the laboratory to do as many things as possible (without overloading the circuits) and simultaneously relate the laboratory training to field operations as closely as possible. The surface has only been scratched here.

A more basic objection that was feared in the early attempt to set up laboratory training was the notion that a police officer, as a personality type, would be resistant to this kind of "groupy" training, seeing it as "instant sociology", "a setup to make him look foolish", "too much like social work, and not job related", and a luxury "police cannot afford" in these days of spiraling crime rates. This notion, it now appears, has no substance. After doing a number of laboratory intensives, it became clear that officers will indeed not only accept, but welcome laboratory training. The evaluations of the program given at the end of each week-long session indicate enthusiastic response to both content and presentation of the laboratories. Further, the evaluations, in almost all cases, state a commitment to "transfer" the learning from the laboratory into the field situation, and a concomitant commitment to promote collaborative models wherever appropriate.

This suggests that there are two variables that tend to produce such a heartening response: one, that laboratory training is such a distinct departure from routine police training that the novelty and excitement of being part of something new had an effect of the evaluations; or two, that men see the applicability of laboratory training and the collaborative model in their own operations and that applicability is its own reward. If the latter is true, then laboratory training can be a successful program. Probably the truth lies somewhere in between. The point, however, is that acceptance of laboratory training did not become as large a problem as was predicted.

In New York, at least, the door is beginning to open. It would be presumptuous to predict the long-range effect and the future of this kind of training. It is suspected that there will be more laboratory training time allotted all over the country, especially as the techniques and methodologies begin to build toward their potential and a momentum is generated. It seems apparent that the challenge that faces team policing and laboratory training in the near future is to pool the techniques and resources in all of the related training programs, and forge from the collective experience a viable methodology to confront the requirements of laboratory training and the collaborative style of policing and authority that is beginning to emerge in the United States.

ABOUT THE AUTHORS: *Mr. Boer (deceased) received his Bachelor of Arts from Macalester College and his Master of Arts in English from the State University of New York at Stony Brook.*

Previously he worked as Director of Research and Curriculum Development in the State University of New York's Wyandanch Project in the use of group process and non-lecture techniques in dealing with the problems of minorities in the education system.

Mr. McIver graduated with a Bachelor of Science from Columbia University in New York City.

He previously worked as an assistant to the director of the Correctional Management Training Program administered by the National Council of Crime and Delinquency. Mr. McIver has also worked in the training of volunteers for the Domestic Peace Corps.

Mr. McIver is currently, as was Mr. Boer previously, a consultant to the New York City Police Department's Neighborhood Police Team Training Program.

A look at human relations training
for police organizations.

Sensitivity Training and the Police

DONALD BIMSTEIN

The Problem

Today, the forces of law enforcement in this country have reached a crisis point in their relationships with the communities in which they operate. The newspapers are filled with front page stories of police battles with organized groups comprising substantial numbers of the population of this country. Violent physical confrontations are taking place throughout our nation, with angry epithets being hurled by both sides. The erosion of respect for the forces of law and order can be noted by the derogatory terms now being used by various groups to denote minions of the law. Many a police officer, when off duty, is reluctant to reveal his vocation to other members of the community because withdrawal by the other persons often results from such revelation. Although there has recently been a slight rise in the esteem accorded the police by many of the more substantial members of the community, it is often fear for their personal safety and the safety of their property which causes these members to turn to the police as allies. Accordingly, salaries are being raised and strong recruitment drives are being launched in order to obtain protection from the lawlessness that is so rampant in this nation.

The economic and social ills of this country are many, and into this cauldron of seething emotions on both sides, the police are thrust to act as buffers and barriers to physical violence. Being unable to satisfy either side without offending the other, the police usually end up receiving abuse from both. It is an unhappy situation for the individual members of the many police departments in the United States. Since they are physically present at the scenes of demonstrations and prevent groups from doing things they feel they are entitled to do,

---

From "Sensitivity Training and the Police," by Donald Bimstein, from POLICE courtesy of Charles C Thomas, Springfield, Illinois.

the pent-up frustrations and anger from the condition against which these groups are demonstrating are often transferred to be vented against the police.[1] The police officers, in turn, reacting in anger against the physical and oral abuse to which they are subjected, sometimes lose control of their emotions and respond in kind. They become emotionally involved, and the confrontations turn into a vendetta of "Them against us." This results in further polarization between groups and a hardening of the mistrust and suspicion felt by all members of the aggrieved population. Also, few police officers are consciously aware of their scapegoat role as recipients of the frustrated anger felt by many members of the ghetto area against the wrongs of society. Thus, it is difficult for them to understand why, in those neighborhoods, resentment and open hostility greet even minor police actions taken during routine patrol. The police, in turn, respond with resentment of their own, and an unhappy, uneasy atmosphere of wary hostility prevails in those areas.[2] It often feeds upon itself and, through constant aggravation in daily contacts, builds up to a festering climax completely out of proportion to the basic causes. Minor incidents of little importance in themselves heighten the tension and solidify the antagonisms felt on both sides. Eruptions occur frequently, and the resulting violence increases the schism.

Compounding these difficulties are the problems of the built-up prejudices that all officers bring with them when they are sworn into office. They are human beings like everyone else and do not, by the mere donning of a uniform, shed all the prejudices that have come to be a part of their daily lives. These are of all kinds and encompass every race, religion, social condition, and other aspects of the social environment. Although instructed in the need for impartiality in the daily performance of their duty, and bound by the rules and regulations of their departments to so comport themselves, it is a difficult task they are called upon to perform. They are required to repress their prejudices during their hours of duty but are free to express them during the rest of the day. Since these feelings have not been eradicated, the mere denial of the right to express them while on duty does not alter the inner reaction of the individual officer and often unconsciously affects his performance. This, in turn, causes resentment on the part of the members of the community against whom this prejudice is directed. Since there are several hundred thousand police officers in the United States there isn't a group in the country against whom some officer does not have a blind aversion. Thus, it is very readily

---

[1] Edwards, George: *The Police on the Urban Frontier*. New York, Institute of Human Relations Press, 1968, p. 23.

[2] *Ibid.*, p. 24.

apparent that it is a potent source of disruption to harmonious relations between the police and the public.

By the very nature of the police officer's job there arises many occasions in the course of the day when he is required to take some action of a repressive nature against some members of the community. It is in this area that personality conflicts very often arise, and what would ordinarily be a routine encounter escalates into a violent verbal or physical confrontation. It is also in this area that the vast majority of the illwill is engendered among the respectable, law abiding segment of the population. It is not caused by what is done, but rather the manner in which it is done.

These are some of the problems that confront the conscientious administrators of police departments today. Public alienation has escalated to the point that it demands immediate and drastic steps to remedy it. The purpose of this paper is to point out a possible path of action.

Standard Solutions

The top administrative echelon of the various police departments across the nation are well aware of the deleterious consequences that can accompany continued erosion of public cooperation and respect. They have taken strong, positive steps to seek out the basic causes of conflict and win back the support of the American public. Today it is a rare department which does not have a program in effect to accomplish this end. However, the intensiveness and the scope of the programs vary with the different departments.

Some departments, seeking to get at the root of the conflict, have been attempting to eliminate potential causes of conflict with the public by screening applicants for the department on the basis of their emotional stability. By rejecting those of unsuitable temperament, it is hoped that the incidence of clashes with the police due mainly to personality differences can be decreased. To that end, psychological testing has been employed in pre-entrance examinations to weed out the unfit. Standardized tests for police personnel are now available which delve into this area. One such test, the "TAV Selection System," seeks to test the personal makeup of the applicant by exploring several aspects of his personality.[3]

After entrance, many departments have incorporated intensive programs in human relations into their recruit training courses. Coupled with this has been a heavy emphasis on the importance of good community relations if the department is to function effectively. One

---

[3]Hankey, Richard O., *et al.*: Evaluating patrolman performance. *Police Chief*, January, 1967, p. 23.

big city department, New York, utilized the facilities of a local Educational Television Station to broadcast a training program to the members of the force stationed in different precincts throughout the city. This program, which could be viewed by the general public, demonstrated practical situations in human relations and community relations and how best to deal with them.[4] To date, most training in these areas for members of the departments has consisted of standard type lecture or discussion sessions conducted by department officials or guest lecturers. Heavy reliance has been placed on showing, telling, or demonstrating. Some departments have gone beyond this into areas which will be discussed later on. It is the contention of this paper that the utilization of new innovative methodology is required if meaningful learning and attitude change is to be brought about.

To further enhance the police image in the public eye, some departments have turned to the area of public relations. Many in the field, as well as leading criminologists, are of the belief that if a good public relations program is established early and promoted vigorously over the years, then community relations would not present a problem.[5]

Another area that is being promoted very vigorously by many police agencies is that of police-community relations. Most such programs attempt to establish channels of communication with the community by initiating a two-way dialogue wherein mutual understanding can take place between members of the community and the police.[6] In this manner problems can be brought out in the open, explored and analyzed with respect to the community desires and the police department's capabilities. Precinct community councils have been established whose purpose is to involve the residents of an area in the local community problems. They promote among the citizens an awareness of the limitations of the powers the police possess and their inability to accomplish all that the people wish. In addition, they help to point up the responsibilities of the citizens in the maintenance of peace in the community. They also act as a channel to make known to the police the grievances the people feel so that some positive action can be taken in time to prevent little shortcomings from growing into major divisive factors. Open meetings are held to which all are invited to attend and voice their complaints and have them resolved. From

---

[4]Hamilton, Lander C.: Some functions of a police community relations program, *Police*, Vol. 14, 3:74, Jan.-Feb., 1970.

[5]Moore, Charles E., Jr.: Public relations: Public responsibility, *Police Chief*, March, 1967, p. 14.

[6]Brown, Lee P.: Dynamic police-community relations at work. *Police Chief*, April, 1968, p. 46.

this public interchange of ideas both sides receive a greater insight into the problems of the other.

Along similar lines are the programs initiated by some departments to involve the police officers and the community residents in mutual projects in all areas of community life. Working together, visiting together on each other's home ground, meeting each other as people rather than under impersonal official circumstances has the salutary effect of cementing relations and achieving friendly acceptance as individuals. This usually results in a beneficial improvement of the atmosphere for enforcement.

Up to now I have listed the more conventional methods being employed today for improving relations. I should like to stop at this point and consider the area of human relations set forth in the title of this article.

Sensitivity Training

What is "sensitivity training?" To many the name is strange and, since it is a relatively new concept, most people have an unclear idea of just what it means. Thus, I should like to explain what it is before considering the advantages that can accrue from its utilization.

To begin with, its basic unit is the small group. A small group has been defined as "a number of persons engaged in interaction with one another in a face to face meeting or a series of such metings in which each member receives some impression or perception of each other member distinct enough so that he can give some reaction to each of the others as an individual person."[7] It utilizes the psychological finding that whenever two or more people are gathered in a social situation sooner or later one of them will feel impelled to say something or at least react to the others.[8]

The basic idea is to conduct intensive human-relations training under "laboratory" conditions for a sufficient time for results to be meaningful. Most authorities date the start of this idea as 1947 when the National Training Laboratories (then known as the National Training Laboratory in Group Development) conducted the first such session at Bethel, Maine. Although the National Training Laboratories conducted several other such laboratory sessions in subsequent years, it was not until the early fifties that similar laboratories were conducted by others.[9]

---

[7]Hopkins, Terence K.: *The Exercise of Influence in Small Groups,* New York, Bedminster, 1964, p. 15.

[8]Berne, Eric: *Games People Play.* New York, Grove Press, 1961, p. 29.

[9]Bradford, Leland P., Gibb, Jack R., and Benne, Kenneth D.: *T-Group Theory and Laboratory Method.* New York, Wiley, 1961, p. 3.

The usual size of a group involved in a training laboratory is from six to twelve persons who usually meet in a temporary residential setting removed from everyday activities for a period ranging anywhere from three days to four weeks. The term most commonly applied to this group is *T-Group* with the "T" standing for training. It is comprehensively applied to groups of many types of composition, though the use of the term "encounter group" is currently in favor on the west coast to denote groups which are specifically seeking individual growth and development. However, the term "sensitivity training groups" is broadly used to encompass both groups.[10]

The participants conduct their sessions under the supervison of a trainer who is a member of the staff and who usually has a social science background and special training in the methodology of conducting these gatherings. Many are psychologists or sociologists who have made a study of this field. However, even though there is a trainer, his function is not to lead or direct the group. There is no pre-set schedule to follow nor outlined course of action. The setting is completely unstructured and whatever does arise is the result of the feelings and reactions engendered by the interaction of the group members. The trainer's role is merely to render procedural help or offer an occasional interpretive commentary or brief analysis of something which has surfaced during the course of the session.[11] The atmosphere is completely permissive and all are encouraged to put aside restrictive conventions, rigid formalities and polite niceties, and to relax completely into any mode of behavior that to them is most comfortable and natural. The honest expression of their feelings is the goal, and each is encouraged to express what he feels and thinks so that the other members of the group might better understand him as a person. There is no way of knowing at the start of the session what subject matter will be discussed. Usually, until a group rapport is established and a mutual sense of trust is created, meaningful group intercommunication is inhibited. Thus, strong effort is made to achieve this sense of group solidarity, the feeling of belonging, the enhanced concern for each other's welfare.

The above bears a striking resemblance to group therapy and it does contain elements of it. But there is one very important difference. In the T-Group we are dealing with normally adjusted people who are merely seeking to learn more about themselves in their relationships

---

[10]Schutz, William C.: *Joy-Expanding Human Awareness.* New York, Grove, 1967, pp. 21-22.

[11]Weschsler, Irving R., (Ed.): *Issues in Human Relations Training.* Washington, D.C.: National Training Laboratories, 1962, p. 5.

to others rather than mentally ill people who are trying to find the causes of their ailments.[12]

How do these groups function? Usually the members and the trainer sit in a circle so that every one has a clear view of every one else, and face to face conversations are possible for all. Any member can initiate a discussion on any topic that interests him, but idle conversation is discouraged. During the discussion which ensues, each member of the group is vitally interested in helping every other member understand just how he sounds and comes across to other people. If a member has some irritating mannerism, it is the function of the other members to acquaint him with this. If any other facet of his personality has a tendency to irritate or arouse antagonistic feelings in any of the group members, those members are supposed to state openly this negative reaction. This process whereby the group acts as a sounding board for each of its members by openly verbalizing negative or positive reactions is called "feedback." Meaningful feedback is best achieved when the group arrives at a point where group unity, a sense of belonging, and a mutual feeling of respect and trust have arisen within the group. It is not as easy to accept criticism or suggestions from those with whom a relationship is distant or casual as it is from one who is close. Conversely, it is much easier to be frank and express one's true feelings and reactions when the recipient is one with whom a very close relationship has been established. Then there no longer is the fear that the recipient will misinterpret the motives or resent the language. Freed from these inhibiting restrictions it is much easier to express what is in the heart. It is in this frank, open atmosphere that each can learn about himself, the reaction he produces in others, and can pinpoint those flaws which interfere with proper communication and interaction with other members of society.[13] He can then experiment with behavioral changes designed to overcome the shortcomings pointed out to him, or to reinforce those aspects which have produced a positive effect. Secure in the bosom of his little group he is free to make mistakes and make alterations based on the group feedback that is a constant part of the progress. During this interplay each member develops a greater insight into himself, his motivations, his prejudices, his ideas.[14] Through this experience he builds up a sensitivity toward himself and the feelings of others. Listening to the others pouring out their thoughts and fears he becomes

---

[12]Bradford, *op. cit.*, p. 2.

[13]*Ibid.*, p. 2

[14]Weschler, *op. cit.*, p. 16.

increasingly aware of and concerned for the needs of others. This cannot help but have a beneficial effect on his ability to accomplish the highly complex process of truly communicating with others. To really get an idea or thought across to another person it is necessary to consider it from the other person's point of view, and to sense what his interpretation of the meaning of the expressed thought will be. This entails the necessity of a feeling of empathy and concern for the other person if a proper understanding is to be reached. This is especially true in situations which are highly emotional, and strong feelings are involved on both sides. Unless this concern for the other person's frame of reference is present, no meaningful communication will result.[15] This is especially important for the law enforcement officer whose daily work brings him in contact with people of completely different socioeconomic backgrounds from his own. It is a barrier of which he must be aware and which he must overcome if respect and ungrudging compliance is to be obtained.

The composition of the membership of the groups involved in the training session can vary greatly depending on the objectives desired. Although, usually, there is some degree of homogeneity or similarity in some aspect of the group's membership, excellent results have also been obtained from training sessions wherein the membership was composed of representatives from different cultural and ethnic backgrounds. The purpose of these sessions is to improve the relationships and close the gap between the groups involved by exposing them to each other in a situation where intimate intensive personal interplay can afford each the opportunity to rid himself of stereotyped prejudices and see the other person for the human being that he is. The rapport that is established allows for the better understanding of the other's views and why he holds them. A report evaluating such type of training laboratory states, "Experience indicates that such a laboratory experience, short as it is, may do more to bring about realistic understanding of similarities and differences among groups than a year or more spent in formal campus or work situations."[16]

One method of achieving such a result is by the use of dyads or the pairing of two members of the group. In longer workshops the group members are placed in dyads early in the training session and requested to meet together for a specified length of time each day. No matter how uncomfortable the relationship may be, they are requested to continue it. Often a quicker rapport is reached through

---

[15]Rogers, Carl R.: *On Becoming a Person.* Boston, Houghton, 1961, p. 331.
[16]Bradford, *op. cit.*, p. 21.

this intimate relationship than would be possible at sessions of the entire group.[17]

Another technique sometimes used is called "doubling." Under this procedure a person is selected to stand behind one of the other group members and try to project himself into the other's thoughts. From time to time he reports how he thinks the other person feels.[18]

There are values other than those discussed to be derived from sensitivity training, and there are other purposes for the training sessions, but in this brief summary I have considered only those that would be of primary importance to the police officer. The concept of sensitivity training has been tested in the crucible of time and its success has been such that its acceptance has been worldwide.

Suggested Course of Action

As it must be obvious by now, the purpose of this paper is to suggest that the law enforcement agencies in this country incorporate the use of sensitivity training in their programs for bettering their relations with the public. It is not such a radically new proposal, since at this very moment within the community relations programs of many departments elements of sensitivity training are already taking place. Thinking administrators in the police field are well aware of the need to resolve conflicts by involving the public itself in the program. Thus constant meetings are taking place where, in face to face confrontation, all sides gather to listen to each other, hear the other's side and make suggestions for improving relations. This involves give and take and a need to alter procedures and behavior in consonance with the suggestions advanced. Community irritations are revealed and, in often times heated exchanges, specific shortcomings on both sides are pointed out. Sometimes these proceedings even evoke personal interchanges which lay bare the personality shortcomings of the participants. This is all good and provides the information and feedback which the enforcement agencies so vitally need to formulate corrective measures.[19]

Within the departments themselves, as I have previously indicated, intensive human relations training is the order of the day. An attempt is made to get the officers to see and understand better the groups with whom they come in contact in their official capacity.

The Houston Police Department, for example, has set up a series

---

[17]Schutz, *op. cit.*, pp. 77-78.

[18]*Ibid.*, p. 61.

[19]*Police-Community Relations in St. Louis.* New York, National Conference of Christians and Jews, 1966, p. 7.

of human relations training laboratories wherein, eventually, every member of the force will be involved in small group interaction programs with members of the community they are serving. The goal is to study and bring about changes in the stereotyped views each has of the other.[20]

In setting up a similar program for the Grand Rapids (Michigan) Police Department, the men chosen to implement the program and act as trainers for the other members of the department participated in a three-day residential T-Group session as part of their preparation.[21]

One organization which has been very active in this field is the National Conference of Christians and Jews. Among the many institutes it sponsors at colleges throughout the country is the National Institute on Police and Community Relations at Michigan State University, which is an annual event. It also takes an active role in helping local police departments formulate and conduct recruit and in-service community relations training programs. Today there are many such organizations, groups, agencies, and police departments working together under the combined banner of community relations and human relations whose activities fringe on the area of sensitivity training. My thesis is that the police departments should take the next logical step and plunge whole-heartedly into the process itself. It is fine to conduct departmental programs covering human relations, but merely telling or explaining can never carry the impact exerted by experiencing. Many police organizations have strict rules and regulations against the employment of racial slurs or epithets and some even go so far as to issue lists of words that are not to be used. But it is not until the officer knows at first hand what it is like to be on the receiving end that the program will accomplish meaningful results. One result a true sensitivity laboratory training session can help to bring about is that an officer will develop an empathy for the people with whom he deals during his working hours. It will be a rare officer who can emerge from these sessions unchanged in any way. At the very least he will become conscious of the fact that his personal behavior can stand improvement. At its very best the end product will be a more efficient officer who will be constantly garnering goodwill for the department and enhancing its prestige. Since the majority of the

---

[20]Bell, Robert L., *et al.:* Small group dialogue and discussion: An approach to police-community relationships. *J. Criminal Law, Criminology and Police Science,* June, 1969, p. 242.

[21]Allen, Robert F., Pilnick, Saul, and Silverzweig, Stanley: Conflict resolution—Team building for police and ghetto residents. *J. Criminal Law, Criminology and Police Science,* June, 1969, p. 254.

public contacts are non-criminal in nature, any monies spent in preparing the members of the force for their daily activities in this area will be returned a thousandfold in the increased cooperation and respect, and the lessening of tensions. The amount of time and manpower needed now to carry on community relations programs will be appreciably reduced since many of the problems necessitating such programs will be eliminated.

I realize that the logistics of implementing a program of this nature will be a problem in a large department. However, by confining it initially to line officers and only those staff officers who deal with the public it can be kept to manageable proportions. A valuable tool is available. The police of this nation owe it to the public they serve to make use of it.

ABOUT THE AUTHOR: *Donald Bimstein is a former member of the New York City Police Department from which he retired after twenty years of service. For several of those years he was assigned to the Police Academy as an Instructor and, as such, participated in every area of recruit, in-service, specialized, and refresher training.*

At present, he is an Associate Professor in the Police Science Program of the Northern Virginia Community College where he has been teaching for the past five years. He has a Bachelor of Social Science degree from City University of New York and is currently completing a Master's program at George Washington University in the field of Adult Education and Training.

New interdisciplinary programs are needed to train specific types of criminal justice personnel.

Training Programs for Treatment Specialists in Corrections: A University-Based Model

ALBERT R. ROBERTS

What types of courses and workshops need to be specially planned and implemented in order to fill the international void of education and training programs for correctional educators and counselors? What are the personal and academic attributes of the most successful correctional educator and counselor? Are these attributes any different from those needed by any other effective teacher or counselor? What kinds of knowledge and skills should pre-service and in-service training of correctional educators and counselors impart? These are just a few of the important issues facing the select group who are concerned with educating and training the correctional educator and/or counselor.

This article intends to serve as the resource and program catalyst needed to fill the information gaps recognized by (1) university faculty members who are planning educational programs (pre-service and in-service) for correctional treatment specialists, and (2) students and practitioners who are interested in participating in the program which best meets their individual educational needs and aspirations.

The recent developments in a small number of undergraduate and graduate criminal justice programs have begun to focus on filling the extensive manpower shortages of trained specialists in corrections. This newly-developed interest in criminal justice programs grew out of a two-fold root—the increased dissatisfaction of a number of correctional administrators with traditional practices, combined with

---

From *Public Personnel Management,* March-April 1974, pp. 149-154. Reprinted by permission of the International Personnel Management Association.

the universities' growing wish to take an active stance in the field of corrections.[1]

There has been a decline recently in enrollments at private colleges and universities throughout the United States. But in contrast to this trend, criminal justice education programs (most of which are located at public institutions of higher education) are experiencing continued increases and unprecedented growth in their student enrollments. This increase provides the basis for the hiring of additional faculty, and the expansion of program offerings to meet existing and future needs. The new types of interdisciplinary correctional training opportunities recommended in this article are essential to meet the personnel needs of corrections.

Education and Training

Specialized education and training in criminal justice is necessary to provide increased insight-producing experiences, knowledge, and skills to enable the correctional treatment practitioners to be effective change agents in the rehabilitation process.

Correctional Educators and Counselors

To operate effective correctional treatment programs, careful consideration should be given to the best ways of recruiting and selecting competent job applicants, as well as to training and motivating teachers and counselors to upgrade their skills.

The correctional teacher, counselor, caseworker, or classification officer must understand the needs of each offender. The problems which are related to the needs of convicted felons can be identified as follows: lack of self-confidence in one's ability to learn; unwillingness to work toward long range goals; need for immediate gratification; insufficient knowledge of where the community and institutional resources for seeking help are located; lack of family and interpersonal relationships; lack of job training and unstable work history; obstacles caused by past memories and criminal associates; and conflicting orientations between custodial and administrative personnel and counselors/teachers.

The competent teacher's primary concern must be the student. This teacher must have the ability to improve the inmates' self-confidence. The teacher as a person needs to be basically people-oriented, displaying a sensitivity, understanding, and acceptance of students from disadvantaged environments. He or she must be highly

---

[1]Elmer H. Johnson, "Personnel Problems of Corrections and the Potential Contribution of Universities," *Federal Probation* (December, 1967), p. 57.

perceptive, a good listener, a quick thinker, and a capable innovator, with a diverse array of teaching methods and strategies readily at hand in the exploratory correctional setting.

The correctional counselor or caseworker should also be people-oriented, sensitive and understanding of the inmates' attitudes and hostilities, and capable of establishing rapport with his or her clients. Active involvement is a prerequisite to real understanding. However, inmates do not usually want sympathy; they are searching for an honest and supportive relationship geared to understanding their own personal feelings and goals. As a treatment specialist, it is all too easy for a counselor or teacher to become overly involved. A critical eye is needed to distinguish between and be aware of that fine line between offering objective assistance, and reacting on an emotional level. The teacher, counselor, or caseworker does not do something *to* the inmate, but *with* the inmate; then together through cooperative problem-solving efforts, the inmate will grow as a person, learning to cope with and to solve his or her own problems. The teacher, counselor, or caseworker with this rare combination of qualities will encounter great success in establishing the necessary rapport with the offender.

A relatively small number of persons have had experience teaching or counseling prisoners. Those teachers and counselors known as correctional educators and counselors, have not, for the most part, had the opportunity to be given any special preparation for their job. In the past, correctional specialists have learned by trial and error. Thus, the need for pre-service training and education is self-evident.

Training Corrections Staffers[2]

There is presently a scarcity of qualified correctional teachers and counselors to meet the needs of inmate populations. Education and training opportunities therefore must be developed *now* to provide the necessary specialists to treat future inmate populations. According to the *Task Force Report on Corrections* (1967) of the President's Commission on Law Enforcement and Administration of Justice, it is estimated that the average daily inmate population under correctional supervision in the United States will *increase* in the period from 1970 to 1975 *by over 300,000* to a projected 1.84 million.

The 1968 survey on correctional personnel conducted by Louis Harris and Associates gave evidence of the shortage of treatment specialists in corrections. It was reported that there are 5,359 correctional educators and 4,638 counselors out of a total of over 75,000

---

[2]Parts of this section were adapted from Albert R. Roberts, "Introduction to Section III," *Readings in Prison Education* (Springfield, Illinois: Charles C Thomas, 1972).

persons employed by juvenile and adult institutions.[3] This small number of treatment specialists is given the task of providing special treatment services for over 400,000 inmates in state and federal juvenile and adult institutions.[4] Comprehensive surveys must be connected with the full cooperation of each correctional agency before a more accurate picture of the obvious shortage of correctional treatment staff is obtained.

Pre-Service Training

Pre-service training should be required for all beginning teachers and counselors in correctional facilities. This training could be part of an undergraduate or graduate major in a state certified program leading to a degree, or a special orientation workshop of several weeks to several months' duration.

The educator as well as the classification counselor, social worker, psychologist, employment counselor, parole agent—in fact, the whole treatment team in corrections—would benefit from recognition by correctional agencies of the importance of university-based training. Peter P. Lejins has emphasized the need for college or university trained personnel in corrections:

> Correction, as one of the major contemporary methods of dealing with crime and delinquency, broadly means the removal of the causes, reasons, motivations or factors that are responsible for the criminal or delinquent behavior. Thus correction can be properly identified as behavior modification. In line with the prevailing conceptions in our modern society about behavior modifying practices and in the setting of our contemporary educational systems, it is quite apparent that the proper educational base for personnel involved in correction is a college or university-level education.[5]

The corrections curriculum should include training in the types of methods and materials applicable to inmate populations. Intensive pre-service training should provide the new correctional educator or counselor with a number of skills. Of paramount importance is the

---

[3]See unpublished data from *Joint Commission on Correctional Manpower and Training* (Washington, D.C.: Louis Harris and Associates, 1968). See also: *The Challenge of Crime in a Free Society*, A Report by the President's Commission on Law Enforcement and Administration of Justice; (Washington, D.C.: U.S. Government Printing Office, 1967).

[4]"The National Profile of Correction," *Crime and Delinquency*, adapted from the President's Commission Survey: *Correction in the United States*, (January 1967), pp. 229-260.

[5]Peter P. Lejins, "Content of the Curriculum and its Relevance for Correctional Practice," *Criminology and Corrections Programs: A Study of the Issues*. (Washington, D.C.: Joint Commission on Correctional Manpower and Training, July, 1968), p. 28.

growth of human relations skills for understanding, establishing rapport, and motivating inmates; also important is knowledge of grouping techniques, audiovisual aids, and information about institutional and community resources.

Teachers and counselors in corrections need the same skills as any successful teacher/counselor, but they need these skills to a more intense degree. In addition to relevant methods courses, they need courses in all phases of (1) English and speech; (2) learning theory; (3) education, and its measurement and evaluation; (4) human development; (5) counseling psychology; (6) group dynamics; (7) abnormal psychology; (8) etiology, treatment, and prevention of crime and delinquency; (9) race and ethnic relations; (10) urban sociology; (11) community services and resources; (12) sociology of deviant behavior; and lots of expertise in the particular field(s) in which they are to be teaching or counseling.

Field trips, practicum experiences, and student teaching in correctional facilities should be considered an essential part of pre-service training. Field trips can complement classwork by giving students an opportunity to observe firsthand what they have been studying about and discussing in class. These trips help the student to build upon the facts he or she has gleaned from lectures and published material, and they also can foster increased awareness about day-to-day problems encountered in correctional programs. Field trips can assist students in making more realistic requests for practicum-based assignments which interest them as preparation for specific careers in corrections. In addition, the students who pose provocative questions during field trips can serve to stimulate the thoughts of correctional administrators toward new program experimentation. Practicum and internship differential experiences should include practice teaching or group counseling in juvenile, adult felon, and county institutions, individual counseling or tutorial work with confined offenders, and attendance at and participation in interdisciplinary staff conferences at residential settings. A competent corrections teacher or counselor needs to encounter these experiences through a variety of pre-service and in-service internships in areas such as a mental hospital, a rehabilitation hospital, a residential setting for emotionally disturbed youths, a community-based correctional facility, a probation department, an inner city adult education program, as well as a maximum-security correctional facility.

In-Service Training

Internships and field placements are important to the integration of theory and practice for students. As Vernon Fox says about those enrolled in his program at Florida State University:

> ...the student is required to do enough thinking and reporting in written assignments concerning his internship so that his professors are sure that he does not view the classroom and the field of practice as two unrelated experiences.
>
> Internships in criminology and corrections have been served throughout the United States, in Canada, and in the Panama Canal Zone. Candidates for the Master of Social Work degree, with emphasis in corrections, have had field placements in probation departments in New York City, the Juvenile Court in Tampa, the Federal Correctional Institution at Tallahassee, and the Dozier School for Boys at Marianna.[6]

In order to recruit competent students for careers in all areas of correctional work, including teaching and counseling, these needs must be met:

(1) Provisions must be made for internships, part-time jobs, and for volunteer work opportunities for students during the academic year and summer employment in correctional agencies.

(2) Financial assistance in the form of stipends, tuition grants, and traineeships for pre-service students must be available as well as educational leaves of absence of one to three years (undergraduate and graduate work) with full salary and/or fellowship aid for in-service workers.

(3) There must be improved pay scales and merit systems with entry specifications and examinations that reflect requirements for college and university coursework. Personnel administrators must change the nonprofessional policies which have been in existence for many years. They should begin by allocating lots in corrections which require specific education and training, such as a position for the man who has two years of teaching or counseling experience and a master's degree in adult education, correctional education, guidance and counseling, social work, special education, or urban education.

(4) Depending upon the job they are performing correctional teachers and counselors should be given the same opportunities as public school teachers and college-level instructors. Most corrections people work a twelve-month school year with only a two-week vacation, yet their salaries are usually lower than those of the public school teacher and guidance counselor who works ten months.

Lack of Available Programs

Most of the courses mentioned are given at the major universities in the United States in such departments as adult education, criminology

---

[6]Vernon Fox, "Universities and the Field of Practice in Corrections," *Criminology and Corrections Programs: A Study of the Issues, op. cit.,* pp. 59-60.

and corrections, counseling psychology, education, guidance and counseling, public administration, social work, sociology, and special education. However, only a small number of colleges and universities have pulled together their departmental resources and implemented the multidisciplinary approach needed by those individuals who have chosen the correctional profession as their life's work.

In the first comprehensive textbook on inmate education, *Sourcebook on Prison Education: Past, Present, and Future* (1971), Albert R. Roberts has commented on the dearth of educational opportunities available to correctional educators and counselors:

> In the United States and Canada, education and corrections have yet to collaborate to any extensive degree. Very few educators have been exposed during their education and training to the internal parts of correctional institutions and the associated educational problems of the individuals who live and work within them. Higher education programs in state and private universities and colleges for teachers, counselors, and educational administrators have in a few rare instances included involvement in the educational treatment, staff training, and research needs of the field of corrections.[7]

Under grants from the U.S. Office of Education, teacher corps programs have been developed at Fordham University and Montclair State College. These graduate programs combine coursework with internships in urban and prison schools. The National Teacher Corps students take part in special internships which have been designed to provide meaningful work experiences for the corpsmen in inner city schools and the community, and in several cases, in prison schools. These corpsmen are exposed to teaching through such experiences as tutoring, teaching small reading and arithmetic groups, constructing materials, counseling, and by engaging in before- and after-school educational experiences for children and youths. The corpsmen work with federally funded agencies such as the Neighborhood Youth Corps, Basic Skills Program, and Operation Outreach. They work with local action councils and parents in the community. These programs' main thrust is to train educators for urban schools; their involvement in prison schools has only recently emerged.

The departments, institutes, and programs in criminology and corrections at the following universities have offered a sequence of courses on the etiology, treatment, and prevention of crime and delinquency.

---

[7] Albert R. Roberts, *Sourcebook on Prison Education: Past, Present, and Future.* (Springfield, Illinois: Charles C Thomas, 1971), p. xiii.

American University	San Francisco State College
Anderson College	San Jose State College
Auburn University	Southern Illinois University
Ball State University	State University of New York at Albany
Bowling Green University	Trenton State College
California State College, Long Beach	University of Arizona
Chico State College	University of California, Berkeley
Coppin State College	University of Colorado
Flordia State University	University of Georgia
Fresno State University	University of Illinois
Indiana State University	University of Iowa
Indiana University of Pennsylvania	University of Kentucky
Iowa State University	University of Maryland
John Jay College	University of Minnesota
Kent State University	University of Pennsylvania
Michigan State University	University of South Carolina
New York University	University of Southern California
Northern Illinois University	University of Tennessee
North Texas State University	University of Toledo
Pennsylvania State University	University of Utah
Pepperdine College	University of Washington
Sacramento State College	Utah State University
Sam Houston State Teachers College	Valdosta State University
San Diego State College	Washington State University

This list of colleges and universities offering degree programs with concentration in criminology and corrections is complete at the time of writing. It is hoped that new institutes and departments will be developed each year.

Students in degree programs at these institutions study the kinds of issues and problems that constitute the subject matter of criminology. Many of these programs include courses which examine the following:

(1) Etiology (theory and research on causation) of criminal and delinquent behavior.
(2) Establishing the fact of crime (police, courts, etc.).
(3) Research and theory on the punitive, institutional, and community treatment and management of the offender.
(4) Prevention—elimination of the causes of criminal behavior (punitive, mechanical, and corrective prevention).

Conclusion

For the important years ahead this author is recommending the continued growth of these programs, and the development of new interdisciplinary programs geared toward training specific types of criminal justice personnel. This plan aims at training teachers and counselors for careers in corrections. Other model programs are needed to train correctional administrators; law enforcement officers as community and human relations specialists; skyjack marshals in the detection of explosives through the most advanced technology; criminal and juvenile court judges in human behavior, and the psychology of crime and delinquency; and para-professionals as crisis intervention workers for people with problems in the areas of alcohol, drugs, suicide, mental health, and family relations.

The shortage of competent correctional treatment specialists can be remedied effectively only through the growth and collaborative developments of specialized criminal justice education programs, and the concomitant upgrading of recruitment, hiring, promotion, and working standards and conditions in corrections.

ABOUT THE AUTHOR: *Albert R. Roberts is assistant professor and chairman of the Criminal Justice Studies Department, Coppin State College, Baltimore, and a consultant to the Maryland Division of Correction. He received a B.A. in Sociology from C.W. Post College, an M.A. from Long Island University, and has completed doctoral courses in sociology and criminology at the University of Maryland. Roberts is the author and editor of articles on criminology and social disorganization and has written three books on corrections.*

The internal training function as an active force in planning and implementing organization change.

Is External Management Training Effective for Organizational Change?

YORAM ZEIRA

Off-the-job management training by external training organizations has recently become a big industry. The number of institutions which conduct external training programs is constantly increasing, and the scope and number of their training programs is ceaselessly expanding.

This means that their clients are making substantial financial investments in formal outside management training. The question is: during periods of planned organizational change, can such off-the-job external training bring about the needed change?

The answer is that it apparently cannot. While it may achieve many important goals relevant for updating the management teams, it usually cannot bring about the specific required changes in managerial behavior to meet the organization's specific goals of changes.

Introduction

Nancy G. McNulty, in her book *Training Managers: The International Guide,*[1] describes management training programs in about 1500 training institutions which conduct courses in general management, functional management and personal skills. Excluded from this guide are programs which are a part of a regular academic course, programs restricted to employees of one organization or industry, programs of less than five days' duration, and academic institutions not accredited by the American Association of Collegiate Schools of Business. The catalogues of the civil service commissions, the productivity centers, the extension university courses, the institutes of the professional

---

From *Public Personnel Management,* November-December 1973, pp. 400-407. Reprinted by permission of the International Personnel Management Association.

[1] Nancy G. McNulty, *Training Managers: The International Guide* (New York: Harper & Row, 1969).

management associations, the UNESCO World Survey of Education, and the programs organized by the International Labour Organization and the United Nations Industrial Development Organization can also help the reader get acquainted with this tremendous and diversified field of study.

The wide range of formal external training methods can be grouped under the following headings:

1. University executive development programs
2. Management workshops
3. Professional conferences
4. Sabbaticals

Common to all these training methods is that they are off-the-job and that they are organized by external agents. Otherwise, they differ greatly from one another. Even within a category, there might be a wide range of differences with regard to content of training, level of instruction, prerequisites for participation, type of training methods and aids, type of trainers, kind of participants, and length of training. The following descriptions of these training methods are very brief, and discuss only the general characteristics.

UNIVERSITY EXECUTIVE DEVELOPMENT PROGRAMS

University executive programs are very popular[2] and influential.[3] Usually, executives trained by this method are top-level managers, or upper-middle managers with the potential for becoming top managers. Some of those programs are very progressive and dynamic.

---

[2] For an international guide to university executive development programs, see N. G. McNulty (ibid.). For a detailed description of programs in the U.S., including objectives, organization and administration, costs, requirements for admissions, content, teaching process and physical facilities and annotated bibliography, see Jude P. West and Don R. Sheriff, *Executive Development Programs in Universities,* (New York: National Industrial Conference Board, 1969), SPP 215.

[3] For an evaluation of university executive development programs, see Kenneth R. Andrews, "Reaction to University Development Programs," *Harvard Business Review,* Vol. XXXIX, No. 3 (May-June, 1961), pp. 116-34; K. R. Andrews, *The Effectiveness of University Management Development Programs* (Boston: Division of Research, Graduate School of Business Administration, Harvard University, 1966); Reed M. Powell, "Business Looks at University Executive Development Programs," *Business Topics,* Vol. X, No. 4 (Autumn, 1962), pp. 60-64; Fred E. Case, "The University View of Executive Development Programs," *Business Horizons,* Vol. VI, No. 3 (Fall, 1963), pp. 8-11; Malcolm S. Knowles (ed.), *Handbook of Adult Education in the U.S.* (Chicago: Adult Educational Association, 1960), see especially Robert F. Risley, "Adult Education in Business and Industry," Robert L. Craig and Lester R. Bittel (eds.), *Training and Development Handbook* (New York: McGraw-Hill, 1967), Chapter 23; M. Anshen, "Executive Development: In-Company versus University Programs," *Harvard Business Review,* Vol. XXXII, No. 5 (September-October, 1959), pp. 83-91.

The training is conducted mostly by university professors, whose presentations of their viewpoints to the participants are based on their knowledge, research and consulting experience.[4] Universities have off-campus programs, and use a wide variety of teaching methods.

The better programs offer famous faculty members who are experts in their fields and contribute to its development by their research; a heterogeneous group of participants from similar and different organizations who can compare problems and solutions, and make friends with other participants of the same profession; up-to-date training facilities that include laboratories, computers and audio-visual training aids; tested, well-planned training; the prestige of participating in outstanding and famous programs; and an atmosphere of objectivity, research and creativity.

WORKSHOPS AND SEMINARS

Workshops that cover a great variety of subjects are organized by such bodies as universities, professional associations, civil service commissions, private training institutions and international bodies.[5] Generally, classes are confined to a limited number of participants, and the leaders of the workshops are experts in their fields. The participants have an opportunity for speedy cooperative learning through an exchange of knowledge and experience with the experts and the other managers. In most instances, the particular subject of the workshops is narrowly defined, so that it can be handled effectively in a short period of time (2 to 6 days).

CONFERENCES

The conference technique is another widely used training device. Conferences are organized by many professional associations, training institutions and international organizations. This method enables a public of interested managers with a broad and varied background to be exposed to ideas developed by the speakers and the institutions

---

[4]G. Strauss and L. Sayles point out that "the authors' experience is that management trainees work considerably harder than the typical undergraduate and derive tremendous stimulation from dealing with difficult intellectual problems." See G. Strauss and L. Sayles, *Personnel* (Englewood Cliffs, N.J.: Prentice-Hall, 1967), ch. 24, p. 584.

[5]For international information regarding management workshops, see the publications of the UN, UNESCO, BIM, ILO, UNIDO and the publications of the civil service commissions of the U.S.A. and the U.K. In the U.S., the better known workshops, managed by professional associates, are those organized by American Management Association, American Society of Training and Development, National Industrial Conference Board, Industrial Management Society, National Council of Industrial Management Clubs, Society for Advancement of Management, the National Management Association, and the American Association of Industrial Management.

they represent. It is a direct and economical method of transmitting information that applies to the participants. Generally, this method can be effective in bringing new ideas to a large, interested population.

Conferences usually enable some discussion among the participants, so they can analyze and compare the viewpoints and approaches presented in the conference. This method is especially suitable for experts who wish to broaden and deepen their knowledge.

SABBATICALS

The system of granting sabbaticals to executives is quite a new one, and is not yet widely used.[6] If it is well planned, this method can be an excellent developmental technique, especially for persons in the higher levels of the organization. To be effective, these leaves should last at least an academic year, and should be organized in advance according to the managerial field in which the executive wishes to specialize. This prolonged period is required in order to refresh the managerial approach of the executive by giving him an adequate opportunity to study and assimilate new knowledge, skills and attitudes.

ADVANTAGES AND LIMITATIONS OF EXTERNAL OFF-THE-JOB MANAGEMENT TRAINING

The proliferation of external training institutions indicates that organizations tend to spend tremendous amounts of resources on formal outside training. In view of this situation, a legitimate question may be asked: is this huge investment in manpower and resources justified? Can off-the-job external management training bring about the expected changes in managerial behavior according to each organization's specific goals of change?

In order to answer this question, we have to analyze the advantages and limitations of this method.

Advantages

Following are the more important advantages of formal external management training:

(1) Being away from the job and its immediate environment permits the manager to concentrate more on the subject matter. He can study without the conflicting pressures of his daily work. This change in atmosphere is usually stimulating and contributes to the process of learning. Day-to-day immersion in the details of the job, especially at

---

[6] Roger O'Meara, *Combatting Knowledge Obsolescence* (New York: National Industrial Conference Board, 1968), SPP 209.

higher levels, makes it difficult to undergo major changes in behavior and to understand complex problems. The daily pressures prevent managers from analyzing the relationships of broad principles to specific problems. Off-the-job training makes it possible to achieve a wider and more objective perspective. This "moratorium" from daily pressures gives the managers, perhaps for the first time, an opportunity to re-evaluate themselves and their performance on the job.[7]

(2) Meeting people from other units of the organization or from other organizations permits the managers to hold a productive exchange of ideas. External training makes it possible to present some of the daily problems to an objective study group. By discussing those problems with people from other departments or organizations, the managers can achieve new approaches or even original solutions.

(3) When managers study with people who manage similar kinds of organizations, a comparative approach emerges. People in different organizations face and solve similar problems in different ways. During the learning process, the participants can compare attitudes, techniques and systems. The process of comparing managerial behavior can help broaden the participants' approaches to their specific problems, and even cause certain changes in managerial behavior.

(4) High-quality external training usually makes it possible for the participants to be exposed to the most recent management theories and viewpoints, presented by qualified instructors. It helps to close the gap that quite often exists between theory and practice: between theories and interpretations of research findings known to experts and university people, and their implementation in organizations. Through this type of training, the participants are exposed to the latest theories and concepts which have not yet been incorporated in their organizations. The managers may influence their organizations to implement these new approaches.

(5) Some of the in-house training courses and seminars of an organization's own training department tend to emphasize the point of view of the organization. This is a kind of indoctrination which has, of course, its organizational advantages. But outside training makes it possible for the manager to get away from the confinements of the point of view of his organization, and to compare it with other approaches. In this manner, he is trained in an environment which is conducive to objectivity. The consciousness of objectivity and freedom can stimulate the participants to question, discuss and criticize the subject matter. Outside training can eliminate the danger of excessive uniformity

---

[7]Kamla Chowdry, "Management Development Programs: Moratorium for Executives," *Human Organizations,* Vol. XXIII, No. 3 (Fall, 1964), pp. 254-59.

of thinking and behavior, the frequent side effect of internal training and indoctrination.

(6) The sending of a manager to an outside training institution usually means that the organization finances the study and grants him a leave of absence to attend the program. This gives the participant a feeling of importance, prestige and status: his organization is ready to finance his managerial development and enable him to leave his daily work. If the outside program has a good reputation, his important personal needs of learning, prestige, development and recognition tend to be satisfied. In this manner, personal needs and organizational goals tend to become integrated.

(7) Outside programs are usually cheaper than a one-time internal course. Rates per man seem high, but the installation of the same program in-house would be even more expensive when all the costs of training are considered. If the number of managers being sent is small, and the organization does not feel the need to repeat the program for other groups of managers, then outside training is usually more economical.

(8) In-house training programs of small and medium-size organizations cannot provide the variety of topics and approaches which are developed outside the organization. Neither can they afford the same caliber of experts invited to the better outside programs. Furthermore, the cross-fertilization and stimulation which takes place in external programs are very important for the participants and their organizations, and only very large and complex organizations can provide this development experience within their facilities without using outside training.

(9) Training departments which try to initiate organizational change usually face skepticism and criticism from the participants. Sending them to outside programs for study, conference or research reinforces the subject of change by objective means. Outside training can decrease resistance to change, and gain support for change. The saying that "a prophet is not without honor save in his own country" is relevant to the process of initiating change. Reinforcement is thus provided when the managers, exposed to ideas of change in their own organization, find themselves subjected to the same ideas in the new environment.

(10) There are always some problems which cannot be solved by in-house training because the need is very specific or the number of managers in the organization who are interested in this problem is very limited. Outside programs, which are much broader in scope and variety, may be better able to provide the specialized training that is needed. In the process of looking for managerial solutions to unique problems, outside knowledge cannot be ignored.

Limitations

(1) External off-the-job training is more general than internal training,[8] and usually attracts managers from various organizations. Therefore, it cannot be programmed to the specific goals of any organization nor to the specific needs of any trainee. Well-planned internal training, utilizing the system approach,[9] can be designed around the specific organizational and individual requirements.

(2) External management training usually consists of *ad hoc* training groups which can be quite heterogeneous in abilities, interests, scope of responsibilities, professional expertise and past experience. This heterogeneity may be a major obstacle to effective training, especially if the program is for a short period of time. The participants in in-house training are employees of the organization, and are more apt to be familiar with the organization's problems and needs than are heterogeneous groups composed of managers from different organizations. In-house training enables the trainer and the trainees to concentrate on the organization's internal and specific problems; since the subjects are relevant to the daily work of the participants, they tend to be more involved in the learning process. One of the most important learning conditions is the concentration of the training process on problems and behavior which are related to the trainee's job, so that he can apply his new knowledge in his job situation.[10] This condition can usually be achieved more easily in a well-planned internal course.

(3) External management training is usually conducted by experts who are not familiar with the specific problems of the trainees and their organizations. As external experts, they cannot follow up the trainees with advice and guidance after the completion of the training.

---

[8]"Internal Training" refers to courses, seminars, workshops and special tailor-made programs organized by the internal training department of the organization.

[9]The term "system approach" refers to a new theory in the field of training. It presents a model of a training system aimed at achieving its goals in the following stages: needs analysis (of the gap between the present and desired managerial behavior); development of a plan to eliminate this gap; implementation of this plan; and evaluation of its effectiveness. The main function of this system of training is to achieve "predefined behavior changes required by the other systems in the organization to carry out their mission" (Warren, p. 26). For a detailed discussion, see M. W. Warren, *Training for Results* (Reading, Mass.: Addison-Wesley, 1969). R. J. House, *Management Development: Design, Evaluation and Implementation* (Ann Arbor: Graduate School of Business Administration, The University of Michigan, 1967).

[10]B. M. Bass and H. Vaughn, *Training in Industry* (Belmont, California: Wadsworth, 1966); W. McGehee and P. W. Thayer, *Training in Business and Industry* (New York: Wiley, 1961).

Internal training has the benefit of instructors who are very familiar with the subject matter. Since some of the instructors take part in the need analysis, and plan the training according to those specific needs, the learning process and the solution of management programs can be very effective. A well-balanced internal program will use some of the organization's executives and line managers for at least part of the instruction. This has the advantage of adding the influence of the boss to the authority of the instructor; thus, the message is put across in a more actuating way. Another very important benefit of using executives as instructors is that it helps to eliminate the conflict and gaps between behavior taught in the classroom and that practiced in the organization.[11] An executive who is training his immediate or secondary subordinates is more likely to practice on the job what he preaches in the classroom. Furthermore, internal training handled by line executives can forestall a certain kind of frustration which is common in external training; this frustration occurs when a trainee is unable to put into practice what he has learned because of the opposition of his superiors.

(4) The planning, control and evaluation of internal formal training is much easier and much more effective than that of external training. Appraisal of the effectiveness of outside training programs is usually limited to the distribution of questionnaires to the participants immediately after training to measure the satisfaction gained from the learning experience. Internal training enables the planners to prepare specific measurement tools before, during and after the training (including questionnaires, interviews and observation). If the "during" measurement techniques are sufficiently sensitive, the form and content of the training can be changed according to the reactions of the participants or the organization's changing situation and needs. A pilot study, to determine the effectiveness of an in-house training program, can be held only if the training is internal. Systematic follow-up is also easier when the training is planned and conducted by an internal training department.[12]

---

[11] E. A. Fleishman, "Leadership Climate, Human Relations Training and Supervisory Behavior." *Personnel Psychology*, Vol. 6, No. 1 (Summer, 1953), pp. 205-222, A. J. M. Sykes, "The Effect of a Supervisory Training Course on Supervisors' Perceptions and Expectations of the Role of Management." *Human Relations*, Vol. 15, No. 3, (August, 1962), pp. 227-244.

[12] For a discussion of those evaluation problems, see J. P. Campbell, M. P. Dunnette, E. E. Lawler III and K. E. Weick, Jr. *Managerial Behavior, Performance and Effectiveness* (New York, McGraw-Hill, 1970) ch. 12 & 13. M. H. Steel, "An Organized Evaluation of Management Training." *Personnel Journal*, (October, 1972), pp. 723-7. D. L. Kirkpatrick, "Evaluation of Training" in R. L. Craig and L. R. Bittel (eds.) *Training and Development Handbook*, (New York: McGraw-Hill, 1967).

(5) Effective learning permits newly acquired managerial behavior to be exercised in the classroom before being practiced in daily organizational situations. According to Schein, in the course of classroom training,

> The new responses studied (a) can be successfully generalized from the learning situation to other situations and can be appropriately used; (b) the new responses are 'reinforced' in the sense of being followed by some reward or information that the response has been made correctly; (c) the learner is an active participant in the learning process, trying out new responses, rather than a passive listener only; (d) the learning situation provides opportunities to practise the new responses and allows for 'plateaus', periods of little improvement which often precede marked improvement.[13]

Practicing of the new specific behavior acquired in class can be achieved more easily in internal training programs than in heterogeneous external programs.

(6) External training might subject the trainees to up-to-date managerial theories which their organization is not yet ready or willing to adopt. In such a case the trainees are likely to criticize their organization, lose their trust in its management and create dissatisfaction among other members. Furthermore, external training helps managers to find out about the activities and trends in other organizations, and leads to personal contacts among the trainees; this information and these social relations might be used as bridges to jobs in other organizations where more modern theories are applied. In addition, if the professional level of external training is higher than that of the internal one, the participants in outside training may criticize the internal training and refuse to participate in its future activities. Finally, participation in prestigious outside training could be interpreted by the trainees primarily as a status symbol to satisfy their need for recognition, rather than as a means for changing their managerial behavior.

CONCLUSIONS

It is commonly agreed that the major goal of management training and development in the process of planned change is to bring about a change in managerial behavior. This point was clearly expressed by G. S. Odiorne: "Of all the personnel and industrial relations functions, the training function alone has the function of being a change

---

[13]E. H. Schein, *Organizational Psychology* (Englewood Cliffs, N.J.: Prentice-Hall, Inc., 1965), p. 35.

agent."[14] This activity is usually planned and financed by the organization and is intended to further the organizational goals. Hence, management should clearly define the goals of organizational change, and the training activity should be evaluated according to its contributions to these specific goals.[15] Since the training goals are different in each organization, the training programs should also be different; the programs should focus on the specific organizational goals and the specific required behavior of different managers in different organizations, units and levels.

The objective of management development is not only the promotion of organizational goals. It is also directed toward the satisfaction of personal needs for human growth, in order to increase the fit between organizational goals and personal requirements.[16] And, since the personal needs of managers in different organizations and at different managerial levels are not identical, the training programs should be adjusted both to the specific goals of change and to the specific human needs of the managers who are being trained.

A way to cope with the problem of specific behavior change is suggested by the system approach in the training field. In summary form, this approach recommends the following steps: analyzing present managerial behavior; defining the required managerial behavior; building a model to eliminate the gap between present and required behavior; preparing specific training goals; choosing the right composition of training and development methods; implementing the training program; evaluating its effectiveness; and presenting feedback and recommendations for future training activities. It is hoped that by taking these steps, the training function will be able to contribute to the process of planned organizational change.

There is no doubt that off-the-job external training programs have many impressive advantages and comprise an essential sector of management development. The question is whether this method is effective when the organization is planning changes in order to reach a better state of adaptation to its environment.

It seems that the foregoing analysis of external management training makes it clear that internal training utilizing the system approach has a better potential for bringing about the expected changes

---

[14]G. S. Odiorne, *Training by Objectives* (New York: Macmillan, 1970), p. 8.

[15]H. H. Hand, "The Mystery of Executive Education," *Business Horizons,* (June, 1971), pp. 35-38; P. R. Cone and R. N. McKinney, "Management Development Can Be More Effective," *California Management Review,* Vol. 14, No. 3, (Spring, 1972), pp. 13-19.

[16]P. R. Lawrence and J. M. Lorsch, *Developing Organizations: Diagnosis and Action* (Reading, Mass.: Addison-Wesley, 1969).

in managerial behavior. External training can be an important and sometimes even vital prerequisite for updating the managerial teams. But during periods of planned changes, internal training should be preferred for bringing about the specific changes. Organizations which tend to invest huge amounts in external training, hoping that this approach will assure a better process of adaptation, should reconsider.[17] In most cases the conclusion will be that the internal training function should be strengthened and that it should play a much more active role in the process of planning and implementing organizational changes.

To sum up: the internal training function can play a critical role in the process of organizational change if:

a) the training is based on an analysis of training needs;
b) the participants focus on their specific problems, both present and future;
c) the in-house training is conducted by an experienced staff which is familiar with learning theories, present managerial problems, future goals of the organization and the specific problems of team training;
d) the key executives of the organization take part in the training activities as trainers and participants in the group discussions and decisions;
e) the training department is constantly engaged in evaluation studies and in the implementation of changes in the program, consistent with the participants' reactions and the changes in the organizational environment.

The more opportunities the internal training function has to take these steps, the higher will be the probability of its success as a change agent.

ABOUT THE AUTHOR: *Yoram Zeira teaches organizational development and human resource development at Tel Aviv University. He did his undergraduate work at Hebrew University and earned his master's degree at the University of California and his doctorate at New York University. Dr. Zeira has served as a consultant to governments and multinational corporations.*

---

[17]J. Sterling Livingston, "Myth of the Well-Educated Manager," *Harvard Business Review*, Vol. XLIX, (January-February, 1971), pp. 79-89.

Using FIRO-B in assessing police leadership.

Measuring the Qualities of Police Leadership

EDWARD E. PEOPLES

The needs of contemporary society demand that those selected to manage law enforcement agencies and supervise police personnel have the best qualities of leadership. For the most part, selecting police leaders has moved beyond seniority, friendship, or politics as determining factors, but ironically enough, that move has left a vacuum. How does one determine "best"? In the past, defining wanted leadership qualities, and then measuring the existence of those qualities in an individual, has been the assumed charge of academic theoreticians whose concepts, unfortunately, frequently lacked objectives for meaningful application.

This seeming dichotomy between theory and application no longer needs to exist. Given the high state of the art in blending the behavioral sciences with traditional management theory, we can define the qualities necessary for leadership in objective and tangible terms. We can measure the degree to which an individual possesses those qualities; and both the definitions and measuring instruments have been validated sufficiently to allow for their application in the field of law enforcement.

This study represents one of many experiments by the author to measure the behavioral needs relative to the leadership styles of over 400 police managers in an effort to test a hypothesis about the ideal police leader. It also represents one example of the continuing effort to refine the selection-interpretive process and validate the measuring instrument known as FIRO-B.

Reproduced from *The Police Chief* magazine, May 1974 issue, with the permission of the International Association of Chiefs of Police.

THE MEASURING INSTRUMENT

The FIRO-B is a 54-item questionnaire designed to measure the expressed and wanted dimensions of the behavioral needs of inclusion, control, and affection. Its initials stand for Fundamental Interpersonal Relations Orientation—Behavior. William C. Schutz developed the questionnaire from research on a theory of interpersonal behavior while at Tufts College, and later at Harvard University, which indicated that these behavioral needs are basic components of human interaction.[1] Inclusion is the need to establish and maintain a relationship with people in general—a social relationship. Control is the need to establish and maintain a relationship with others relative to power, dominance, or authority. It also reflects the degree of one's internal comfort with responsibility and decision-making roles. Affection is the need to establish and maintain a comfortable dyadic relationship based on friendship, personal warmth, or intimacy.

Each of the three areas is assessed on two dimensions, expressed and wanted. Expressed scores project the overt behavior one originates with others, while wanted scores project the behavior one wants from others. Each category is measured nine times, and the intensity of each need, or the degree to which each need is characteristic of one's behavior is rated from zero to nine. Each need area is evaluated individually, then in combination with the other five areas to arrive at a behavioral, and in this case a leadership, profile.

THE IDEAL POLICE SUPERVISOR

In measuring aspects of human behavior, and particularly in evaluating those measurements in terms of an ideal police supervisor, there are no absolute criteria against which the results of the questionnaire can be validated. However, after extensive research, this writer has constructed an ideal profile against which other profiles are compared. In the experiment described below, the following police leadership profile was hypothesized as the ideal projection.

He will project a moderate expressed inclusion score, with a low wanted inclusion score, indicating that he is socially skilled and comfortable with people, but not compelled to feed upon their recognition; a high-average expressed control score with a moderately low wanted control score, indicating that he is confident, self-assured, and comfortable assuming responsibility. And, though willing to listen, he will dominate the final decision process with firmness, yet without any

---

[1] William C. Schutz. *FIRO: A Three-Dimensional Theory of Interpersonal Behavior* (New York: Holt, Rinehart and Winston, 1960), reprinted as *The Interpersonal Underworld* by Behavior and Science Books, Inc., Palo Alto.

compulsive need to exercise power; and he will express a moderately low affection score, combined with a low wanted score, suggesting a preference for quality rather than quantity in dyadic relationships.

Combined, these scores project an individual who is comfortable assuming responsibility and making decisions, but who does not thrive on power, who relates well to groups and to individuals in a natural way, without a personality overkill, and who controls his own level of involvement. His concern for people will be a consideration, but it will not inhibit his primary role obligation.

THE EXPERIMENT

Twenty police officers participated in the experiment, unknowingly at first. All were students in a two-week middle management training program, and each one held the rank of lieutenant or captain. The sizes of the departments represented ranged from 25 to 1800 sworn personnel, and the average time in police work was 15.3 years.[2]

On the third day of the program, the FIRO-B questionnaire was administered. They were scored and assigned letters to identify each student. Each profile was interpreted and compared against the hypothesized ideal, then rated on an ordinal scale, and the top three were placed in order relative to that ideal. Plans called for each participant to rate the others on leadership potential and to compare their ratings with the three selected, and to provide each individual with an interpretation of his own profile.

Two assumptions were made, based on findings documented in the management literature: (1) that in an informal group the leadership qualities of an individual will emerge naturally, and be recognized by others in the group; and, (2) if the construct of the measuring instrument is valid, individuals in the group will be able to confirm or refute the interpretations made of their own projected profiles and leadership styles.

RESULTS

After scoring and interpreting the questionnaires, student "C" was ranked first as being closest to the ideal leader, student "D" was ranked second, and student "A" was placed third. At the end of the program each participant selected from the group the three officers he thought emerged as the most natural leader, and rated those three in priority. Their rankings were compared with the three selected interpretations

---

[2]This writer has conducted so many similar experiments in middle-management programs that it is unlikely that participants in the one described will be able to recognize themselves, or the group involved.

with the following results: fourteen students placed "C" first and six placed him second; nine placed "D" second and six placed him third; and five placed "A" third, while twelve placed "A" among their top three choices. The number of votes cast for other students was negligible.

Additional validation, although on a more subjective level, was obtained by discussing with each individual, and with the group, a detailed interpretation of their leadership profiles. Fifteen students agreed almost completely with the evaluations, three agreed with only minor exceptions, while two completely rejected the validity of the projections.

CONCLUSIONS/IMPLICATIONS

Significantly high agreement resulted when comparing the students' selection of leaders and those chosen in relationship to the hypothesized ideal. These results lend strong support for the continued use of FIRO as one method of measuring behavioral needs and their bearing on leadership qualities. Actually, what was measured and proven in this experiment was one's preference for, and internal comfort with, the leadership role in the group situation described. Although FIRO is extremely accurate in its ability to project, one must remember that it is only *one* method, not *the* method suggested for selecting leaders. Behavior profiles change and can be changed; they are never absolute.

One must also bear in mind that different leadership styles can be equally effective, and the effectiveness of one over another depends upon a number of other variables. Without discounting the validity of the experiment, the composition of the group tested and the environment in which they were tested are variables to consider. And, though an ideal was hypothesized, what makes one the ideal may be situational and relative to the political and social climate in which he will lead.

In this regard, FIRO has shown favorable results in assessing need compatibilities with groups, from entire departments to police teams to pairs in a patrol car. It has also been useful for purposes of staff development during the selection and training process. Research in progress hopefully will isolate more specifically various qualities of leadership and relate them to the organizational roles desired.

The application of FIRO has received extensive use in business and the military. Law enforcement agencies also are increasingly making use of it in selection of new recruits. However, its potential for evaluating leadership has received only recent attention. It is in this area that concern for quality is most important, and where the application of FIRO can provide a basic framework of understanding in the selection process.

ABOUT THE AUTHOR: *Edward E. Peoples is Assistant Professor, Administration of Justice Department, California State University/San Jose, San Jose, California 95192. Now in his fourth year in this position, he also lectures in middle-management programs and serves as consultant to local law enforcement agencies on personnel selection and staff development. He holds the B.A. and M.A. in social science and is presently working toward his doctorate in public administration.*

An evaluation on the use of leaderless group discussion as a tool for selecting personnel for promotion.

Leaderless Group Discussion as an Assessment Tool for Supervisory and Command Promotions

PRESTON HORSTMAN

The essence of selection, whether it be for employment or promotion, is making a "correct" choice. If this were not true, then selection systems would be quite superfluous to any organization. We strive to be right; we want to make a "good" decision, particularly about whomever we put in supervisory and command positions. Our intentions are quite noble, but let us consider for a moment how we generally go about selecting those individuals who have a profound influence upon our police organizations—our leaders.

In a vast majority of departments, promotions are made on the basis of competitive examinations, usually containing questions aimed at measuring the individual's depth of knowledge in law enforcement. In other words, we find those who are doing the best job where they are, and promote them on that basis to a job to which they may be entirely unsuited, thus hurting the organization, and, just as important, forcing a failure situation on a formerly good employee.

If we are to develop a rational and valid method of making promotions, it is extremely important that we identify good indices of satisfactory performance in the position to which we are promoting officers. Until then, there is no way selection can function but in a trial and error fashion, hurting both organization and officer.

The second step is to find and test tools to predict successful performance on these indices. If a department is too small, it may need to utilize the findings of others in lieu of its own experimentally derived measures. It is far better, however, for a department to develop the

---

Reprinted by permission of the *Journal of Police Science and Administration,* Copyright © 1974 by Northwestern University School of Law, Volume II, Number 1.

system within its own organization due to individual differences that always exist between departments.

The measurement or assessment tool to which this article is devoted is a process called "leaderless group discussion." The basic scheme of leaderless group discussion is to ask a group of examinees to carry on a discussion on one or more job relevant topics for a given period of time. No one is appointed leader, and no structure is given for the interaction. Due to the lack of structure, one or more leaders must emerge voluntarily to give structure and guidance to the discussion in order for it to achieve the objectives set out before the start. The examiners do not participate in the discussion, but remain free to observe and rate the performance of each examinee. The raters are asked to make judgments based on specific criteria about each examinee from their observed performance. It is extremely important to use a great deal of discretion in the choosing of rated criteria due to the fact that invalid criteria destroy the utility of the method.

According to published reports, leaderless group discussion has been used to assess candidates for many professions and occupations. The examinees have included military officer candidates, OSS agent applicants, advanced Naval, Air Force, and Army ROTC cadets, industrial management trainees, industrial executives and supervisors, shipyard foremen, and many others, but to the knowledge of the author the technique has never been validated in a police promotion setting. The method, however, has been used in a published study to aid in the initial selection of police applicants for the Honolulu Police Department.[1]

The originator of the method was allegedly J. B. Rieffert, who directed German military psychology from 1920-1931. The German Army used the procedure until about 1939, while the Navy continued to employ it in its selection programs until late in World War II. Influenced by the German developments in situational testing, the British War Selection Board in 1942 introduced the method for selection of Army officer candidates, and a similar program was established by the British Navy. At the end of the war, the leaderless group discussion technique was employed as a device for screening British management trainees, and for testing British Civil Service applicants. The OSS assessment staff appears to have initiated the use of leaderless group discussion in the United States late in World War II. American state and federal Civil Service examiners began trying out the technique at the end of the war. In 1950, approximately 25 percent of 190

---

[1] Kiessling and Kalish, "Correlates of Success in Leaderless Group Discussion," *Journal of Social Psychology*, Vol. 54, p. 359-365 (1961).

Civil Service agencies surveyed reported using leaderless group discussion. Leaderless group discussion has also been employed by many American industrial and business firms.

The spread of leaderless group discussion has been attributed primarily to its relative ease of administration compared to individual interviews, especially where large numbers of applicants are involved, as well as to its face validity compared to paper and pencil tests. Leaderless group discussion appears to share with real world situations such elements as the need to choose a leader to communicate effectively, to overcome inertia, to solve various interaction problems, to meet deadlines, and to reach consensus.

The higher up the organizational ladder an officer climbs, the more important these types of behavior become to his success. He must be able to communicate effectively to motivate those who work under him, to effectively handle interpersonal problems, and meet deadlines. For those reasons, leaderless group discussion holds a great deal of promise for the selection of supervisors and command staff.

Although the process is quite easy to administer and score, the mechanics of setting the system up should be handled by a professional in the area. Cost, however, is quite reasonable due to the relatively short period of time needed by a consultant to individualize the process to the specific department and try out a validation design.

The technique was investigated experimentally by the planning and research section of a Southwestern United States police department. Using an experimental rating form of uncertain construct validity, the technique successfully identified two candidates from a field of eight who were promoted independently of the technique into the next two first-line supervisors' slots. Although possessing obvious bias, the results give definite support to the utility of the technique.

SYSTEM IMPLEMENTATION

There are a number of factors which should be kept in mind in the implementation of such a system.

1. *Size of the group.* The optimum number of examinees per session has been found to be six. Two- and three-man groups should be avoided. Eighty-three percent of the variance in ratings where members come from groups of 2, 4, 6, 8, and 12 is accounted for by the size of the group.[2] The average participant score was reduced 50 percent when the number of participants was increased from 2 to 12. Therefore, all groups used in the same evaluation should be the same size in order to allow for intergroup comparison of members.

---

[2]Bass and Norton, "Group Size and Leaderless Discussions," *Journal of Applied Psychology,* Vol. 6, p. 397-400 (1951).

2. *Location of seat and seating arrangement.* Although the effect was found to be small, it was significant at the .01 level that participants seated at the ends of seating configurations obtained slightly higher mean scores.[3] To control this effect it is recommended that a round table be used whenever possible.

3. *Pre-test Coaching.* Coaching tends to help those who without coaching would score high, and has no significant effect on initial low scorers.[4]

4. *Extrinsic motivation.* Varying motivational levels external to the testing situation have been found to have little effect on performance in the discussion.[5]

5. *Amount of participation.* High correlations (.64-.96) have been found between the sheer amount of talk by the participants and their ratings.[6] This finding should be expected due to the necessity to attempt in order to succeed.

6. *Kind of participation.* It is reported that qualitative differences exist in the kinds of participation engaged in by the successful leader and by those who participated and attempted leadership acts, but who nonetheless earned low scores as successful leaders. Leaders were much more likely than nonleaders to diagnose the situation, ask for expressions of opinions, propose course of action, support and define their proposals, give information, express opinions, and argue with others.[7]

VALIDITY

In order to approach true predictive validity—the ultimate objective in promotional testing—the technique must be laid out so as to allow an assessment of those particular on-the-job types of behavior that are responsible for success or failure. For example, when using leaderless group discussion to assess a group of lieutenants for the position of assistant chief, one of whose responsibilities would be to hold staff advisory meetings, it would be highly valid to use a situation that might arise in one of those meetings dealing with manpower acquisition.

---

[3] Bass and Klubeck, "Effects of Seating Arrangement on Leaderless Group Discussions," *Journal of Abnormal and Social Psychology,* Vol. 47, p. 724-727 (1952).

[4] Klubeck and Bass, "Differential Effects of Training on Persons of Different Leaderless Status," *Human Relations,* Vol. 7, p. 59-72 (1954).

[5] Bass, "A Psychological Theory of Leadership," unpublished manuscript, Louisiana State University (1953).

[6] French, "Verbal Output and Leadership Status in Initially Leaderless Discussion Groups," *American Psychologist,* Vol. 5, p. 310 (1950).

[7] Carter, *et al.*, "The Behavior of Leaders and Other Group Members," *Journal of Abnormal and Social Psychology,* Vol. 46, p. 589-595 (1951).

However, the same situation would be hardly related, and therefore highly invalid, if used in a leaderless group discussion aimed at selecting first line supervisors. For sergeants, it would be more appropriate to use disciplinary situations or district deployment exercises.

The less the leadership situation for which we are selecting leaders requires verbal communication, or verbal problem-solving, the less likely it is that leaderless group discussion will be useful as a measure or predictor of the tendency to exhibit successful leadership in the object situation. It is, however, difficult to conceive of any supervisory or command position in law enforcement that does not rely heavily on verbal communications and problem-solving.

Whenever possible, the situation should be avoided in which the examinees are tested among others of different rank. In such a case, status and not esteem or personality will determine who succeeds in leaderless group discussion.

To maximize the reliability and validity of leaderless group discussion, as well as other situational tests, scoring techniques should minimize reliance on the ability of observers to infer differences in personality traits and future tendencies among examiners. Observers should merely report or evaluate the immediate behavior they observe.

SUMMARY

Leaderless group discussion has been used with a good deal of success in many situations, but has aparently been ignored by police. Police promotional selection appears to be an ideal place to utilize the technique, test its specific validity, and reap its obvious benefits.

ABOUT THE AUTHOR: *Preston Horstman is the executive director of the National Association of State Directors of Law Enforcement Training (NASDLET), Gaithersburg, Maryland. He formerly was a staff psychologist for the Human Resources Development Bureau of the Dallas, Texas, Police Department. He holds a B.A. degree in psychology and an M.S. degree in industrial/organizational psychology from the University of Oklahoma, and is currently completing requirements for a Ph.D. He served as a police officer in Norman, Oklahoma, for eight years.*

*Goals differ for the craftsman,
the company man, the gamesman,
and the jungle fighter; what
turns you on?*

"Winning" and "Losing" at Work*

MICHAEL MACCOBY

What do you want from your work? Money? Promotions? Interesting challenges? Continual learning? Membership in a high-powered team at the cutting edge of technology? The opportunity to develop your own ideas?

Have you ever thought about how your work influences the kind of person you are becoming? How possible is it in a highly competitive corporation to develop yourself emotionally and spiritually as well as intellectually while achieving your work goals?

We are all individuals and so our answers will differ. To find out just how they differ, my colleagues and I have been interviewing engineers and managers for the past few years in an attempt to understand them and the nature of their work: what it means to them, how it affects them, and how it may be related to their character.

The psychoanalytic concept of character refers to emotional attitudes that determine what satisfies or annoys an individual—what he finds attractive, exciting, or frustrating—and how he relates to himself and to others. Essentially, what we look for in the context of character is what *energizes* a person, what turns him on, what gets him up in the morning. Among people in electronics, particularly in management, two elements stand out: the desire to win, and an interest in problem-solving, building, and gaining knowledge. Naturally, we find various mixes of these two elements among people.

---

*See "The Organization Man: Insights into Motivation," p. 87.

Reprinted with permission of the author and *IEEE Spectrum* from *IEEE Spectrum*, July 1973, pp. 39-48.

The relationship between work and character is vital as well as complex. In exploring it, we have learned that the successful individual is the one who does what needs to be done to meet his organization's particular goals, *not* because he has been *told* to do it, but because he *wants* to do it, he *enjoys* doing it, he feels *impelled* to do it. This may seem reasonable, but it is by no means obvious, and I shall consider its implications in the course of this article.

Once it is established that a person does his job well when his character is adaptive to his mode of work, the well-known Peter principle can be redefined to say, quite seriously, that people do not merely rise to the level of their intellectual incompetence; they rise only to a level permitted by their character. Successively promoted until their personalities no longer fit the requirements of work, even the most brilliant engineers and scientists are likely to fail. Furthermore, a character type adaptive to a high level in one kind of organization may not fit another. For example, a fast-moving aggressive manager, ideally suited to working at high levels in a computer company, might well fail in a small instrument company; whereas a responsible and respectful craftsman might succeed at a small instrument company, but not in the semiconductor industry.

In the course of our study (which is described in some detail on pages 160–162), we have identified four major character types among electronics engineers and their managers, and we have learned about the relationship between these character types and different kinds of work environments. As we gain a deeper understanding of such matters, it should become possible both to help managers better understand which kinds of people will perform best in their organization, and to help individuals see how they will adapt to different kinds of companies. Beyond these practical considerations, we expect the study to show the effects on mental and emotional health of adaptation to an organization. Such knowledge can be the first step toward organizing work in order to optimize the healthy personal development of the individual.

Four Character Types

It should be obvious that in considering types of people we must really deal with a concept social scientists call "ideal type." No individual fits an exact type—everybody is a mixture of personality traits. But just as we can speak of one person as stingy and another as generous, so can we speak of types in terms of dominant tendencies. In high-technology electronics we have identified four basic types of people. I call them the craftsman, the company man, the gamesman, and the jungle fighter.

CRAFTSMAN: "I turned down jobs $300 to $400 more per month because I didn't like the work. I wanted a job like this, with the satisfaction of putting something together and seeing it work."

The craftsman. Holding all the traditional values—thrift, belief in the work ethic, and respect for people as well as for craftsmanship and quality—the craftsman is rather closed and hard to get close to, but he's a man of his word and a person who can be trusted in the crunch. He is highly independent, and doesn't generally like to compete against others. One highly respected craftsman noted, "The natural stimulation for me is my interest in the work; the competition seems to me unnatural. For others, it might be different." While the craftsman loves work, he also likes to get away from it and tinker with cars or pursue other hobbies.

The craftsman is rarely satisfied in large organizations and feels more at home working in a small group or on a project with a defined and understandable structure. He wants to stay with the product from conception to completion. One craftsman remarked that for him "electrical engineering is a great hobby, but I wonder about it as a profession. I'm not strongly motivated by money; I turned down jobs $300 to $400 more per month because I didn't like the work. I wanted a job like this, with the satisfaction of putting something together and seeing it work."

When he rises in the organization it is usually not above what I would call an administrative maintenance position—a laboratory or project director, for example—unless he is one of the rare entrepreneurial craftsmen-builders who create new industries. In any case, the craftsman is absolutely essential to the creation of advanced technology.

COMPANY MAN: "By myself, there's not much I can do to change the world, but by having a high position in this corporation, I play an important part in creating products of the highest quality."

The company man. Unlike the craftsman, the company man is much more likely to identify with the large organization and to be satisfied within large, hierarchical projects. He tends to be a submissive bureaucrat in many ways, although he is generally courteous and more concerned with people than is the craftsman. Much of his satisfaction in life comes from belonging to a powerful, important company and, unlike the craftsman, he would not like to be off on his own. He derives a certain security from knowing where he fits in the structure and perceiving that he can rise within that structure by being responsible, and loyal, and doing his job right.

A very ambitious company man is also driven by fear of failure. In his dreams, he is typically chased or is in danger of falling from heights. (One manager actually told us he dreamt he was a spinning top.) The successful company man is both modest about himself and energized into compulsive activity by his fear of falling behind or just losing his momentum. Further, he often displays elements of what the psychoanalyst Erich Fromm, who first developed the theory of social character, describes as the marketing character. This is a person who relates to others by making himself an attractive package, who molds himself into what people want of him; he is a kind of centerless person who is very malleable but who also makes a good salesman. The prototypical marketing man is less adaptive to high technology than he is, say, to an advertising agency. Nevertheless, one often finds such people in certain middle management positions where they serve as mediators.

GAMESMAN: "My goal is to win and to be known as a winner. What I like most is being the boss; what I like least is taking orders. I want to call the plays."

The gamesman. This individual is in some ways uniquely a product of the U.S. He appears at the beginning of the Republic, yet is very much a modern man. Even though the gamesman comprises only 10–15 percent of our sample, certain game attitudes seem to be increasingly characteristic of the younger high-technology managers. For this reason, and because he has not been adequately recognized, the gamesman deserves an extended description.

Alexis de Toqueville noted the penchant in the U.S. for treating business competition as play when he wrote in the early 19th century:

"The whole life of an American is passed like a game of chance, a revolutionary crisis, or a battle. As the same causes are continually in operation throughout the country, they ultimately impart an irresistible impulse to the national character."

Later, in the middle of the 19th century, a group of scientists interested in developing technology in the U.S. called themselves the "Lazzaroni," after a society of Italian workmen whose goal was to make work into play, and that goal continues to be uppermost in the minds of many scientists and engineers.

Today, however, most scientific "play" in the corporation is no longer indulged in by individuals, but has been structured into a kind of game, where teams compete against time, other projects, and the market. Consequently, there is a special need for people who can integrate many specialists into a unified team, working at a fast pace.

Those who do the job best are the ones who experience this kind of work as a game.

The gamesman often aspires to be a kind of quarterback; professional football is his favorite game as it is increasingly the favorite spectator sport in the U.S., replacing the slower, less aggressive, less innovative, and more individualistic game of baseball. The gamesman often sees his work in terms of the metaphors of football and its technology—he will speak of the "game plan," of making "the big play"; he'll say, "we're going to have to punt now," or "let's try an end around and see if we can corner a few more yards of the market." Indeed, this language has become part of the jargon of the high-technology business world.

Like a successful quarterback, the gamesman is innovative, flexible, detached, and aggressive in a controlled way. He likes to take risks and is fascinated by technique and new methods. He sees the developing project (and his career) in terms of options and possibilities, as in a game, and tends to be turned on, energized, by competitive pressures and crises.

Often rather bored and passive when deprived of competition, once the game is on, once he can feel he's in the Super Bowl, he comes to life, remains cool, and thinks hard. While others such as the craftsman may find such high-pressure competition enervating, the gamesman's goal in life is to win and to be known as a winner. (Significantly, while many of the people we interviewed tended to repress or deny their interest in personal power, some of the gamesmen admitted that what they liked most about their job was being the boss and what they liked least was having to take orders from someone else. They want to call the plays.)

The gamesman and the craftsman often feel frustrated trying to communicate with one another. (You might say that if the gamesman's idea of play is football, for the craftsman it is tinkering, hiking, or sailing—that is, competing against himself and nature with the overriding goal of perfecting his technique.) The gamesman thinks the craftsman is a stick-in-the-mud, is too cautious, is not ambitious enough, and does not understand the real market. A gamesman told me that he managed a group of scientists who were like children, with neither a sense of business nor the motivation to win; he even called his lab "the sandbox." The craftsman, on the other hand, thinks that the gamesman is unsound, grandiose, superficial, pushy, and not respectful of others.

Increasingly, these gamesmen fill the top positions of middle management. They are the project leaders and marketing directors, and they like to integrate, direct, and motivate a team of highly talented specialists who are all working interdependently to win, to be number one—goals that for other character types are irrelevant. (After all, why should winning be more important than creating something of the highest quality, asks the craftsman, or, we would add, of making people's lives better?)

Significantly, the game character is less prone to suffer from the emotional problems that we found to be especially common among the craftsmen and some company men we interviewed. These problems are rooted in what Fromm calls the hoarding orientation, by which he means a tendency to retreat behind an emotional shell, thus finding it difficult to communicate with others. Practically every engineer we interviewed reports as problems the kinds of symptoms that psychiatrists describe as obsessive-compulsive—keeping his feelings to himself, avoiding other people, being overly anxious and finicky, being a perfectionist, and even having difficulty making decisions. Although these problems are sometimes encountered in the gamesman, they are generally less significant for him, and that is one reason he is better able to rise to high levels.

Seldom, however, do the gamesmen rise to the very top, even though an increasing number of company men have elements of the gamesman's character. Many gamesmen have mixed feelings about authority, and more than a little adolescent rebelliousness. Consequently, they are often considered too free-wheeling for top management positions. While they like to run the team, they also like to circumvent the rules. Furthermore, the gamesman cannot create his own team. He lacks patience and commitment to people, principles, and goals beyond winning. He is not an independent person and tends to lose sight of realities beyond the game he is currently playing. Indeed, he can be looked upon as creating a secondary reality for himself. If life is not interesting enough for him, he makes it a game and enters a semifantasy world.

Some negative consequences. The character of the gamesman is not easy to evaluate. Besides the importance of his role in advancing technology, he supports some positive social values; he tends to be very fair, to believe that everybody should be allowed to play who is good, and that neither race, sex, nor religion nor anything else besides contributing to the team matters. But we can see a number of elements that inhibit both his self-development and his effect on others. He is excessively competitive and aggressive. Since he makes life a game, he expects everyone else to do the same. For him, it is enough that everyone gets a "fair" chance to play the game, and he ignores the fact that some people, due to their background or temperament, never have a fair chance to compete. He has a tendency to put people into categories of winners and losers, and to be contemptuous of the losers. Beyond this, his detachment and need to win blind him to the effects of his actions on real people, so that he never seriously considers the social values of the products he makes.

Nor is he sufficiently concerned about himself. Somebody with such a character may remain happy so long as he's a winner and so long as he is young and vigorous, but once he loses his vigor and his thrill in winning, he becomes depressed and goalless, questioning the purpose of his life because he hasn't sufficiently developed the ability to love and understand and create. This is borne out by the successful gamesman in his forties who admitted he no longer had a goal in life and felt worried and apathetic. Another gamesman whose big project "failed" has become a depressed alcoholic. In contrast, we have met craftsmen aged 70 and older who are still energetic and interested in new ideas.

In common with the company man, the gamesman also tends to report another symptom. He often feels that he gives in to others too easily, that he doesn't control his own destiny, that he is too malleable. Even at the highest levels, such personality types may feel a kind of unconscious self-contempt that they've given in, that they are performing for others rather than developing their own goals.

The sense of guilt and self-betrayal they feel over having to sacrifice some of their independence is usually not conscious, but it comes out in dreams and projective tests—particularly on the Rorschach test where they report self-images of humiliation and castration. Their negative self-image tends to be related to a certain suppressed anger and hardening of the heart that occurs when one gives up a part of oneself or betrays one's convictions in order to get ahead.

In contrast to this unconscious guilt, I have observed that some of the most creative businessmen–engineers do not repress their guilt, but act to alleviate it. These individuals are deeply concerned with the effects of their actions and recognize that their behavior has sometimes been destructive to themselves or others. But rather than hiding from their conscience, rather than hardening their hearts, their guilt spurs them to better themselves and their organizations. One corporation president told us, "I saw myself as a slave owner, ripping off the work of other people, and I knew I had to do something to change working conditions.

JUNGLE FIGHTER: "My company needs me to get rid of the 'dead wood.' So what if I'm feared? Fear stimulates better work. Survival of the fittest—that's the name of the game!"

The jungle fighter. This fourth character type is less frequently encountered, but nonetheless often plays a key role in advanced technology. The jungle fighter experiences the corporation as a battleground where survival and advancement depend on crushing enemies both within and outside the company. Like the gamesman he wants to be a winner, but for him the struggle is not a game but a life-and-death contest. The Rorschach images of the jungle fighters are full of lions, tigers, and panthers; sometimes pictures of these animals are hung on their office walls.

Many jungle fighters have strong sadistic tendencies, although it is rare that they will admit this. Nevertheless, some do admit they enjoy crushing the opponent, and seeing his ego crack. They are likely to take pride in being feared by others, but rationalize this by claiming such fear stimulates better work.

Sometimes a talented and brilliant jungle fighter will be brought into a corporation in trouble and given the task of reorganizing the company and getting rid of the "dead wood." (It is notable that the other types—craftsmen, game characters, and company men—deeply dislike having to fire anyone.) Consequently, in some corporations, jungle fighters rise to high levels, though they often eventually fail because others become disgusted by their hard-hearted and self-serving conduct. Speaking of the fall of a jungle fighter, one of his associates pointed out that he had "left a trail of bodies behind him and he became a victim of revenge."

To get ahead in the corporate world of advanced technology, it is necessary to be competitive. But the competitive urge is very different for each of these four character types. The table on page 168 summarizes these differences and the contrast between competitive behavior and its various meanings in character. A key element is that each type is energized differently: the craftsman by his interest and pleasure in his work; the company man by his fear of failure and desire for acceptance; the gamesman by the glory of victory in the "contest"; and the jungle fighter by his need for power over others. Each character has a strong need for achievement, but achievement means something different for each character type.

How the study is being conducted

In order to study social character within the corporate structure, Dr. Maccoby is employing techniques he developed in conjunction with the well-known psychoanalyst Erich Fromm for an appraisal of peasant life in Mexico (*Social Character in a Mexican Village*, Englewood, N.J.: Prentice-Hall, 1970). The study of engineers, which began in May 1969, and is expected to be completed in 1974, is based on a series of interviews conducted at a dozen corporations throughout the U.S.

More than 250 executives, lower-level managers, and engineers have been interviewed in sessions lasting as long as six hours. Roughly half of the sample was drawn from two of the largest and most successful companies in the electronics industry; the remainder of those interviewed were also employed by what might be called elite companies—that is, companies which, unlike some of the aerospace firms, generally hire people right out of college and expect to keep them.

Through an extensive questionnaire of 150 items, which is administered during the interviews and supplemented by both dream interpretation and Rorschach tests, the members of the study team (including Dr. Maccoby, Douglass Carmichael, Rolando Weissmann, and Dennis M. Greene) have been individually interviewing presidents, top executives, and representatives of all levels of the technostructure including the project engineer). Dr. Maccoby points out that "the result is not a random sample, but a strategic one based upon the recommendations of corporate officials as to who played the key roles at each level in the company."

The questionnaire developed for these interviews is divided into five parts and deals with the work situation, attitudes to work, personal problems and values, sociopolitical attitudes, and family life.

As an example of the interview process, one question asked is, "What do you most like as well as dislike about your work?" The gamesman is likely to respond that he likes "the excitement" and the "new options," or "directing a high-powered team." One gamesman stated he most liked "the challenge of a wide range of problems and the interface with many types of people and situations," whereas he least liked "not winning all the games." Another stated that he least liked "the controls, because I want all the options."

The craftsman, on the other hand, stresses "doing high-quality work," "maintaining high standards," and "working with knowledgeable people." He dislikes such things as "being pushed around" and "not having a chance to build anything." One craftsman said he most enjoyed "the technical involvement and learning about new things" and least liked it "when we have disagreements, because I like to see everybody happy."

The questionnaire interview generally lasts about three hours, and it was further conceived to probe the individual's relationships with those closest to him both inside and outside of work. To produce the most valid results the interviewers enter the work situation directly, checking the individual's description of himself and his work against the views of his colleagues about him and their shared situation.

The material gathered in this manner is then analyzed, often in a group, to arrive at a diagnosis of character. These discussions are like psychoanalytic case conferences where interpretations of character dynamics are carefully checked against the evidence. In some cases, the analysis leads to second interviews of key individuals in order to obtain further data crucial to deciding between two different but plausible interpretations. Thus, as many as five to six hours are spent on the average subject, and 20 or more hours have been spent on cases deemed to be of exceptional interest.

Dr. Maccoby observes that in order to know another person deeply, that person must be willing to be known. Otherwise, the input will be "closer to that gained by an FBI investigation" than to profound human understanding. The study team acknowledges natural suspiciousness and is as open as possible about its aims. It often holds a meeting at the outset in which the purpose and methodology of the study are discussed and questions answered. Many of the most intelligent and gifted managers, engineers, and scientists exhibit a deep dislike for what they consider mechanistic social science studies; in contrast to those studies, Dr. Maccoby encourages a dialogue with the individual. In some cases, this has led to a continuing process of interviewing in which he describes what he has seen in the interview and asks the individual for his reaction. Such a process often refines understanding and increases confidence in the findings.

The Concept of Psychostructure

As our project developed, we found that different character types fit particular organizational roles and we found it useful to develop a new concept, one that brings together sociological–anthropological data and psychological–psychoanalytic data. We have called that concept *the psychostructure*.

To understand the psychostructure we must distinguish two of its elements: the dynamics of character and the mode of work. Character has already been discussed and we have seen that seemingly similar behavior, like competitiveness, may be rooted in different character traits.

As for work, it is by no means simple to define. When we asked the managers and engineers what their work was, most of them responded in a very conventional, abstract way: "I manage projects," or "I'm in marketing," or "I design memory systems." You have to ask them: But what do you *really* do? And then you find that the *real* work can be described more precisely. Besides typical engineering tasks, meetings, and reading, the work may include dramatizing new ideas in order to sell them to the company. (In some corporations, the culture is such that nobody can progress within the structure unless he is able to put on a "good show.")

The work may also comprise such delicate but crucial activities as sensing someone's doubts and lack of enthusiasm about a particular assignment which he hasn't attempted to talk about because, as with most engineers, he is rather inhibited. Practically everyone agrees that one of the problems is the difficulty in communicating and truly opening up to other people (you might say that this hesitancy characterizes electrical engineers as a group). An important part of a manager's work, therefore, is to stimulate confidence, to be able to offer others confirmation, and to be enthusiastic about a good idea. Some people find this very difficult—they are deeply afraid to say "Gee, that's good, I like that." They would rather say, "uh huh," noncommittally.

On the other hand, a manager must sometimes dampen overenthusiasm and inject caution. This can be done either coldly or with a friendly penetrating concern that teaches the other person to be more self-critical. I could go on at length in this vein, but the point is simply that if you want to understand the character traits that are adaptive to work, you must first understand work in this larger sense of stimulating another person, of sensing attitudes, and of being able to communicate. (One distinguished engineer–executive told me, "The major part of my work is understanding character.") Thus, it becomes clear that the reason certain people can do these things and certain people cannot is not just a matter of intelligence but of emotional attitude as well.

In these broader terms, it is also apparent that the work success depends on the fit between character and one's role in a particular kind of organization or work culture. It makes a difference whether you are in a structure where you have to report daily to a superior, or whether you are in a place where you are given a large amount of leeway to do something without being watched all the time. In makes a further difference whether the work is fragmented, so that each person feels like a highly specialized part of a huge machine, or whether the work role calls for cooperative relationships with other engineers, with other parts of the organization (like marketing), and with customers.

And lastly, work varies depending on the rights and privileges accorded to the worker, including his participation in decisions, his sense of equity in terms of fair rewards for his work, and the opportunity for his continued learning to avoid obsolescence. Thus, it is both the task, in the larger sense of activity, and the role, in terms of duties, responsibilities, rights, and privileges, that define the work and the kind of character that is selected and molded.

In analyzing technical work, we have found three interrelated factors that influence and color all work roles and activities, and which, together, determine the nature, or the shape, of the psychostructure. The first is the technology itself, the second is the market, and the third is the corporate culture.

Technology. By technology, I am referring to the fact that a person's work role and his relationship to the total product are, in some part, shaped by the type of product being developed, particularly its size, the division of work required (including the number of people), and the length of time required to make it. Because of these differences, the development of different electronic products calls for different qualities of mind and emotional attitudes on the part of those who work on them. Consider, for example, the following products: small electronic measuring instruments such as oscilloscopes, large computers, and semiconductor components.

Measuring instruments are typically developed over a one- to three-year period by groups of three to eight engineers working closely together. Each member of the group shares in varied craftsmanlike activities. Depending on the culture of the company, some may even spend time with the customers, who are generally engineers like themselves, in order to understand their needs. In such a situation there is not likely to be a strong hierarchy—at most a group of people carrying out a project together, and the immediate "boss" who may be scarcely different in rank from the other people on the project—a "first among peers."

What kind of person does this kind of work best? A gifted craftsman who likes to work with hardware; he is a self-starter who can work cooperatively with a few people and who is most satisfied when he can relate to all aspects of a limited, concrete product with a well-defined market.

On the other hand, the development of a large computer takes much longer and requires a pyramid of highly specialized roles. Output is directed and integrated at various levels, and there may be 200 people or more, all highly specialized and filling different roles. Most of the engineers developing the computer have little sense of the total product and its ultimate uses. Those working, for example, on the memory, may even have little idea of what the CPU people are working on. In contrast to the small-instrument engineers, even the top development managers know relatively little about who the customers will be. Moreover, many who work on a computer only do so for brief periods in the development cycle.

What kind of person is attracted to these conditions? High-level computer work attracts engineers who are satisfied with a highly specialized role on a high powered team, preferably at the cutting edge of technology—that is, the company man. It also attracts those who like to manage, control, or at best teach, other people, because it requires a large number of coordinating and middle management roles. And it appeals to gamesmen who like to be inspirational, or who enjoy being tough Vince Lombardi types, pushing the troops to beat the deadlines with ever-better performance.

In fact, it is interesting how frequently one finds photographs of football players and sayings of famous coaches on the walls of computer companies, in contrast to those in a lab making small electronic instruments where one is more likely to find a picture of a lone pine on a New England hillside.

The computer company also attracts people who are very ambitious, as well as those who like to speculate in abstract terms about the unlimited possibilities of the product. It attracts a lot of people who enjoy fantasizing about the unlimited possibilities of the computer. In contrast, an oscilloscope doesn't lend itself to grandiose fantasies about social control or superbrains.

The market. The second factor is the nature of the market. This includes everything connected with the selling of a product, particularly the structure of competition in the industry, and the company's position in this structure. An adequate description of the market would require a fuller treatment than is possible here, but an illustrative example of its effect on character is provided by the semiconductor component business.

Here, executives who are highly imaginative and who have a real gambler's character and instinct (ideally, the instinct of a gamesman or even a jungle fighter) are valued. They must constantly weigh two variables that determine success or failure. One is the level of design sophistication and the other is the capacity to produce large numbers of components. The overly cautious executive (the company man) may produce an inferior component too hurriedly, while the more scientifically oriented executive (the craftsman), driven by the hope that he will soon have the ultimate design, may hold off developing production facilities until it is too late.

As a result, the spirit of intense competition for high stakes that pervades the whole industry and is felt on all levels of the technostructure lends itself to the kind of people who thrive under great pressure, and the top managers of these companies see it this way. They are gamblers.

Some of these top managers have the instincts of jungle fighters. As if they did not have enough excitement at work, they tend to enjoy playing poker, a game in which they conquer others by capitalizing on their weaknesses. And they discuss one another in "game" terms, seeing themselves as President Kennedy probably saw himself in conflict with Khrushchev or Castro. They think, "I know this guy; he will tend to do this, and this, and this, and therefore I'm going to do this, and this, and this." They say, "He tends to bluff in this kind of situation," or "He's going to think he'll get a scientific advantage here and so he's not going to produce in time, and I'm going to cut in here because I know I'll beat him."

This climate arises only partly because the industry is a young one and most of the top people know one another; it exists also because the tiger instinct is less adaptive to the market of the computer or small-instrument companies we studied. In those businesses, product lead times are much greater and decisions to buy are not made solely on the basis of cost or technical performance; rather, servicing and other considerations enter strongly, with the result that the nature of the competitive struggle is considerably more relaxed.

This does not mean the competitive spirit is absent from such companies, however. All high-technology companies believe they must continue to grow or they will lose their position in an expanding market so that, eventually, their profits will diminish. They also believe a growing company attracts the best young people because growth allows greater opportunity for advancement. The desire for growth and the selection of ambitious young employees are mutually reinforcing and increase competitive pressures, even where the market is far less competitive than the semiconductor industry.

The man in the study

The interview used by the author included many open-ended questions and check lists that dealt with the individual's work situation, his attitudes toward work, his sociopolitical attitudes, his personal values, and his family life. In some cases, it also included the Rorschach test. The results of these tests helped delineate a picture of character types and responses to different work environments from which a sketch of the study's typical EE can be drawn.

He is a second-level manager in a development project supervising some ten people. He is 38, has three children, and has never been divorced. (Only 7 percent of the sample had been divorced, and almost all the more successful managers report closely knit families—a finding consistent with the Defense Department's Hindsight study of key contributors to defense research.) He earns between $15,000 and $25,000 a year and holds a master's degree in electrical engineering. (Most engineers in the sample earned their degrees from schools other than the "leading" universities.) He has worked for ten years at his present company, which he joined right after his military service (usually, the Navy).

He is a conservative, family-oriented person who grew up in a small town and has inherited traditional values of hard work, self-sufficiency, and thrift. His parents were middle class (native American or Northern European). His father was either a manager, a white collar worker, or a skilled worker in some technical or technically related work such as railroading, engineering, surveying, or technical sales. It is likely that his grandfather was a farmer, although in many cases he was an independent professional or semiprofessional, such as a contractor, clergyman, lawyer, or elected official.

The typical EE studied tends to be a father-oriented person, admiring his father and sharing many of his values even though in many cases he has outdistanced him economically. His mother, in many cases, worked for a time as a bookkeeper, secretary, schoolteacher, or nurse.

The typical EE states that he works with advanced technology, either creating it or using it in new ways. Not surprisingly, he considers this work "extremely important" in his life and he would rather do what he is doing than any other job he can imagine. His work is, therefore, central to his life, to his view of himself, and to his sense of fulfillment.

His main function is to develop new projects and coordinate the work of others. He spends his time talking to both superiors and subordinates; he must judge others' work and, in turn, have his own work judged. He works 40 to 45 hours a week, including a few hours at home. Although some study subjects indicate that they work as many as 50 or 60 hours, among those who don't exceed the normal week, some label the 50-hour week as "overactivity," leading to lessened effectiveness. They take pride in *not* working so much.

Most subjects interviewed frequently dream about work, or think about it as they're driving to and from the job. They keep up with the "state of the art" and participate in company retraining programs. Although most say they consider their work technically interesting, creative, and important to the company, they are nagged by thoughts of being merely part of a huge machine, of becoming technically obsolete, or of being bypassed for promotions. Many engineers and lower-level managers don't feel they possess much power to affect the policies of the company and would like to have more say in how products are developed. If they had the choice, said over half of the people interviewed, they would rather run a small company of their own than reach a high level in a large company. For many, the ideals of individualism persist within the large organization.

The corporate culture. The third factor influencing the nature of the manager's work is the culture of the corporation. This includes the principles, both business and human, that shape an organization, and which are only partly determined by the product and the market. Differences in corporate culture can be quite great. For example, there are Japanese corporations that are organized on the principle of total job security—a cultural principle determined neither by the market nor the product, but by human goals and sociocultural patterns.

Other elements in the corporate culture are the degree of internal competition allowed, the quality of authority, the degree of self-management, the attitude toward dissent, the concern for health and safety, and moral concerns, including attitudes toward hiring and promoting racial or ethnic minorities or women.

In addition, the culture of the corporation is influenced by particular historical conditions. A corporation developed by a single family and dominating a geographical area may have aspects of a feudal barony in the sense that loyalties are personal, meritocracy is constrained, traditions and rituals are important, and so forth. By contrast, another company in the same technological area may be totally without tradition, meritocratic, and nonpaternalistic; it may thus allow bright young people to advance more quickly than in a traditional company, but it may also be more ruthless about firing nonproductive employees. Here again, it should be clear that a person's character will affect his performance.

Roots of competition

Character Type	Craftsman	Company Man	Gamesman	Jungle Fighter
Typical meanings of competition	Drive to build the best	Climb or fall	Win or lose	Kill or be killed
	Competition vs. self and the materials	Competition as price for success	Triumph or humiliation	Dominate or be dominated
Source of psychic energy for competitive drive	Interest in work, goal of perfection, pleasure in building something better	Fear of failure, desire for acceptance by authority	The contest, new plays, new options, pleasure in winning	Lust for power and pleasure in crushing opponent

The Selection of Character Types

We can now begin to integrate these concepts of work and character, and consider the function of the psychostructure in terms of selecting and developing character types. The organization obviously does not form the character from scratch, but it selects certain kinds of character from the available population.

You might say that, overall, we are dealing with a threefold process of social (in contrast to natural) selection that includes organizations, individuals, and internal psychodynamics. One part of the process has to do with which organizations survive and prosper in the marketplace. The second has to do with which character types are selected to man these organizations. (Over time, the adaptive companies tend to be the ones with the structures, culture, and the kinds of people—i.e., the psychostructures—that best fit the requirements of the technology and the market, and which best succeed in creating an atmosphere that encourages productive work.) And the third part involves an internal selection process, whereby those traits that fit the psychostructure are reinforced while others tend to be suppressed and underdeveloped. For example, an individual in an authoritarian firm must stifle his democratic side if he is concerned solely with advancement.

This, of course, suggests that those people who prosper in an organization are adaptive to their roles and tasks, not just in behavior but in emotional attitudes and impulses as well. This is what many managers are really recognizing when they tell us that they claim to have the "right attitude." They mean they must have that attitude which best fits the particular social role to which they aspire.

But there are many cases of brilliant and innovative engineers and scientists who have the "wrong attitude" and therefore fail. A scientist may try to manage a project, but be unable to delegate authority because he doesn't have the attitude of *liking* to see other people do things and develop themselves. He is so suspicious that he wants to recheck everything himself and control everybody's activity, making sure there is no carelessness or wastage. Such a person has an attitude that would be fine for a "lone wolf" research scientist—but within the industrial technostructure, it would be disastrous.

In our study, we have so far identified two contrasting psychostructures that exist within a number of corporations making similar products: (1) the pyramidal psychostructure of the large computer development project which, because of its many specialized roles and management functions, tends to *have* to be pyramidal; and (2) the much more cooperative project organization of the manufacturer of small electronic instruments. Both are in competitive markets and seek to produce an innovative product in the most efficient way possible.

As an example of how this adaptation process works, consider first the "mature" computer company—that is, the one run by professional managers. At the top of such a company we are likely to find a talented and loyal company man. At the top of the project group, however, we find the person who has the kind of character that allows him to manage many people, to respond to pressure, and to deal with many different things; in short, the generalist, who is most often a gamesman. He's the one who is in charge of making sure everybody is integrated into the team, that schedules are met, and that everyone is motivated by a go–go spirit.

On the lower levels we find craftsmen, company men, and a few young gamesmen. (We find more than a few older company men, authoritarian bosses who serve as first- or second-level foremen and like to control others and keep them to a tight schedule.) Young, aspiring game characters seldom stay at these levels for long, for they quickly look for jobs that allow more opportunity for both excitement and advancement—positions such as assistant to an executive, or leader of a small development project. The company man frequently rises to the middle levels and higher of a computer company. He may get further if he is especially talented because he is a person the company can trust to take care of its organizational needs. He might move from the middle of a project into marketing, for instance.

In the psychostructure of the small development group, it may not be necessary to have such strict hierarchical control and there are fewer managerial ranks. We find that the craftsman character is much more likely to advance in the small instrument company than elsewhere. Similarly, we find less evidence of gamesmen, and even company men, in the developmental labs of these companies.

The Question of Work Satisfaction

Our studies show that it doesn't mean much to say somebody is satisfied or dissatisfied unless you know both his character and the nature of his work. The craftsman is satisfied when he has relative freedom to determine the quality of his work, while a more authoritarian company man would be satisfied if his place in the power structure were high enough.

Moreover, what may be quite satisfying to an individual in the short run may not ultimately prove fulfilling for him. Thus, the gamesman, whose way of life leads him in later years to be somewhat depressed and goalless, has been contrasted to those engineers and scientists with a deep interest in building or understanding and who, therefore, remain forever youthful in their attitudes.

Given the foregoing, it is still the case that a work environment can lessen satisfaction for practically everyone if it causes strong negative feelings such as fear and distrust. However, the psychostructure can be constructed so as to minimize these feelings because, while the nature of technology and the market incline the psychostructure, they do not determine its final shape; the culture of the company is also a determining variable, and can be modified within certain constraints.

We can begin to judge such cultures in terms of their influence on the emotional states reported by engineers and managers. Some of them seem to produce more fear and depression in employees, while others show a high percentage of very satisfied employees.

The healthiest company cultures I have seen are those that can be described in terms of four principles:

1. *Security.* Your job is protected so long as you work responsibly, and your pension is portable if you decide to leave. Without security, fear and suspicion are engendered by all new programs since they may lead to reorganization and firings. At one highly successful corporation, where there is an exceptional spirit of cooperation and trust, not only is no one fired during reorganizations, but during the recent recession everyone from the top down took a pay cut rather than separate a single employee. This is in contrast to other companies we studied where the recession was used as an excuse to fire the employees deemed to be the least productive.

2. *Equity.* There is concern for fairness in pay differentials, profit sharing, and promotions; and management rewards individuals equitably for extraordinary ideas and work. Inequity stimulates envy and resentment.

3. *Individuation.* Individuals are not used in such a way that they become technically obsolete, but, rather, each has a chance to develop himself individually through work that is interesting and calls for continual learning and craftsmanship. Thus, no one feels himself to be a replaceable part in a machine. Furthermore, the individual's need for autonomy must be respected. In those companies where engineers are most pushed and their work is constantly audited, engineers report more symptoms of anxiety and depression.

4. *Democracy.* As much as possible, individuals participate in the decisions that affect them, including decisions about how to do the work and the hiring of new employees. Wherever possible individuals should be able to work with other parts of the organization and with customers, and they should have the right to speak out, with appropriate constitutional protection. Without concern for democracy, passive obedience and timidity, rather than active responsibility, result.

The Corporate Culture and Society

One might think that a system most satisfying to the participants and productive for the corporation would also be beneficial for the larger society. But this is not necessarily the case. A corporation that is good for the engineers and managers may not contribute to social well being. Furthermore, in the long run, it may not even lead to the level of human development these individuals are capable of achieving. This point leads to some comments about the sample as a whole.

We see many positive results from the work of the people we interviewed. They report that it often generates greater self-confidence and sharpened ability. And, in working with other people, they have had to develop open-mindedness and flexibility. Many have been educated by the demands of technology and work in the corporation; they have seen the need for planning and for fairness in the larger society. This is a liberalizing process, particularly for those who come from a very insulated, small-town background and who are rather conservative. Some wives we interviewed, with the same backgrounds as their husbands, are more insular and politically conservative than their husbands precisely because they have not had this experience.

Yet minimal concern is reported by the managers and engineers we interviewed about the effect of the work on their own spiritual self-development. They say that the work does not stimulate compassion, generosity, idealism, or even friendliness; and their responses to the questions show little concern with overcoming greed and egotism, and in developing their capacity to love and understand. In their highly competitive environment, they evaluate other people mainly in terms of how well or how poorly they contribute to the work.

Few even mention the goal of increasing their scientific understanding, as opposed to doing something technically effective and being part of a successful project. They are oriented toward personal success first, interesting work second, and a comfortable family life third.

With their energies concentrated on these goals, few take responsibility for bettering their community, or even consider what steps they might take—despite the intelligence and knowledge they could presumably offer—to make a contribution to civic affairs.

Few worry about the social effects of the products they have created, even though a majority believe that advanced technology contributes to dehumanization. This is, in part, because they feel, with some justification, that there is little they can do about these broader issues, but also because they see their small, protected world as an isolated one. They live a privileged life in comfortable surroundings, with stimulating work, and have little contact with people who lack both. Some say the social implications of their work are important to them, but this doesn't translate into practical terms.

The majority consider that the U.S. overinvests in the military and they don't like to think that what they are working on is for the military; they would much rather believe that what they are doing is for education, for medicine, for improving communications in the world, and so on. Most important, they do not make an effort to learn the effects of what they do on others, in the United States and the rest of the world. As long as they remain unaware and unrelated, they avoid having to accept responsibility.

Thus, while the work of engineers and managers stimulates intellectual or cognitive development, the heart remains underdeveloped. They not only tend to become hardened or self-protective and little able to love, but that other quality of the heart—courage of one's convictions—is also underdeveloped. In fact, we found that those engineers who are most concerned about people and spiritual development suffer the most in the corporate environment and report the most psychosomatic symptoms such as headaches, gastrointestinal complaints, and insomnia.

Is this picture any different from that of other workers in the U.S.? Lacking comparable data, I can only speculate. However, comparing my own experience in universities, I would say that although academics generally consider themselves more "humane" than businessmen, the EEs we interviewed are no more competitive and a lot more cooperative with one another than most professors. Furthermore, many of them, especially those with religious concerns, are more open to the issues of human relationships presented here than we had expected. They react as though waking up to truths already half-known. Most of the people we interviewed have seldom, if ever, even talked about these issues, particularly as they affect their inner lives, but many are not so hardened that they are unable to experience the emptiness that results from lack of love and lack of goals beyond success and comfort.

As a result, when I return to report these findings to individuals or at seminars held at the companies we have studied, the question is invariably asked: "What can we do about it?" The best answer that I have is simply to avoid illusions that are debilitating. During the past decade many managers have been sold formulas for improving morale, efficiency, and "self-actualization" that range from sensitivity groups to organizational development programs. Such programs have left considerable disappointment in their wake because they do not take character and psychostructure sufficiently into account.

I would refrain from offering merely another nostrum. Cultural changes such as the ones outlined here can increase work satisfaction and decrease negative feelings. They have a good chance of being adopted because they also increase work efficiency. However, they will not change character. Our study shows that the technology and the market conditions are the major influences in shaping the psychostructure and, correspondingly, those character traits that will be selected and strengthened. Under present industrial systems, companies throughout the world are likely to remain hierarchical and competitive in order to maximize growth and profits.

This brings us to a question we raised at the outset: To what extent is it possible in a highly competitive corporation for the engineer or manager to achieve his goals at work and further his intellectual development while, at the same time, developing himself emotionally and spiritually?

Those whose main goal is continued advancement leading to the executive suite already know the answer. For the most part, they are aware of the costs of moving up in the organization and are willing to pay the price, even to the extent of failing as fathers or husbands. The individual who does not wish to pay this price is left with the alternative of doing his work, but detaching himself from the contest in order to develop those aspects of his self that are suppressed in the workplace. On this final point, I would welcome the views of *Spectrum* readers.

ABOUT THE AUTHOR: *Michael Maccoby directs the Harvard University Project on Technology, Work, and Character. This project, which is sponsored by the Harvard Seminar on Science, Technology, and Public Policy, has been under way since 1969. Its overall aim is to contribute to understanding the managers and engineers of technologically advanced companies in the field of electronics as a social class of considerable power and influence throughout the world. He is now preparing a book titled* The Corporate Individual.

Dr. Maccoby is a Fellow of the Institute for Policy Studies in Washington, D.C., and is in private practice as a psychoanalyst. After receiving the Ph.D. from the Harvard Department of Social Relations in 1960, Dr. Maccoby went to Mexico to study psychoanalysis under Erich Fromm. Their collaboration on the study of social character laid the basis for the project described in this article. Dr. Maccoby has taught at several universities and was a Fellow at the Center for Advanced Study in the Behavioral Sciences when he began the project. He has written extensively on the humanization of work and he is a contributor to the recent HEW report, Work in America.

What you need to know about organization development.

Common Questions and Tentative Answers Regarding Organization Development

LYMAN K. RANDALL

More people in business and government are searching for more meaningful, more effective, ways to get work done. As a result of their search, they are becoming optimistic about initiating creative and purposeful change in work organizations. They label their activities and concepts *Organization Development*. The search for new answers, however, also leads to more questions. Listed are many of the questions commonly asked about Organization Development. The answers which follow are tentative simply because the field is still emerging and the conclusions are not final.

1. Briefly, what is Organization Development?

Organization Development is a reorientation of man's thinking and behavior toward his work organizations. It applies the scientific method and its underlying values of open investigation and experimentation to individual and work group behaviors as they are directed toward the solution of work problems. It views both man and change optimistically. It applies a humanistic value system to work behaviors. It assumes people have the capability and motivation to grow through learning how to improve their own work climate, work processes and their resulting products. It accepts as inevitable the conflicts among the needs of individuals, work groups, and the organization, but advocates openly confronting these conflicts using problem-solving strategies. Its goal is to maximize the use of organization resources in solving work problems through the optimal use of human potential.

© 1971 by The Regents of the University of California. Reprinted from CALIFORNIA MANAGEMENT REVIEW, Vol. 13, No. 3, pp. 45-52, by permission of The Regents.

2. Is Organization Development simply the Human Relations Movement in a new format?

Although related to earlier human relations work, OD differs from it in several ways. Many managers interpreted the message of human relations to be: "If morale is high, productivity will increase; and morale can be increased by 'being nice to people.'" For these managers "being nice to people" eventually meant emphasizing what Frederick Herzberg later categorized as work hygiene factors: employee benefits, working conditions, facilities, administrative policies, and social relationships.[1]

Organization Development, on the other hand, concentrates on the accomplishment of work and the solving of work problems by people. The improvement of relationships between people and work groups is not an end in itself, as it often turned out to be in human relations. Instead, interpersonal and intergroup behaviors are the focus as they are relevant to the successful problem-solving efforts of the work unit.

3. Is Organizational Development primarily concerned with restructuring organizations?

No. Many people assume that the term, *organization development,* is closely related to the organization planning process with its emphasis on organization charts, and the like. Although the restructuring of an organizational unit could be one of the results of an OD effort, this activity might be only one consequence of OD.

4. On what concepts is Organization Development based?

The concepts fundamental to OD can be placed in two general categories: those that apply more often to work groups and large organizations and those that apply to the individual. Naturally, these concepts are interrelated.

OD Concepts Regarding Work Groups and Organizations

- *Systems.* —Organizations are laced together by systems and subsystems such as budgeting, purchasing, inventory and stores, and so on. All subunits or parts of a system are interrelated to the whole. When one part of a system is changed, the total system is affected. In OD, thinking in systems terms is necessary when planning the tactics and strategies of change.

---

[1] For a fuller discussion of Herzberg's theory regarding hygiene factors vs. motivating factors, see "One More Time: How Do You Motivate Employees," *Harvard Business Review,* (Jan.-Feb. 1968).

- *Problem-Solving Interdependence.*—This concept is closely related to *systems.* When individuals and groups are working toward the solution of problems which affect other persons and groups, the problem is said to be interdependent rather than independent. In this situation people and groups have a common stake in the outcome and therefore need to have a voice in the solution. Treating interdependent problems as if they are independent usually leads to resistance to change and win/lose conflict between those who had a chance to have their say and those who did not.
- *Work Climate.*—Research indicates that work climate affects the kinds of results that individuals, groups, and total organizations produce as atmospheric climate affects the quality of crops that a farm produces. Work climate is comprised of the values, attitudes, and underlying assumptions which determine how work gets done. Work climate is closely related to *OD Values* and *Theory Y* discussed later.[2]
- *Force Field.*—This theory states that any given behavior of a work group is held at a given level by two opposing sets of forces: driving forces which push the level of performance up to a certain point; restraining forces which prevent the behavior from rising beyond this same point. Using this concept we can see there are two basic options open to us if we wish to increase any behavior or set of behaviors such as, for example, work group productivity. We can add more driving forces to increase productivity or we can identify and remove some of the restraining forces which keep productivity from going any higher. The first option is more often used, but the second option often holds more promise for results since it removes a force that most individuals see as negative. Although OD focuses on both driving and restraining forces as determinants of job behavior, it often emphasizes the latter since restraining forces are more often overlooked in the analysis of work problems.
- *Process and Tasks.*—Work groups and individual jobs exist to accomplish tasks needed for the organization to survive, remain healthy, and grow. Specific tasks are determined by goals of the group or corporation. Process, on the other hand, is what happens between individuals and groups as they work on their tasks. In the Broadway musical, "Zorba," *life* is described as "what happens to you as you are waiting to die." Similarly, process is what happens among people as they are working on tasks. Typically managers focus on tasks much more frequently than they do on process although process problems usually cause below-standard task achievement. Perhaps the most difficult

---

[2]See George Litwin and Robert Stringer, *Motivation and Organization Climate* (Boston: Harvard University, 1968).

aspect of OD for many managers is learning to deal with process issues. Several specific factors distinguish *tasks* from *process*.

Task (the job to do)		Process (the "happenings" of getting tasks done)
Usually concrete and based on objectives	vs.	More nebulous and difficult to identify
More static and often repetitive	vs.	Very dynamic and fluid
Outside of ourselves	vs.	Involves "tuning-in" to what's going on inside ourselves
Much "There and Then" time orientation	vs.	"Here and Now" time orientation
Usually dealt with intellectually	vs.	Involves much feeling and subjective perception

■ *Data Collection and Diagnosis.* —For years businessmen have been collecting data about such factors as markets, new product performance, and capital expenditures in order to diagnose problems that need to be resolved. These same men have only recently begun to learn to collect data about the human interaction process in their organizations. Problems involving individual and group perceptions, feelings, assumptions, and attitudes often provide the key for improving the accomplishment of work group tasks. Usually data are collected either by using anonymous questionnaires or by an outside resource person who interviews selected individuals. A summary of the data is then fed back to the group for discussion and problem-solving.

OD Concepts Regarding Individuals

■ *OD Values.* —These are values which people must regard highly before an OD effort can succeed in an organization. They are important ingredients in the work climate of an organization involved in OD. Many of these values have a concomitant skill or behavior which can be learned and practiced by individuals. These values and related skills include the following:

Trust and openness: This is perhaps the cornerstone of all OD work. Trust in interpersonal and intergroup relationships is essential if full and open communication is to occur. An open and nonmanipulative sharing of data is required for the effective solving of work problems. In most organizations or work groups, trust does not exist automatically. Traditional work orientations based on the manipulation of people have generated widespread distrust at all levels. This widespread distrust of supervisors, other work groups, and other employees is one of the initial problems often encountered in an OD effort. Building trust and openness throughout an organization is therefore one of the continuing goals of OD.

Leveling: "Tell it like it is!" OD work is usually called leveling. An individual with the skill and courage to share candidly with others meaningful information and how he thinks, reacts, and feels about work issues and co-workers is unfortunately the exception in today's organization. However, leveling skills are essential if OD is to succeed.

Feedback: People tend to make many assumptions about other people—how they feel, what they think, why they behave as they do—without ever checking out the accuracy of what they have assumed. Feedback is simply a communications skill for verifying or correcting these assumptions and thereby providing more accurate data on others as well as on ourselves. To be useful, however, feedback must be shared in a helpful, nonaccusatory manner. Feedback that begins, "The trouble with you is . . ." is generally destructive rather than helpful. Feedback can be given and received successfully only when relationships are based on trust and mutual respect. The result is a deeper and more accurate comprehension of what is going on in the process of accomplishing work.

Confronting conflict: OD values hold that conflict is a natural occurrence between people and work groups. Conflict issues should therefore be dealt with openly and problem-solved. Unfortunately traditional work orientations, perhaps influenced by the military, hold that conflict is negative and should be avoided, denied, or smoothed-over whenever possible. The result of this approach is the perpetuation of unresolved problems. Conflict confrontation skills include such factors as trust, leveling, and ability to give and receive feedback.

Risk-taking: This refers to the ability of individuals to "stick their necks out" in meaningful ways. Examples include taking an unpopular stand in an important issue, conflicting with a superior on preferred solutions to a problem, trying to initiate action on a problem seemingly avoided by others, and sharing with co-workers personal feelings such as commitment, concern, anxiety, or caring.

Owning of personal experience: In today's organizations it is very easy to point the finger of blame or responsibility at others. In fact many, many people have spent years learning how to defend themselves from real or imagined accusors by denying responsibility, concern, and feeling regarding their work experiences. Personal experience also underlies an individual's ability to level about himself, give feedback to others, build interpersonal trust, take risks, and to confront conflict—all of which are essential to OD activities.

■ *Self-Actualization.*—This term is used by Maslow to describe man's highest order of motivational need. It includes his personal needs for learning, growth, achievement, competence, recognition, and the striving toward his fullest potential. These are the elements Herzberg has recently formulated as the Motivating Factors of people at work. Self-actualization is premised on an optimistic view of man. A self-actualizing man is an individual behaving at his most creative and productive level. An individual is most likely to behave in self-actualizing ways if the climate in which he works is characterized by openness, trust, confrontation, and so on, and he has challenging goals.

■ *Theory Y.*—In reviewing the findings of behavioral science research in industry several years ago, Douglas McGregor formulated a set of assumptions about man at work that seemed to be supported by the research. He called this formulation *Theory Y*.[3] It is built on the following premises:

- Work is as natural to man as play and rest.
- Man will use self-direction and control when he is committed to objectives.
- Man learns, under proper conditions, to accept and even to seek responsibility.
- Creative ability is widely dispersed among individuals.
- In industry, man's potential is only partially utilized.

McGregor then contrasted Theory Y with another set of assumptions about man at work. He labeled these *Theory X*, and observed that most organizations behaved as if they believed these assumptions rather than *Theory Y*. *Theory X* assumptions include:

- The average man dislikes and will avoid work.
- He must be forced, controlled, and directed to work.
- He prefers to be directed in his work since he has little ambition.
- He seeks only security.

Obviously, OD is based on *Theory Y* assumptions. Many of the work climate values and organizational practices which are change-targets for OD stem from *Theory X* assumptions.

■ *T-Groups.*—T-Groups are specially designed learning experiences which focus on most of the OD concepts discussed above, i.e. trust, openness, process, leveling, feedback, risk-taking, owning experience, and so on. For many individuals, T-Groups provide unique opportunities to assess themselves regarding where they stand in relation to these values and skills. For this reason, some version of a T-Group is often used as a first step in launching an OD effort in an organization.[4]

5. How do many Organization Development efforts get initiated?

Many OD activities begin when a manager becomes uneasy about the effectiveness of his own work group. Often he is not aware of the causes of ineffectiveness although he can usually point to several symptoms. These might include frequently missed deadlines, conflicts between employees that are never dealt with directly, low-level innovation in

---

[3] Douglas McGregor, *The Human Side of Enterprise* (New York: McGraw-Hill, 1960).

[4] Chris Argyris, "T-Groups for Organizational Effectiveness," *Harvard Business Review* (March-April, 1964).

problem-solving, distrust between individuals or groups, the disowning of personal responsibility, et cetera. In other words, OD begins with a manager looking for more effective ways of accomplishing the goals of his group and the organization. He is usually a man who sees himself as reasonably competent but with more to learn.

6. Is it true that Organization Development must always begin at the top of the organization?

A recent survey by the National Industrial Conference Board found that approximately half of the OD efforts studied had been initiated by corporate presidents or board chairmen. In the other organizations the early OD experimenting and risk-taking was done by managers further down the hierarchy.

"OD must begin at the top!," is sometimes used by a person who wants to deny any personal need or responsibility for change. In this case he is actually saying, "My work group is in fine shape, but it's those S.O.B.'s who always foul-up things!" Pointing to the top of the organization gets him off the hook nicely since there is little he can do personally to make top management aware of *their* need to change.

Eventually OD must include top management. Organizational climate is formed at the top. Similarly the rewards for and restraints against risk-taking, leveling, and confronting conflict issues are established here. The overall quality of teamwork characteristic of the organization is heavily influenced by the behaviors of the top team.

7. Where can an individual find an Organization Development program to fit his needs?

Many managers are accustomed to thinking about their activities in terms of concrete programs that begin at a specific time and end by a preset date. It is therefore natural for them to expect OD to fit this same pattern. Unfortunately, it does not. By definition OD must begin where individuals and the work group are. This requires an initial collection of data from members of the work group followed by a basic diagnosis of restraints that seem to be interfering with the work group's problem-solving efforts and the achievement of its goals. Planning specific OD activities must evolve from this initial diagnosis.

8. Does OD have a beginning, middle, and end like most programs?

This question is closely related to Question #7. As mentioned above, many managers are accustomed to thinking in terms of programs which have clearly defined start-up and conclusion phases. If, however, an OD effort is successful, it will become "a way of organization life" and therefore will have no identifiable conclusion. This is often a difficult and frustrating point to understand. Just as *managing* is a means to an end, OD is also a process rather than an end product. One of its goals is to build into an organization the human dynamics essential for continuous self-renewing change. OD should lead a work group toward continuing purposeful adaptation and away from reactive change.

Several reasonably distinct phases of the OD process can be identified.[5] Initially a key manager must feel some heightened discomfort from internal or external pressures before an awareness of serious problems can occur. If none of his usual options for handling the problem prove effective, he may then look for new ways of attacking it. This is often the point where a behavioral science consultant is included in the work. The organization then goes through what is often called "an unfreezing process." Common psychological and communication restraints are purposely diminished. Because people and groups are now freer to communicate, considerably more relevant data and ideas become available for diagnosing and resolving the critical problems. As increasing degrees of trust and openness are built into the climate, more people become involved with and committed to creating the changes necessary to resolve the problem of the group. This greatly reduces the commonly encountered resistances to change. The next stage of change is characterized by increased experimentation and testing of new ways for working together and solving problems. If moderate to considerable success is experienced, the new work values and approaches to problems become the new work norms. This improved level of reintegrating work resources represents the final phase which makes possible a natural recycling of the whole process. At this point, managers in the group have learned to become OD managers.

9. Must a manager attend a T-Group or Management Training Laboratory before he can undertake OD in his group?

Although attending a T-Group is not a prerequisite for a manager interested in initiating an OD effort, it usually helps to prepare him for the experience in several ways. It enables him to experience what it is like to learn purposefully from his own experience. T-Group experience also helps him to learn more about OD concepts and related skills such as: process, "owning-up," trust, openness, leveling, giving helpful feedback, risk-taking, and confronting conflict. These cannot

---

[5] Larry Greiner, "Patterns of Organization Change." *Harvard Business Review* (May-June 1967).

be learned except through experience, and T-Groups provide a shortcut to this kind of experience.

10. What if a manager cannot afford the time or expense demanded by an OD effort?

This question is also based on the already-examined assumption that OD is some kind of new program that an organization carries on in addition to everything else. As we saw earlier, this assumption is false. Instead OD is a process through which work is accomplished more efficiently and effectively and without the human fallout and contamination often resulting from more traditional orientations toward work. Its payoffs are to be found in the saving of time and resources.

11. If OD is so promising, why aren't more groups or organizations practicing it?

OD is not more widely practiced at the present time for at least three reasons. First, individuals have only started to learn within the last twenty years how to create the process of change and growth within their own organizations. Before this, change was something that happened to them. OD is an attempt to integrate what we have learned in this area, and is a very recent idea. Another reason is that OD is a complex process and requires considerable time to spread throughout a total organization. Finally, OD has not always been an irrefutable success. People and organizations are still learning about OD.

12. Why is it often difficult to get the top executives of an organization involved in OD?

There are many reasons. Many top executives have been successful in their careers, in part, because they have learned to live by the traditional values of the organization. It is difficult for them to contemplate modifying or discarding that for which they have been so well rewarded.

In some cases top executives are among the last to know about some of the serious problems which drain an inordinate amount of time and energy from the organization. As John Gardner recently noted "We have still not discovered how to counteract the process by which every organization filters the feedback on performance in order to screen out the things it doesn't want to face up to."[6]

Other executives may fail to see any interdependence between their own behavior and the problems they identify at lower levels. Some executives believe that they cannot afford the time to engage in OD efforts.

---

[6] John W. Gardner, "We, the People," Millikan Award Address, California Institute of Technology, November 21, 1968.

Finally, most executives are also human beings. They have the same anxieties, or perhaps even stronger ones, about more openly exposing themselves as vulnerable individuals. They have valid reasons to distrust others in the organization who often try to influence them by using distorted information and manipulation. They perhaps even sense some of the seething anger and frustration at lower levels of the organization and hesitate to put themselves in a position to have these feelings dumped on them.

13. If OD encourages people to express their feelings, doesn't it lead toward subjective anarchy and away from a rational and scientific approach to managing?

Feelings and subjective experiences are as relevant to the successes and failures of organizations as are budgets and statistical reports. However, until recently they were largely ignored since they were considered nonrational and therefore inappropriate. It is paradoxical that the more we learn about our own feelings, the more rational we become.

14. What are the most common obstacles to OD?

OD efforts must overcome obstacles that commonly block any other management activity: misusing authority to bring about change; denying or avoiding conflict of central importance; disowning personal responsibility for initiating action or taking a stand on an issue; waiting for someone else to make the first move; resting on early or easy successes instead of pushing on for higher levels of effectiveness; involving only a few people at the top in the planning of change rather than working toward widespread involvement; reacting to failure experiences by finding a scapegoat rather than searching for the real causes of failure; expecting to accomplish new levels of effectiveness without learning essential new concepts and skills from qualified experts; taking action without having clear goals in mind due to an initial lack of data. Fortunately, however, these are all specific problems to which OD efforts are particularly sensitive.

15. How can you evaluate the pay-off of an OD effort?

OD results are extremely difficult to evaluate in a strict, scientifically controlled design for several reasons. OD is a slowly evolving process involving numerous people over an extended period of time. Many variables, such as key personnel promotions and transfers, occur during the OD experimentation period and also have an impact on the results accomplished by an organization. Who is to say whether improvements are attributable to the OD effort or to the change in leadership? Both are likely influences toward change.

Robert Blake and Jane Mouton conducted an OD experiment several years ago at a Humble Oil Refinery which Louis Barnes and Larry Greiner from the Harvard Business School were asked to evaluate. Although Barnes and Greiner argued logically and persuasively that the experiment resulted in several millions of dollars of profit, they were unable to prove the direct cause and effect relationships.[7]

There are two different ways in which the results of experiments can be judged. One approach is called *quantitative validation*. It attempts to demonstrate statistically quantified relationships between experimental activities and the results achieved. To a limited extent OD efforts can be measured by this method. For example, an initial diagnosis might be made of a work group's perception of itself using a written questionnaire. The OD activities which follow can then focus on the problems identified by the diagnosis. Later a similar written survey can again be conducted to determine if the earlier problems have been resolved. The results of the two surveys can be statistically compared.

A second approach is called *experiential validation*. It places importance on judgments individuals make about their own experiences. As an example, research shows that subordinates are reasonably accurate in discriminating between an effective and an ineffective boss. They base their judgments on their own private experiences with the world of bosses. OD results can more readily be judged through this same kind of experiential validation than by quantitative means. Most individuals in a work group that is involved in an OD effort can point to several critical incidents which would probably not have happened if OD had not been underway.

16. Aren't the values on which OD is based somewhat at odds with practical organization realities?

Yes, they are. One of the basic goals of OD is to change the traditional climate of organizations in order to utilize their resources more fully. Often the phrase, *practical realities,* is used by persons who feel the need to defend the status quo against the need for change. Being practical and realistic are two norms frequently advocated in the management-world of organizations. But who is to define what is practical and what is real? OD is built on the assumption that it is more

---

[7]Robert Blake and Jane Mouton, Louis Barnes and Larry Greiner, "Break Through in Organization Development," *Harvard Business Review* (Nov.-Dec. 1964).

scientifically valid to engage a large number of people at all levels of the organization in the investigation and discovery of what is both real and practical.

17. Is Organization Development an attempt to build an industrial Utopia?

In many ways, yes. The goal of OD is to maximize organizational productivity through actualizing the potential of individuals and work groups in which they are members. Certainly this is an idealistic objective, but does this make it an unreasonable one to strive toward?

The focus of OD is on the difference between what we are and what we are capable of becoming. Individual and organizational change are directed toward narrowing this gap. An executive involved in OD recently described the paradox involved in this type of goal: "We will continuously have to be dealing with resistance to change, including resistances within ourselves. People are not standing in line outside our doors asking to be freed up, liberated, and upended. Cultures are not saying: 'Change us; we can no longer cope; we are unstable.' Commitment to trying as hard and as well as we can to implement these (OD) values is not commitment to an easy, soft existence. On the other hand, the rewards we experience can be precious, real, and profound. They can have important meanings for us individually, for those with whom we work, and for our organizations. Ultimately, what we stand for can make for a better world—and we deeply know that this is what keeps us going."[8]

Conclusion

In his recent book, *The Revolution of Hope Toward a Humanized Technology,*[9] Erich Fromm asks: "Are we confronted with a tragic, insolvable dilemma? Must we produce sick people in order to have a healthy economy, or can we use our material resources, our inventions, our computers to serve the ends of man? Must individuals be passive and dependent in order to have strong and well-functioning organizations?"

Organization Development is an attempt to provide humanly affirmative answers to these difficult questions.

---

[8]Robert Tannenbaum and Sheldon Davis, "Values, Man, and Organizations," *MIT Research Report* (Oct. 1967).

[9]Erich Fromm, *The Revolution of Hope Toward a Humanized Technology* (New York: Harper & Row, 1968).

ABOUT THE AUTHOR: *Lyman K. Randall is Corporate Director of Training and Development at American Airlines. He has extensive experience in the field of organization development concepts and department organizations.*

A discussion of the need to evaluate the police training environment and to match the training effort to the organization's need.

Training: A Conceptual Model for Organizational Development

**MICHAEL E. O'NEILL
FRANK R. BENADERET**

There has been considerable progress in recent years in developing training programs. However, when this is related to the complexity of the law enforcement role it is totally inadequate. This inadequacy has stemmed from the fact that no quantifiable data relative to the actual work performed by officers has been available. However, recent studies have indicated that the field officer spends less than ten percent of his time fighting crime while the remainder of the time is spent in "people-oriented" tasks.[1]

To alleviate the recognized deficits in police training, we must know where we have been, acknowledge where we are, and assess what we need. This article will consider those questions, define and identify the training processes involved and explore a positive posture in meeting our complex training needs.

PRESENT STATE

In 1967, the President's Task Force Report on Police expounded on where training was at that time. They indicated that police training programs are fragmented, sporadic, and rather inadequate for the needs of the law enforcement field. It was indicated that the police

---

Reproduced from *The Police Chief* magazine, February, 1973 issue, with permission of the International Association of Chiefs of Police.

[1] Michael O'Neill and Carlton Bloom. "A Comparative Study of the Field Patrolman's Workload in Selected Police Departments of California Cities as Compared with the Long Beach Police Department," *Unpublished Master's Thesis, California State College at Long Beach,* January, 1971. *See also* Michael O'Neill and Carlton Bloom, "The Field Officer: Is He Really Fighting Crime?" *The Police Chief,* February, 1972.

187

are confronted with some of the most perplexing social and behavioral problems we have ever known.[2] However, it was also indicated that the police are not meeting this demand. More recent publications have also noted that police training, when related to need, is woefully inadequate.[3] As a result of the President's Task Force Reports, many police administrators have made a definite commitment to change their training perspectives. In response to the needs of law enforcement, the Omnibus Crime Control and Safe Streets Act of 1968 was created. The funding provided by this act gave law enforcement an opportunity to develop resources relating to training and other areas. With the advent of monies available, academic instructors took immediate note and instituted programs to train and upgrade the law enforcement profession. This disjointed and uncoordinated effort, in many instances, between the police and academicians, has resulted in a sporadic training effort. The impact of this has been training with no identifiable characteristics relative to where we are going. It must be admonished that training cannot be accomplished by occasional, improvised, or purely technical programs. Even with the resources and attention given to police training, it has been noted that police education and training are in a state of acute cultural lag.[4] There have been some honest efforts at bridging the gap between technical training and behavioral-organizational development training; however, most people responsible for those efforts have been relegated to personnel offices and are concerned mainly with limited concepts of training standards and techniques.

PROCESS V. CONTENT

The problem existing in our present-day training concerns itself with a dicotomized philosophy of process v. content. Most police training programs are steeped in "content-oriented" training—that is, training aimed at the technical approach or dissemination of information. There are probably two reasons for this type of training, namely tradition and lack of knowledge regarding process. Content-oriented training consists of firearms training, latest court decisions, evidence collection and preservation, etc., whereas process involves methods, attitudes, and behavioral concepts of police service in relation to organizational development.

---

[2]President's Crime Commission, *Task Force Report: The Police,* U. S. Government Printing Office, 1967.

[3]American Bar Association, "Standards Relating to the Urban Police Function," Institute of Judicial Administration, A.B.A., March, 1972.

[4]Norman Langhoff, "An Essay: Police Education and Training—A Foundation for Change," *Criminal Law Bulletin,* vol. 8, no. 4, May, 1972.

Process can further be defined as culturally oriented with emphasis on purpose, objectives, action steps, and evolution of a training program. One article appearing in recent literature expounds on the concept in defining training as the *how* and education as the *why* of doing the job.[5] In relation to our present approach, we would conceive the *how* as being the content and *why* as the process. This is used in the broadest conceptualization in differentiating the concepts of content v. process as utilized in this article.

ASSESSING THE ENVIRONMENT

Before organizational evolution can take place, one must first sense the training environment in the organization. Training environment is used within the content of where the organization stands in terms of growth. The authors view this as a continuum leading from specific skills or technical training to organizational evolution. The authors view organizational evolution as a biological context whereby you start from an embryo state and progress toward that in which organization and personnel development merge into the organizational framework.

It would appear that training today is not seen in this continuum. Instead, it is usually dealt with in a haphazard, undirected state without any directed end. That directed end can and must be identified by introspection into the organizational environment. Hence, a true assessment of organizational training needs must include valuable input from all strata of the organization. The trainer can draw upon a number of behavioral science theories to gain insight into these organizational strata which permeate any organization. These organizational and behavioral theories must be viewed within the context of the organization environment. This environment is made up of two types, namely the *diffuse environment* and the *focused environment*.

The diffuse environment is defined as the physical, social, political, and economic atmosphere within which the organization is affected and encompassed. It has a pervading influence relating to moral, political, youthful, and revolutionary constraints in the larger society and has a definite impact upon the organizational setting.

The focused environment can be defined as the coalescence of the organization with its effecting and affected clientele. The clientele place demands, have needs, and require resources from the organization. Hence, the elements of clientele demands, needs, and resources affect the organization's goals, personnel, structure, and technology.

The framework set by the diffuse and focused environment will enable the trainer to utilize techniques in effectively exploring the

---

[5] Michael O'Neill and Jerome Lance, "Education vs. Training: A Distinction," *Journal of California Law Enforcement*, April, 1970.

needs of individuals from the organization. One simple technique to illicit individual needs is to develop a "want" and "don't want" list.[6] Have each individual in the organization list his wants on separate sheets of paper. Then have the individuals list on separate sheets of paper what they don't want from training. Once the lists have been compiled, feed back the information to the individuals as a group process. Then have them as a group give priority to the "wants" and "don't wants."

This information can then be correlated with the behavioral theories and the environmental factors of the organization. The trainer should then utilize the needs, theories, and wants of the interphasing entities into a comprehensive training program to provide the satisfying of "human needs," "organizational needs," and "environmental needs," hence you culminate in organizational evolution.

ORGANIZATIONAL EVOLUTION

In order for the trainer to view where his organization is in relation to the organizational evolution continuum, he must draw upon behavioral theories, individual input, and environmental factors.

The authors view organizational evolution as consisting of four sequential phases. These phases consist of: (1) specific skills or technical training (embryo state); (2) laboratory training; (3) personal development; and (4) organizational evolution. Each phase has its own characteristic *approach, assumption,* and methods of *evaluation.*

SUMMARY

Changing times demand changing concepts, programs, procedures, and ideas.[7] Therefore, the entire environment of the organizational setting must be taken into consideration in order to identify where the organization lies on the continuum. It is very critical to identify the job being performed by the police in the community and orient the training to meet the needs of the organization and the community. Therefore, the assessment of your organizational needs and identification of where your organization stands is paramount before you can develop new training programs to culminate in organizational evolution. The key for innovativeness in the future will depend on how well police organizations can identify the type of environment they are

---

[6]For an extensive look into methods of gaining individual input, see J. William Pfeiffer and John E. Jones, *A handbook of structured experiences for human relations training* (Vols. I, II, III, and IV). La Jolla, Ca.: University Associates, 1969 & 1974; 1970 & 1974; 1971 & 1974; 1973.

[7]J. Edgar Hoover, "Professional Training, A Vital Need," *Justice Magazine,* February, 1972.

working in; identify means of assessing its needs; identify where the organization has been; identify where it is at present; and then develop training programs to reach organizational evolution.

ABOUT THE AUTHORS: *Michael E. O'Neill is the coordinator of Research and Training for the Palo Alto Police Department, Palo Alto, California. Prior to this, he was an administrative analyst with the Long Beach Police Department, Long Beach, California. He received his B.S. degree (1969) and his M.S. degree (1971) from California State University at Long Beach, both degrees being in Criminology.*

Frank R. Benaderet holds the rank of sergeant, Palo Alto Police Department, and is presently assigned to the Office of Research and Training. He is also an instructor in Public Administration at Golden Gate University, San Francisco, California. Sergeant Benaderet received his B.A. degree (1972) in Administration of Justice from California State University at San Jose, California. Currently, he is doing graduate work at the University of Southern California, School of Public Administration.

One police department's approach to organization development.

Organization Development: An Action Plan for the Ontario Police Department

REVIS O. ROBINSON II

INTRODUCTION

In recent years a new term—organization development (OD)—has sprung into vogue in professional business and administrative circles. Commonly, the term denotes both a process of planned change and a desired end result. It embraces many component programs and strategies, some or all of which may be combined into a total OD effort: sensitivity training, T-groups, confrontation meetings, data feedback, team-building, task force management, management by objectives, participative management, managerial grid, laboratory training, and group problem-solving.

Each of these OD techniques, irrespective of its procedural diversity, shares the ultimate goal of creating a self-renewing organization. Organizational development attempts to improve an organization's problem solving capabilities and ability to cope with changes in its external and internal environment.

Objectives or organizational development can be summarized as follows:[1]

1. To increase the level of trust and support among organizational members.
2. To increase the openness of communications laterally, vertically, and diagonally.
3. To increase the incidence of confrontation of organizational problems within groups and among groups.

From the *Journal of California Law Enforcement*, April 1974, pp. 177-183. Used by permission of the author and publisher.

[1] Wendell French, "Organizational Development Objectives, Assumptions and Strategies," *California Management Review,* Vol. XII, No. 2, Winter, 1969, p. 51.

4. To increase the level of personal enthusiasm and satisfaction in the organization.
5. To create an environment in which authority of assigned role is augmented by authority-based knowledge and skill.
6. To find synergistic solutions. (Synergistic solutions are creative solutions through which all parties gain more through cooperation than through conflict.)
7. To increase the level of self and group responsibility in planning and implementation.

The above listed objectives focus on an obvious fact: OD invariably concentrates on the values, attitudes, relations, and organizational climate—the "people variable"—as the point of initial change. Thus is is understandable that an external change agent, usually a professional behavioral scientist, is employed at least throughout the early phases of an OD program.

PURPOSE OF THIS STUDY

At the time of this writing all staff supervisory personnel of the Ontario Police Department have attended two three-day OD seminars conducted through the University of Southern California. During these sessions the group was introduced to the concepts and assumptions of OD, and more critically, they *experienced and practiced* various OD techniques as mutual problem identification and solving, self-analysis instruments, and team-building exercises. Initial acceptance of the program was so high among all participants that it was decided not only to continue the program among the supervisory staff, but to expand it into an entire OD effort encompassing the whole department.

This report then is an offshoot of these seminars and is designed to formulate an organization development plan for the Ontario Police Department. There are a number of objectives and sub-objectives of this study which will be addressed in the following pages:

1. To define the nature and extent of an OD program for the department.
    1.1 Is the department ready for an expanded OD effort?
    1.2 What conditions are necessary for an expanded OD program?
    1.3 What specific groups of persons will be exposed to what type of OD strategy?
    1.4 What is the proper time sequence for scheduling the OD programs?
2. To establish an in-house, continuing OD capability in the future.

2.1 What types of refresher courses should be given to which groups?
2.2 Should there be an in-house OD expert and if so who?
2.3 What other changes should be made in the organization to complement and reinforce the OD efforts that have preceded it?
3. To determine a suitable methodology for reviewing the OD program for effectiveness at all levels.
3.1 Review reasons for failures in other OD programs.
3.2 Develop strategies for ensuring program acceptance among departmental participants.
3.3 Identify symptoms of program failures and analyze underlying cause(s).

NEED FOR THE STUDY

Perhaps the best statement as to the need for an OD planning and goal setting program has been advanced by Bennis:

Obviously everyone cannot be in the OD program. This raises the question of priorities and choice. Can OD be isolated in certain components of the organization, leaving other components without it? Or should attempts be made to include segments of all subsystems of the client system in the initial stages of the program? In any case, a careful diagnosis needs to be undertaken in order to trace the most strategic circulation of effects throughout the total client system.[2]

The appropriateness of the Ontario Police Department to conduct this diagnosis is evident from another statement made by Bennis:

... The change agent (outside consultant) should attempt to involve the client system (Ontario Police Department) in planning and goal setting for the change program.[3]

SCOPE OF THE STUDY

Organization development efforts are typically divided into four successive stages:

1. *Diagnosis*—a determination that there is some discrepancy between expected and desired results and actual results and the conversion of the identified trouble into a defined problem capable of being impacted by an OD strategy.

---

[2]Warren G. Bennis, *Organization Development: Its Nature, Origins, and Prospects,* Reading, Mass.: Addison-Wesley, 1969, p. 51.
[3]*Ibid.*

2. *Action-Planning*—development of the plan of action which shows the most promise of altering the performance of the system in the desired direction.
3. *Action-Implementation*—translation of the selected plan into actual behavior.
4. *Evaluation*—comparison of the planned goals with actual results and diagnosing the variance and its causes.

This particular study will focus principally on the first two stages: diagnosis and action-planning. It will provide a general overview of the problems presently encountered within and between major departmental sub-systems (e.g., Investigation, Patrol, Services Bureaus) based upon personal observations of the writer and comments elicited from affected personnel in the concerned sub-systems. In short, it will highlight areas of the department in need of and amenable to change through OD interventions.

Action-planning will be performed inasmuch as OD strategies and tactics most appropriate for system improvement will be identified and evaluated for their potential application.

The sections immediately following discuss these stages in the context of specific operational difficulties (diagnosis) and remedies (action-planning).

ORGANIZATIONAL DIAGNOSIS

1. *Group-to-Group Interface*
   An excessive amount of dysfunctional energy is being spent by organizational units in criticizing and opposing the actions of other units. Much of this conflict can be traced simply to a lack of understanding of the other units' operational needs, although sometimes it is obvious that each unit considers itself and its operations to have superceding importance. These conflicts manifest themselves in one form or another at the following organizational unit interfaces:
   - Records Section—Patrol Division.
   - Patrol Division—Investigations Bureau
   - Patrol Watch 1—Watch 2—Watch 3
2. *Individual-to-Group Interface*
   There are really very few effective *teams* functioning in the department despite the fact that the organizational structure has created numerous fragmented work units. Most work effort is performed by individuals with a highly specialized assignment and who are exclusively concerned with fulfilling

their job requirements. Oftentimes broader team goals have not been defined, or if they have, they are not clear, or shared by all team members.

Organizational processes such as decision-making and problem-solving are generally performed in typical bureaucratic fashion—by deference to the formal power structure through a method best described as "decision by authority rule." Participation in these processes, if provided at all, is probably considered tokenism or mere "window-dressing" to the individual employees.

3. *Individual-to-Organization Interface*
A relatively large number of persons are only minimally committed to the department's goals and only half-heartedly motivated toward diligently applying themselves to their jobs. Apparently individuals' needs for achievement, recognition, and self-development are not being satisfactorily fulfilled, or individual needs are in some ways conflicting with organizational demands.

4. *Individual-to-Individual Interface*
Disruptions at this interface usually surface as interpersonal conflicts between co-employees within the same work unit. Personality clashes, perceived differential treatment by supervisors, and role misunderstandings typify the types of incidents which may spark an open confrontation between two parties.

ACTION-PLANNING

To effectively intervene these organizational problems a number of custom-tailored OD strategies are proposed in this section. The arrangement suggested is essentially a packaged OD program, integrating on a planned and multi-phase basis, a number of program efforts organization-wide.

1. *Team-Building and Personal Development*
It is recommended that five separate three-day sessions be provided to the following groups:
   - Records Section
   - Investigations Bureau
   - Patrol Watch 1
   - Patrol Watch 2
   - Patrol Watch 3

This phase of the OD program is intended to focus primarily on the tasks of the teams and the working processes designed to achieve those tasks. Hopefully, the teams will learn to function more effectively while, incidentally, improving their individual performance.

These programs may begin by having each member complete a series of instruments which give his view of the quality and character of team action and individual efforts. This includes how he sees himself operating as a team member and his own barriers to excellence. What he sees other team members doing or not doing which furthers or reduces the effectiveness of the team is also part of this effort. The completion of the selected instruments provides a foundation from which the members can study and resolve team problems.

The first task of the groups is to ask the question, "What can I (we) do to be more effective on the job?" Because a group can get so involved with what causes problems, it may spend an inordinate amount of time diagnosing and analyzing, instead of solving their troubles. Therefore, the question has to be asked: "Considering what we are doing that causes us problems, what alternative actions or behavior would be more effective?" Another question to be asked is: "What do we need to do to achieve the alternatives we have chosen?"

The major activity in these meetings is the working through of the information produced. The groups solve those problems that can be fully dealt with at the meeting. They make action plans for dealing with those items which need to be handled by the team or some subpart of it after the meeting. They also develop mechanisms for handling items that have to be forwarded on to some other part of the organization. At the end of the meetings the teams usually have a list of follow-up activities, including meetings and a timetable of actions or an implementation schedule.

Two key elements in the proposed team building sessions are (1) the involvement of the groups' supervisor(s) and (2) the technical assistance of a trained third-party facilitator. Inclusion of the groups' supervisor(s) is necessary if a genuine "team" approach to problem-solving is to be initiated and sustained in the department. Further, since part of the problems identified may directly or indirectly involve the behavioral intercourse between the supervisor and his team members, it is essential to confront these conflicts openly in a face-to-face environment.

The services of an outside professional trainer are needed to coordinate the sessions, to serve as a resource and facilitator, and to observe, collect, and feedback useful data to the group to help it reach its goals. This person(s) should be well-versed in small-group behavior and in techniques of behavioral science intervention.

2. *Interteam Development*

The objective of organization development efforts at this interface is to achieve collaboration or integration between these groups of specialized employees so that they can make a coordinated effort toward total organizational goals.

To achieve this end, it is recommended that the manager and several representative members of each functional group in the department attend a three-day interteam development seminar.

The following bureaus, divisions, or units should be represented:
- Records Section
- Patrol Watch 1
- Patrol Watch 2
- Patrol Watch 3
- Detective Division
- Youth Division

Although a number of intervention strategies can be employed at this interface to improve group coordination, a method referred to as the "Differentiation Laboratory" by Lawrence and Lorsch[4] may be appropriate. The design of this laboratory consists of dividing the participants into groups of six—one representative from each functional group. Members of each functional group are asked to talk about what is important in accomplishing their job and what satisfaction they derive from their work. They also are asked to discuss what other functional groups do to block accomplishing their objectives. When these subgroups reconvene in a general session, a discussion develops in which the participants work out problems between functional groups and develop a clearer understanding of their misconceptions and stereotypes of each other and how these inhibit communication and conflict resolution.

3. *Management Team Development—A Continuing Effort*

The initial series of three-day OD seminars for all supervisory, management, and administrative personnel inculcated the values and knowledge necessary to sustain an open, direct,

---

[4]Paul R. Lawrence and Jay W. Lorsch, *Developing Organizations: Diagnosis and Action*, Reading, Mass.: Addison-Wesley, 1969, pp. 53-54.

problem-solving capability in the department. It is therefore recommended that similar once-a-month off-site meetings be continued as an integral part of the total OD program. In fact, one such meeting was held on November 2 as an extension of the formal OD training program conducted by USC. However, a significant number of shortcomings were observed at that session which indicate the need for a more structured approach to improve the group's effectiveness and make the most productive use of available time.

Insofar as possible a monthly agenda should be established by requiring that all persons desiring to discuss a certain problem or situation, submit it in writing to the Chief's secretary two days in advance of the meeting. The established agenda should be distributed to all attending persons at least one day prior to the meeting. In the event no agenda is established, no meeting should be held (highly unlikely). The length of the meeting should normally be no longer than half-day with a certain amount of time left open after coverage of the agenda items for free discussion.

Leadership for the meetings should rotate among all participants every month. The same individual acting as coordinator should take minutes which briefly reflect the discussions that occurred, decisions reached, and most important, action items. Each problem discussed which cannot fully be resolved within the meeting or requires follow-up implementation should be assigned to one or more group members with a definite timetable for completion.

Immediately following each meeting but before the group disperses, a brief post-meeting session should be held to discuss the following items:

- A recapitulation of the actions taken and recommendations made during the meeting recently concluded.
- A clear statement of what is to be done (and by whom) before the next session.
- Any thoughts or contributions a member developed after adjournment.
- The question: What specifically does each member believe could be done to improve the effectiveness of the next meeting?

The setting for these monthly meetings should continue to be off the Police Department premises in order to preclude work distractions and psychologically encourage freer expression of personal thoughts and ideas.

Periodically, perhaps two or three times a year, an external OD consultant familiar with departmental management personnel (preferably one that has conducted previous OD seminars for the department) can be invited to observe the monthly management team meeting. The observer does not participate, nor is the session conducted in any special fashion for his benefit. After the meeting, however, the onlooker is asked to give feedback to the team on what he observed, especially interpersonal processes such as the degree of openness and leveling, conflict resolution techniques, mutual support, and goal orientation.

EVALUATING THE OD PROGRAM

The OD consultant as part of his involvement as observer/evaluator of the management team meetings will decide when professional outside consultation is no longer necessary, that is, when the department is capable of sustaining its own OD efforts. Most likely, the consultant will assess such factors as satisfaction, communications patterns, morale, and mutual trust and support in reaching his conclusion.

With a withdrawal of reliance on external consultants, the department must devote attention to identifying and strengthening internal change resources who can help with group and intergroup training activities, such as team-development programs, intergroup workshops, goal-setting programs, etc.

It is possible that the department's Training Sergeant can assume this new role with minimal specialized training in OD interventions. Another alternative would be to appoint an OD training committee from existing department members already possessing some knowledge of OD strategies and programs.

If needed, occasional direct linkages between department personnel and external consultants working as a "project team" can be formulated. For example, if the department desires to adopt a Management By Objectives (MBO) program the temporary services of an external consultant may be employed to provide technical input and implementation assistance. The advantage of this arrangement, of course, is that a balance is struck between the expertise of external consultants and the extensive knowledge of the organization possessed by the internal change agents.

MEASURES TO INCREASE PROGRAM SUCCESS

The single most crucial condition for ensuring success of the OD program is the commitment of the chief executive to the goals and methods of organization development. However, even ostensible advocation is insufficient by itself in determining whether or not the OD program leads to organizational change. The critical factor is the boss' behavior from day to day. If his leadership does not encompass the new spirit of tolerance and candor, the mood soon evaporates. His behavior thus undermines the program's goals and eventually causes it to fail.[5]

Another factor bearing upon the possible success or failure of the program is the timing with which the effort is expanded throughout the department. The OD program should not be expanded downward in the organization until all management personnel are able to reinforce their new behavioral skills in their interactions with others. When they have internalized new behavioral patterns, they will be better able to influence their subordinates.[6]

The action plan presented herein presumes that all management personnel have internalized the appropriate OD values and, furthermore, have demonstrated a willingness to change their organizational behavior accordingly. If this is not the case, the program will be doomed from the outset; it will be considered by many as the epitome of administrative hypocracy!

In undertaking any planned organizational change utilizing OD techniques, the voluntary commitment of the participants is a crucial factor in the success of the program.[7] Departmental personnel at the operational level (patrolmen, detectives, records clerks, etc.) must undertake the training in a completely voluntary spirit. It is highly doubtful that they will learn if this condition does not prevail.

Voluntary participation of all members can be solicited through sound "selling" methods which are calculated to explain the benefits of the program to all concerned. Trigger words which sometimes carry offensive overtones such as "sensitivity training" should be avoided, although persons should be told that they will be encouraged to freely and openly express themselves in the sessions. In this respect, employees must be guaranteed that whatever they say during the course of the seminars will not result in any reprisals by management personnel. In other words, job security of the participants must be protected at all costs. (It may be advisable for the OD consultant to conduct an informal and preliminary survey of participants at the operational level to determine the nature and extent of sensitive problems which they may be reticent to discuss openly at the sessions. Among other

---

[5]Chris Argyris, "The CEO's Behavior: Key to Organizational Development," *Harvard Business Review*, Vol. 51, No. 2, March-April 1973, pp. 59-60.
[6]*Ibid.*, p. 63.
[7]Bennis, p. 74.

things, the responses will indicate whether a confidential written questionnaire should be employed to elicit problem statements within the course of the OD programs.)

FUTURE OD PROGRAM COMPONENTS

Other programs which can develop as logical offshoots of the basic organization development program (and which build upon the behavioral expertise previously established), should be considered for future implementation within the department.

1. *Management by Objectives (MBO)*—Management by Objectives, also referred to as Management by Results, is an approach to management planning and evaluation in which specific targets for a year, or for some lengths of time, are established for each manager, on the basis of the results which each must achieve if the overall objectives of the organization are to be realized. At the end of this period, the actual results achieved are measured against the original goals—that is, against the expected results which each manager knows he is responsible for achieving.[8]

    Currently, Management by O/R serves many ends, chief among them being organizational planning, management control and coordination, personnel utilization, the evaluation of managerial effectiveness, and management training and development.[9]

    Although the MBO/R approach was originally adopted and is predominately practiced by private corporate enterprises, a growing body of evidence indicates that MBO can be successfully implemented in non-profit institutions (such as police organizations).[10]

    Experience also suggests that the organizational capabilities for a successful MBO/R process are essentially the same as those developed through OD. Therefore, one author strongly suggests that OD become the initial effort, and that MBO/R be phased-in later.[11]

---

[8] Dale D. McConkey, *How to Manage by Results,* New York: American Management Association, 1967, p. 15.

[9] *Ibid.,* p. 22.

[10] See, for example, Dale D. McConkey, "Applying Management by Objectives to Non-Profit Organization," *Society for the Advancement of Management (SAM) Journal,* Vol. 38, January 1973, pp. 10-20; Rodney H. Brady, "MBO Goes to Work in the Public Sector," *Harvard Business Review,* Vol. 51, March-April 1973, pp. 65-74; and T. P. Kleber, "The Six Hardest Areas to Manage by Objectives," *Personnel Journal,* Vol. 51, August 1972, pp. 571-575.

[11] Arthur C. Beck, Jr. and Ellis D. Hillmar, "OD to MBO or MBO to OD: Does It Make a Difference?" *Personnel Journal,* Vol. 51. November 1972, pp. 827-834.

2. *Task Force Management (TFM)* — As a component of its on-going OD program, the department should experiment with the concept known as Task Force Management. Interdivisional teams with temporary, but real authority, tackle major departmental problems under this operation. Major departmental objectives such as producing a policy and procedure manual, selecting and implementing a new management information system, or creating a braintrust to create and explore innovative ideas and programs could all be performed more effectively by the initiation of task forces.

A distinctive feature of the task force is that its responsibility extends far beyond suggesting solutions or making recommendations. The true task force has operational responsibility for what it proposes. Its work is not done until it has implemented its recommendations or created the instruments to carry on its work.[12]

Another trademark of the task force is that it cuts across departmental boundaries (and barriers). It is an instrument of integration and collaboration; it ensures that important functions are performed with the assistance of others responsible for other functions.[13]

POSTSCRIPT

The recommendations of this report may sound like jargon and theory-spouting to some. Charges of faddism may be raised by still others. However, the sincere intent of this report is to introduce modern management approaches into a heretofore traditional bureaucratic management structure. It recognizes the need for experimentation with new administrative theories and models, but it tempers this need with the understanding that these new technological tools are not ends in themselves, but simply means to produce systematic and ordered organizational improvements.

ABOUT THE AUTHOR: *Mr. Robinson received a B.S. and a master's degree in Criminology from California State University, Long Beach, in 1969 and 1971, respectively. Since 1971 he has been employed as the Administrative Analyst for the Ontario, California, Police Department. He has also served as a university graduate assistant; research associate for the Center of Criminal Justice, California State University, Long Beach; and municipal police department management consultant through Marquette University.*

---

[12]Thomas L. Quick, *Your Role in Task Force Management,* Garden City, New York: Doubleday, 1972, p. 55.

[13]*Ibid.*

A team-building experience.

Stress and Tension— Teambuilding for the Professional Police Officer

EDWARD S. ESBECK
GEORGE HALVERSON

INTRODUCTION

Re-Organization

In 1970, Michigan officials acknowledged a need for a central agency to investigate, collect data, and provide statewide coordination of activities concerning civil disorders. Early in 1971, assisted by Law Enforcement Assistance Administration funding, the Michigan Civil Disorder Center was established within the Department of State Police. Nine months prior to this decision, the State Office of Civil Defense was abolished and the duties and functions of civil defense were assigned to the Department of State Police. The State Police Director, in addition to his regular duties, was designated the State Civil Defense Director.

Adding the center provided the opportunity to combine the responsibilities of emergency planning (be it natural, nuclear, or civil disorder) into one administrative division. The Civil Defense Division was restructured; a Civil Disturbance Planning Section (CDPS) was created with a five-member staff assigned to the detection, prevention, control, and recovery phases of disorder within the state. The CDPS staff spent its first year doing research and providing tactical assistance to Michigan police departments. Equipment and manpower surveys were made and model disorder planning guides were developed in conjunction with the tactical training done in target cities, universities, and schools.

An Operational Void

In the course of its research, CDPS identified a large operational void in the area of conflict resolution. Specifically, choosing how to inter-

---

Reprinted by permission of the *Journal of Police Science and Administration,* Copyright © 1973 by Northwestern University School of Law, Volume I, Number 2.

vene and facilitate resolutions was absent. CDPS concluded that this was a serious defect in planning operational procedures for dealing with disorders in Michigan; there is no provision for conflict prevention. Statistically, there is overwhelming evidence that police officers, in their daily routine, intervene and facilitate resolution of conflict as much as any other professional group in the world, but specialized training for doing so is not generally available. Furthermore, resolution expertise is needed because a rational resolution is often endangered by political and administrative officials dragging the police image from the closet to shake it at dissidents threatening, "the cops will come and get you if you don't behave."

A Changing Social Role

Current societal confusion about the police role during social change partially explains the void. The image of the law enforcement officer, at one time the man who appropriated apples and moved his lips when he read, has changed. Today, responsible segments of society rely on the police officer to act as a primary buffer during the upheaval that accompanies social change. Current active middle class resistance to re-alignment of social values often creates a "monster" in modern-day police functions. CDPS identified explosive examples in the physical confrontations of large groups subscribing to opposing philosophies. For example, a confrontation positioned the police between two factions of a school bussing dispute. The anti-bussing faction included the wives of several of the police officers and the pro-bussing faction included a number of respected community leaders and citizens.

Problem: Updating Police Professionals

A changing social role necessarily changes the professional requirements for police officers. Therefore, the criteria used in the selection and training of today's police officer are and must continue to be of primary concern to administrators who recognize the changing role. In a recent paper prepared for Project STAR, Harvard's James Q. Wilson offered a set of standards for police officers designed to meet the current demands:

> A recruitment program must have the tested capacity to identify persons who:
> 1. Can calmly handle challenge to their self-respect and manhood;
> 2. Are able to tolerate ambiguous situations;
> 3. Have the physical capacity to subdue persons;
> 4. Are able to accept responsibility for the consequences of their own actions;

5. Can understand and apply legal concepts in concrete situations.
The object should be to develop an inner sense of competence and self-assurance so that, under conditions of stress, conflict, and uncertainty, the officer is capable of responding flexibly and in a relatively dispassionate manner rather than rigidly, emotionally, or defensively.[1]

Many police departments have recognized that the changing criteria have an impact on current personnel. There are numerous instances of training programs designed to prepare officers presently in service. Sociology and psychology courses, human relations training, sensitivity training, teambuilding, and conflict resolution are *not* new words in the vernacular of police training. However, in the CDPS experience the evidence indicated that despite current efforts, experienced officers were inadequately prepared to cope with the role change. Unfortunately, the proof of the inadequacy surfaced on the street during volatile situations. Too often police intervention had an unpredictable (usually untimely) effect on the entire community. The fact that extenuating circumstances and overt provocation has an influence upon the police officer seems to be of little concern to the average citizen; he expects the police officer to act dispassionately to *all* situations. Many publications deal with the expectations, anxieties, feelings of inadequacy, and related fears police officers experience. James W. Sterling of the International Association of Chiefs of Police has described the psychological qualities of the experience and relates them to the changing police role.[2] CDPS felt that Sterling's work substantiated the need for a relevant and innovative training program—one that was perhaps not available within the United States, or for that matter, probably not in the world.

Educational Goals

CDPS reached the conclusion that the needs and capabilities of each individual police officer had to be emphasized. The staff devoted its effort to developing a training program that would prepare officers for the role changing process. A priority emphasis was assigned to the stress and tension of confrontation situations because so much of the ambiguity and apprehension of social change becomes concentrated at those points in time. The pressures of verbal and physical abuse aimed at police officers dictated a second priority. Since conflict reso-

---

[1] Wilson, "The Future Policeman," *Future Roles of Criminal Justice Personnel: Position Papers* (Marina Del Rey, California: Project STAR, American Justice Institute, November, 1971).

[2] Sterling, *Changes in Role Concepts of Police Officers*, Washington, D.C.: International Association of Chiefs of Police (1972).

lution more and more requires a team response, two additional qualities for the "contemporary" police officer were added to James Q. Wilson's five item list:

   1. Exhibit a willingness and propensity for participating as a team member;
   2. Display basic skill with group intervention, or facilitating teambuilding.

Of the seven items, five refer to the qualities of the inner-man and his ability to cope with himself. Inner qualities, however, have to somehow become accessible to fellow officers if the training is to be applicable in disorder situations. Thus, learning to participate as a team member and being able to facilitate team development became training needs. Four goals for research and training were developed and submitted to professionals in several educational institutions. CDPS sought:
   1. A means by which police officers could learn to recognize and understand their tension and predict subsequent personal reactions.
   2. A learning experience that would improve a command officer's ability to recognize tension levels in subordinates and develop practical means of lowering such tension.
   3. Instructional material that would assist police officers to recognize high tension levels in groups.
   4. Basic skills for intervening in confrontation situations.

STRESS AND TENSION-TEAMBUILDING SEMINAR
Design
After several months of discussion and counter proposals, CDPS selected the Hillsdale Center for Management and Organization Development (HCMOD) of Hillsdale College in Hillsdale, Michigan, as its consultant organization. The HCMOD staff recognized that techniques currently used in industry and the military were too time consuming to be practical for the police. Nevertheless, the staff felt that a team process was needed for countering the tension and loneliness of facing hazardous situations. To make team concepts relevant to command officers, the building process simply had to be accelerated. Team members needed to learn how to use one another in a matter of minutes, rather than days. For example, a common practice is to mobilize officers from several, often diverse, communities for assignment to disorder situations. They are thus often complete strangers to each other, but tactically required to work together soon after arrival at a disorder scene. Forming "instant" teams, therefore, is actually dictated by the situation.

To design a program, the Hillsdale task force spent several months doing field research and study. It insisted that each member accompany police officers on a variety of regular patrol shifts across the state. In addition, training manuals, training films, and literally hundreds of pages of printed material from confidential after-action reports were jointly researched by the Hillsdale and CDPS staff members during the preparatory period. Ultimately, this joint approach produced a program which fulfilled the requirements.

Format

The pilot seminar included twenty police officers from city, county, and state police departments. In order to provide long-range impact, officers who had displayed a high potential for advancement and with varying degrees of experience and educational backgrounds were selected.

Table I portrays the five days of seminar training in outline form. Approximately nine hours of activity were planned per day. In addition, the evening sessions extended themselves into the night as the staff and participants developed common interests and/or questions. The Instructional Format responds directly to the four goals in two categories and thus divides the seminar into two 2½ day blocks. The first block focuses on *Grasping and Interpreting the Effects of Stress;* the second on *Teambuilding.* Stress and tension is integral in both blocks. Based on a general theory advanced by Karl Menninger[3], stress and/or tension is analytically described as the set of conditions in the *system* surrounding the individual at any point in time. Conditions, as they were defined for the police officer involved in a civil disorder, result from the ambiguity of the situation. For instance, his orders are to establish and maintain order in a civilian population. However, that population has, by definition, already disregarded established orderly processes. Thus, in reality, the task is to intervene in a highly charged emotional climate *without* the assistance of customary law enforcement practices. The effect amounts to psychologically "stripping" a performing officer of dependable, practiced behavior. Such conditions constitute a stressful or anxiety-evoking system for the officer.

Integrated Objectives

Four major educational objectives appear sequentially in the Instructional Format. Reading horizontally across the center blocks of Table I, the sequence follows from a premise that perception, with correlates of self-perception and self-image, initiate any process of learning new

---

[3]Menninger, *The Vital Balance* (1964).

behavior. Each officer completes a battery of psychological inventories and then carries that information along to the next learning event. The result of the first two units is an increased awareness of stress and a capacity to differentiate among probable causes and effects on self-image.

With awareness and the ability to be specific, the sequence moves to using self-disclosure as the behavioral activity for tension reduction. It is emphasized that disclosure, in order to be effective, has to be self-initiated. For example, an officer, after a shift on a restraining line, is aware of being angry and prone to an aggressive outburst. He needs to describe his feelings in order to reduce the level of stress. If he can choose to do so, the act of disclosure becomes a way of coping with the tension of the situation. Disclosure, however, requires a human recipient and thus the sequence includes learning how to observe the behavior of colleagues involved in the stressful situation.

So that the application of the learning would be situationally realistic, observing and listening to others is done in the context of teams. The first emphasis is placed on the critical interpersonal activities of team members. The integration of self-perception and self-disclosure begins with non-tactically-oriented incidents which set the stage for later simulated tactical team activities. The final portion of the sequence systematically escalates the training into simulated applications developed from police experience in disorder situations. The incident headings describe the training from the standpoint of problems facing a team. For instance, "Gathering and Using Information" presents a team with the situation of investigating the report of an incendiary plant in an urban disturbance area. Specific bits of information are given to each role assignment of the simulation. The plan and action by the team depends on the collection of the bits of information. The leader's process of soliciting information and the way the team members handle the information become the learning ingredients of the exercise.

RESULTS

At Seminar Completion

Table II, The Summary of Responses, displays the participants' evaluative responses to usefulness of the seminar. The frequency data were collected anonymously as a concluding event of the seminar. Depth and specificity with respect to the transferability of the training to operational situations was ascertained in the form of evaluative reactions ninety days after the seminar experience. The consistency of the high ratings at seminar completion shows that the concepts are relevant and perceived useful to the participants.

TABLE I.
INSTRUCTIONAL FORMAT STRESS & TENSION—TEAMBUILDING SEMINAR

SUNDAY	MONDAY	TUESDAY	WEDNESDAY	THURSDAY	FRIDAY
	PERCEPTION —Principles of . . . —Interpersonal Perception & Communication	INTERPRETATIONS OF SELF —Self Description Feedback —Effects of Stress on Self Image	COPING WITH STRESS —Models for Coping —Characteristics of Interpersonal Stress	CRISIS IN TEAM PROCESSES —Crisis Events —Experience with Team Processes	TEAMBUILDING FOR BACKHOME USE —Designing an Activity —Trying Out —Conference Review Feedback to MSP Staff Evaluation Checklist
	LUNCH
PRE-CONFERENCE QUESTIONNAIRE —Registration	SELF-PERCEPTION —Self Image —Use of Tests in Describing Self	STRESS & SELF DISCLOSURE —Models of Individual Under Stress —Stress and the Disclosure Process	OBSERVING TEAM PROCESSES —Process Observer Skillbuilding —Introduction to Incidents Method	TEAMBUILDING EXPERIENCE —Incident: Gathering and Using Info. —Incident: Assessing and Assigning Personnel	GRADUATION

	OPTION HOUR	
	—Sports Activities —Tour of Campus	—Conference Library —Civil Disturbance Films	—Personal Interviews With Staff

	SOCIAL HOUR & DINNER	
INTRODUCTIONS	PERCEIVING OTHERS	TEAMBUILDING DISCLOSURE	EXPERIENCE IN TEAM PROCESSES	TEAMBUILDING (CONTINUED)
Staff Goals Each Other	—Self Disclosure Model —Others-Building Blocks of Teams	—Small Group Self Descriptions —Team Experience with Disclosure	—Competition Vs. Collaboration —Team Process Feedback	—Incident: Intervening in an Ongoing Team Process

TABLE II.
SUMMARY OF RESPONSES TO TOPICAL USEFULNESS SCALE
N = 17, April 14, 1972

	LOW 0	1	2	3	4	5	6	7	8	HIGH 9
Perception							1		4 3	9
Self Perception									4	13
Perceiving Others							1		2 2	12
Interpretations of Self									1 4	12
Stress & Self Disclosure									1 4	12
Teambuilding Disclosure								1	4 5	7
Coping With Stress									3 1	13
Observing Team Processes						2	1	2	7	5
Experience In Team Process									1 6	10
Crisis In Team Process				1	1	1	2	6		6
Teambuilding Experience									1 6	10
Teambuilding For Back Home							3	2	5	7

The Ninety Day Longitudinal Results

As just stated, the impact of a seminar emphasizing behavioral change can be best understood from longitudinal evaluation of its transferability to real situations. In other words, the extent to which participants in a seminar learn the concepts they are exposed to is the extent to which they make use of them in daily work patterns following the seminar. This final section consists of a set of statements documenting retention and use of seminar ideas. The object is to show sufficient samples of change in behavior directly related to the seminar to judge its impact on participants. The statements result from interviews with participants ninety days after completing the seminar. To avoid biasing participant recall, a set of open ended questions were prepared and the interview was taped. Excerpts from the tapes provide the evidence of retention and use of the material offered during the seminar.

Overall, the seminar has definite and significant learning impact. Without exception the interviews show the choice of and attempt to implement changes in on- and off-the-job activities. The staff predicted that it would be beneficial to emphasize how individuals respond to situations *instead of* preparing them for "all possible" situations. Evidence of this is reflected in:

> I've run into a couple of people that were in the program. One of them I knew prior to the program. There has been somewhat of a change in his overall attitude. I think because of self-perception. The reaction that person gave me during the program and his interpretation of it since, I think, helped him very much.

Furthermore, the seminar apparently increased the desire to experiment to improve working situations. This is reflected (along with some impatience in doing so) as personal insight in the following comments:

> I'll tell you right now there wasn't anything that wasn't useful. But, it is frustrating in a way because I know now that the mechanics are there for making a lot of people's jobs easier and their lives more enjoyable.
>
> The problem is that you see a lot of times when it is possible, but you can't do any good. It is tempting to just forget it. But, if you try, remembering that it isn't going to work every time, but it will in the long run, then the only problem is to keep trying.

Many additional examples of overall impact are available in the transcripts. Evaluation, however, needs to be pointed if it is to be useful. To organize in that respect, the preliminary (seminar completion) conclusions of the staff are examined to see if there is evidence of participant's transferring the learning. There are three areas brought forth as questions. A collection of participant statements is presented under each question and followed by the staff conclusions.

Did the seminar teach participants how to change daily work or life patterns if they chose to do so?

> I like to think that control of myself is better, even with the little things at home. For instance, where the kids don't mow the grass the way it should be, I try to understand that they had other things on their minds.
>
> I feel real confident in this. There are some things that I'm going to do with this. Right now I'm searching for the vehicle to present this information, and trying to dig up more to follow that will lead us someplace as far as teambuilding is concerned.
>
> I've been able to talk to people much better.
>
> I've tried to change myself so that even though I know what the right way should be, at least I think I know, I try to let someone else bring it out, to let them get involved. This changes me because I find out that I'm not always right. It also makes a much smoother operation. Even at home, some of the things that were brought out, it changes things.
>
> I've learned, for example, that you get apathetic in your feelings toward people, that you treat all people that you meet as though they are in a certain category. You don't try to put yourself in their place. I try to look behind the crime a little bit more now. I try to determine the causes rather than the effects of it.

Clearly, both work and living patterns were affected by the seminar experience. The content of the excerpts indicates a wide range of impact. It is concluded that the transfer of learning is significant. It should be noted that individual capacities such as changing attitude, increasing self confidence, improving communication ability are mentioned. Thus, not only is there transfer, but what transfers is also comprehensive and specific.

Did the theoretic stress and tension model make sense to experienced officers?

One of the things that really comes to mind is the classes that we had on stress coping devices. I don't know how many hours I've actually talked to people about this same thing. Since then I have quit smoking. Every time I lit up a cigarette, basically, I have thought of the coping device instead of the cigarette. I did eventually quit. I have no problems with it. I just said I was going to quit and quit. The first few days were kind of, lots of mints and gum, but now I don't even have that problem.

I'm sure that by identifying the fact that stress was the big problem certainly helped out in my decision. Knowing that stress was causing this particular problem, I knew how to handle it.

I was really impressed with the portion of the education that had to do with coping with your stresses. This left a real impact on me as to the necessity of getting a decent amount of sleep and in the variation of activities after a hard day's work.

Identifying stress in other people is a lot more difficult than identifying it in yourself. However, there has been several occasions that I have had an opportunity to move into a situation that could have led into more serious consequences. I find that the people you deal with are more stressful than you are yourself.

You could see from the crowd that they weren't all belligerent. Some of them were there as curious onlookers and some were agitating. As you thought back to the seminar you could remember them telling you about people under stressful conditions. You more or less put yourself in the place of those in the crowd. You came up with answers to why they were acting the way they were and it gave you better insight about how to cope with the one with the loudest mouth and going over to him and talking with him and trying to explain or show him the reasons behind your actions, he became, at least for the moment, a person on your side of the story rather than the other.

It explained the systems that we all have, that a lot of our stress comes from outside sources but a great deal of it comes from our own feedback. Being aware of that, I can help them with their system.

Since the stress concept is a keystone of the seminar, it is obviously critical that it be understood. The excerpts show that the concept is understandable and, more importantly, that it lends itself to behavioral change in stressful work and living conditions. It is an understatement to conclude that the concept makes sense to participants. Not only did they learn how to understand themselves and others as systems with stress, their comments show that they learned that such a system has many dimensions for each individual. The stress model is transferable, in significant ways, to daily patterns. In other words, participants do learn how to identify stress as well as how to change their own and others' behavior relative to stress conditions during the seminar.

Did the other major supporting concepts and processes (Teambuilding, Self-Perception/Image, Self-Disclosure) transfer?

Probably self-perception and perceiving others in a teambuilding process is what I remember best. I've always liked to get into a win-lose situation and I really haven't since then. I've watched myself because I really don't think I help anything when I do.

I think you look back and say, well, how much can you really stand? If you've had the benefit of going to your seminar, I think you subconsciously—maybe consciously—think back and say, well, you've gotta remember that you're getting a little bit quick tempered and that student who is coming up to talk to you—he doesn't know whether you've been on the street for four hours or out here for 16 hours. You take that into consideration and try to control yourself.

The perception of others, yourself, and some of the things in the way of reactions brought out on coping with stresses were very valuable in the first part.

I had the five sergeants on my staff, each list the men at the post being rated. They put No. 1, 2, 3, right down with about 14 being rated that way. This gave us, with my own, six lists of men from one to fourteen. I then combined these lists to arrive at a composite from one to fourteen. For this, I involved the sergeants. Now they had a definite, positive, place in the selection of the potential of the man. Surprisingly, or not surprisingly, everyone had pretty close to the same evaluation. It was excellent not only from arriving at a fair way to evaluate the troopers who work here, but also from the involvement and morale point of view from the staff.

I can think of one that has worked out very well and this is not just with the staff situation that we talked about, but with a total post teambuilding effort. Recently, we remodeled our garage out in back into a squad room and we use that space as such. When we started on this we had quite a bit of negative thinking that here we were losing our garage space. We were able to work on this and change the feelings around.

It was really helpful. Now when I get into a group, this is what I look for. I watch for someone to fold their arms, fold out of the picture so to speak. I bring up to someone, do you agree or don't you agree? You know whether you have to sell them again or not. These are very valuable parts of the program.

The excerpts identify the concept or process along with the evidence of transfer. The self-disclosure process is not as evident as others, but there are indications of the value of being more direct and at the same time being collaborative. The conclusion of the staff is that the disclosure concept and experience with disclosing was recognized and used. To find specific evidence of transfer to work and living routines, a more direct inquiry method needs to be used.

In summary, consider the total potential for learning during a five-day seminar event and then note how much of that potential appears to have been grasped and became transferable to operational and daily life activity. This is, of course, the goal of seminar education. It is thus concluded that the right collection of concepts has been made and that a seminar process that achieves considerable learning transfer for police officers has been created and tested.

ABOUT THE AUTHORS: *Edward S. Esbeck is Director of Organization Development, The Hillsdale Center for Management and Organizational Development, Hillsdale College. He holds a Ph.D. in Organizational Behavior from Case Western Reserve University.*

Captain George Halverson is Commander of the Second District, Michigan State Police.

An in-depth discussion of a violence prevention unit.

Change Through Participation (And Vice Versa)[1]

HANS TOCH

Police officers who are experienced in violent involvements can contribute to police professionalization while undergoing personal change and development. These officers can be enlisted in work aimed at the promotion of more effective and constructive police-civilian contacts. Participation in such efforts produces both individual and organizational change.

The Oakland Police Department contains a Violence Prevention Unit, composed of patrolmen and a sergeant. This unit is concerned with research and action programs in training and communication, related to violence.

The project started with seven patrolmen, who met (part time) in the summer of 1969. Among the achievements of this group was the creation of a violence tape library, the completion of a critical incident survey, and the design of a new training officer program for the department.

In the summer of 1970, the 1969 group trained seventeen other officers, who engaged in projects such as family crisis intervention research, and self-analysis interviews.

Late on a Wednesday evening, a fleet of motorcycles turned into a parking lot in Oakland, California. Several Hell's Angels dismounted and crossed the street, heading for the lobby of the Oakland Police

---

Reprinted, with permission of the National Council on Crime and Delinquency, from *Journal of Research in Crime and Delinquency,* July 1970, pp. 198-206.

[1] The project described in this paper is supported by the National Institute of Mental Health; it is entitled "Training Police Officers for Violence Prevention." Raymond Galvin is co-director of this study, and J. Douglas Grant is consultant.

The work is made possible through cooperation by the Oakland Police Department, and its chief, Charles Gain. Throughout the project, Chief Gain has provided support, counsel, and encouragement.

217

Building. Five minutes later, the men entered a meeting room, shook hands with seven police officers, and helped themselves to coffee. The group then settled down to serious business.

The cyclists were serving as consultants to an unusual team of policemen, who work as change agents, groping for ways to solve a complex social and practical problem. Their problem area, of concern to both society and professional police, is that of conflict between police and citizens. Their mission involves finding ways of eliminating avoidable confrontations, and creating an atmosphere that reduces risks of violence.

FROM CHANGE CLIENTS TO CHANGE AGENTS

The unique feature of the project lies in its choice of personnel. Other things being constant, we seek to employ officers who have participated in more physical conflict than their peers. We assume that these men can become not only personally effective, but especially powerful agents of police professionalization.

The argument for this strategy is similar to the advocacy of sinning as a prerequisite for sainthood. In this latter case, it can be argued that when sinners-turned-saints discuss humanity, they know whereof they speak. It stands to reason that such men (and women) can easily put flesh on the bones of their theological concerns; that they can address themselves to the spiritual struggles of their fellows with empathy and credibility. Moreover, it is obvious that they must have reason to care. Having (as they see it) faced the abyss of their own destruction, they become motivated to save others from a comparable fate.

The same logic applies to more mundane transitions. The police officer who has over-eagerly responded to hostile citizens accumulates experience with degenerating contacts. If we can induce such an officer to adopt a more sophisticated perspective, he can draw upon a wealth of data about human interactions not possessed by less agressive officers. Moreover, he may be uniquely able to see the point of the violence prevention effort. He can think back to his own narrow escapes—the near-riots, injuries, courtroom inquisitions, and reprimands from superiors. He can recall the necessary deceptions and their risk.

Of course, the question is whether—and how—we can convince a problem person to abandon habits of a lifetime and to modify his premises and goals. Why should he cooperate? He may not only feel comfortable with his pattern of conduct, but may derive deep-seated satisfactions from it. He may see no "problem," and he may view himself in favorable terms.

What counts is the fact that a demonstrable problem *does* exist. We need only help the person to discover the (for him) undesirable consequences of his acts. We need to also offer attractive rewards on our side of the fence. What is involved is not material incentive, but more intimate psychological gain such as an important role in life or increased grounds for self-respect.

In all of this, I think the fundamental rule to remember is Lewin's adage that you cannot induce change through frontal assault. A person moves if and when he wants to, and he must arrive at this juncture himself. The best any of us can do is to provide an atmosphere that facilitates innovative thinking.

THE POLICE PROJECT

What we have done in the Oakland Police Department is to create an environment in which violence-experienced officers can become experts on violence. In this environment, the officers can evolve ways of reducing conflicts for themselves as well as for others.

We have started modestly. We have brought together seven patrolmen and assigned them (half time) the task of educating themselves and of training others.[2] Our first group is exceptional (for us), because it is not one of problem policemen, although several members have backgrounds of violence involvements. The men were chosen on the basis of group interviews, so as to insure that they could handle themselves constructively in a group setting.

Our team represents a solid variety of resources. The senior member is Bob Prentice (41), who joined the police department in 1951. Bob is physically imposing, direct, and resourceful, with qualities that bring him to the fore in any situation. He is a natural politician and leader. Bob's personal experience extends into "rough and ready" days of law enforcement, and this experience makes him a forceful and sophisticated advocate of flexible police discretion.

Next to Bob in seniority is Mike Weldon (32), who has spent seven years on the job. Mike is a policeman's policeman, thoughtful, firm, consistent, and immensely patient. Mike personifies stability, and his interventions in our group are measured, pointed, and tempering.

Carl Hewitt (28), has five years of police work to his credit. He has an inventive command of language and a spontaneous capacity for mimicry. He is intuitively skilled in human relations, and flexible in the management of interpersonal encounters.

---

[2] As this paper goes to press, our group has expanded to 24. Our first seven officers are working as planners, leaders, and trainers. The 17 new men, all of whom have records of violent involvements, are engaged in research and action programs.

Two of the group who have four years on the force are Roy Garrison (29) and John Dixon (28). Roy has accumulated numerous college credits. His academic work includes several subjects of relevance to the project, including group dynamics and management. John Dixon has no college training, but is an omnifarious reader, and successfully self-educated. John is quiet, perceptive, and thoughtful.

Larry Murphy (31) has spent two years in police work. He is a mature person, having been discharged by the Navy as chief. Larry is invariably able to focus group attention on priorities, and on the means necessary to reach them. Larry provides a reservoir of technical skills (communications and electronics), and much leadership experience.

The comparatively young member of the group is Mike Nordin (26) who joined the department over two years ago. Mike packs power into a quiet, even, soft-spoken approach to others. He is insightful in his dealings with fellow officers and civilians, and is able to skillfully reduce tensions and prevent conflicts.

The Oakland Police Department Violence Prevention Unit (as we called ourselves) started functioning July 2, 1969. Ten of us, seven police officers and three staff, met for two eight-hour days each week. The officers in the group led double lives. Half their working time was spent in uniform, answering calls and responding to routine police business. The rest of the time, in casual attire, they engaged in discussion and research, similar to that of graduate students and professors.

What did the group do? To provide some flavor of their activities, I shall try to describe one or two of the Unit's projects.

THE VIOLENCE TAPE LIBRARY

During our first meeting, an officer (Prentice) brought up the idea that we could record live incidents of potential violence. He suggested that tapes of real confrontations could provide research data, and could permit informed review by others. The group noted the suggestion (among others), but let it drop.

Several sessions later, the tape recording idea was brought forward again. This time, the group worried over ethical and practical implications. What of police who might arrive on the scene? What about the Unit's image if the men were known to carry concealed recorders? How could one run such a project to avoid repercussions? The group decided the idea might be worth the risk, perhaps on a one-shot trial basis.

Next, we examined a miniature recorder, purchased by the police department for other uses. We decided to give the machine a field test. A week later, the recorder reappeared with a successfully captured incident. This incident, discussed in detail, seemed potentially useful as training material. The group decided to add recorded comments to the tape, and to listen to it. This package—in modified form—led to the creation of a violence tape library.

The tapes we produce are spontaneous documentaries. In each of them, an officer confronts citizens in an explosive situation. We hear screaming and cursing, furniture crashing into walls, and people rushing about. We hear recriminations, challenges, and demands for help. We hear the police placed in the vortex of sometimes irreconcilable pressures. And we hear the officer trying to appease, to pacify—to somehow prevent an extreme act. The officer may use various strategies (there are no rule books here) and he may succeed or fail. Whatever happens, there is a lesson, both for him and other police officers faced with like problems.

In the tapes, each officer takes a look at his own experience. In the relative calm of an impromptu studio (Murphy's workshop), the man edits his tape, provides background information, and adds a running commentary as needed. His talk is added "on sound," so that the action evolves as the man talks.

The tapes include an analysis section, in which our officer second-guesses or criticizes himself; that is followed by comments from other group members. The "package" is a lesson drawn from life, of applied human relations. It can be used as is, ready-made, as raw material for comments, or as a model for others if they are equipped with tape recorders on the street.

The prospective market could include officers who permit street situations to degenerate because of poor self-control or bad judgment. Such strategies (or non-strategies) could yield to systematic review of failures. Memory is no help here because even with honesty, errors blur. The tape recorder preserves the moves of the game (in sequence), and it details (inescapably) their sometimes tragic consequences.

Positive alternatives, featuring constructive approaches, can also be dramatized. To illustrate such options, as seen by our group, it might help to review excerpts from a tape. These record one of our officers (Hewitt) responding to a family disturbance call.

THE PROBLEM SITUATION

Few people realize that police officers do not typically deal with crime in process. Only infrequently do they confront a burglar in the act of burglary, or a fleeing mugger or car thief. More routinely, the police deal with emotionally aroused citizens—with persons who are angry, fearful, excited, resentful, or upset. Officers sometimes arrest such persons, but they have other choices of action, and they must carefully assess individuals and circumstances before deciding what to do. A technical violation of the law is a factor they must consider, but there are more human considerations—and they must be weighed.

Hewitt's encounter is instructive in this regard because it shows the options, and resolves these without the use of sanctions. As Hewitt calls—

> I received a call about 10:30 in the morning, Saturday, of a family fight that had just occurred on . . . Avenue, involving a husband and wife. It had occurred in the street and he (the husband) had allegedly beaten her and torn her clothing off. I responded to the call being covered by wagon officers.

The opening conversation on the tape is with the wife, who makes it repeatedly clear that she wants her husband arrested:

> Woman: I want to take care of him for tearing off my sweater! That's what he done two weeks ago, and then he threw a knife at me again last night. I'm tired of this!
> Carl: Didn't you have him arrested?
> Woman: Yeah, but I had to go to the District Attorney. But now I mean it!
> Carl: You mean it this time?
> Woman: I do. I want him picked up!

While this sort of dialogue is going on, the husband appears, unnoticed at first; the situation at this point becomes potentially explosive:

> The lady lunged past me, grabbing for the baby, in an attempt to get it from her husband's arms. My main concern now was keeping them apart to prevent physical contact.
> Carl: Why don't you go inside? All right, go inside!

Hewitt takes the opportunity to question the husband in detail, in an effort to get his side of the story. The man represents himself as a Rescuer of Infants from Irresponsible Intoxicated Women, and describes the ripping of the sweater as an accidental consequence of an unstable hold:

> Carl: Now, how did you happen to tear her sweater off like that without hurting the baby?
> Man: Well, I asked her to stay there. You know, she started out of the car. Then I reached for her and she just ripped. You know, jumped out. She was standing by the car, and she jumped out of the car. And I had my hand on her sweater like this and it ripped when she jumped.

At this juncture, while the officer talks to the husband, the wife re-enters the scene, and new conflict threatens. This time, the officer engages the wife:

> Woman: I mean it! I'm tired of this! Look what he done to me . . .

> Carl: Do you think it might be a good idea to go inside rather than let everybody in the neighborhood know your problem? Huh?

While the other officer distracts the husband, Hewitt takes the wife into the house. He reports that this strategy pays off in some respect (peace is temporarily restored), but brings him new problems. Mainly, the lady welcomes the opportunity for what she regards as a gripe session. Hewitt listens, but tries to turn the conversation back to the marital difficulty:

> She's beginning to tell me things that happened a week ago, two weeks ago—things that have happened the night before, things that are completely irrelevant to the problem at hand. This leads me to believe, at this point, that she may, in fact, just need somebody to talk to.
> Woman: We had a bottle in here . . . (some incoherent sentences)
> Carl: The baby can upset you a great deal, huh? Sometimes?
> Woman: Sometimes he does. I'm getting too old to take care of little babies. And Jim don't help me. If he'd help me, wouldn't care.
> Carl: How old are you now?
> Woman: I'm 45.
> Carl: Forty-five. How long have you and Jim been married?
> Woman: Six years.

As the conversation progresses, Hewitt comes to feel that the wife wants to invoke him "as a threat to her husband." He says:

> At this point I feel she doesn't want an arrest. She merely expects me to scare the man, or to bring to his attention that she, in fact, does have the power to have him arrested.

Having sensed the lady's reluctance to prosecute (despite her vigorous demands for her husband's arrest), Hewitt explores the consequences, and works out a solution that seems satisfactory to the lady:

> Carl: . . . It's kind of tough for a young man like myself to come in here and have to tell people you and Jim's age— you know, how to get along with each other. We don't want to arrest people unless we absolutely have to. You say it's going to mess up his check. Now I'm going to have to leave it up to you.
> Woman: Well, we get $124 and I ain't got no money.
> Carl: You think it's going to worsen the situation to have to put up bail?
> Woman: It will, cause when he gets out it will be worse.
> Carl: Well, financially, anyway. Besides that, he's going to have to pay bail, which is going to cost money.
> Woman: Right.
> Carl: So maybe arrest isn't the answer, do you think?
> Woman: I know, but when you guys leave, that's when I'm really going to get it!
> Carl: Do you really believe that? Do you really believe the guy will work

you over if I tell him that if I have to come back here today or anytime, he's going to go to jail, and I'm not going to even talk about it? That he's just going! You don't think that'll do any good?
Woman: It might, if you talk to him real stern.
Carl: Do you want me to try it?
Woman: Yeah.
Carl: All right, fine! And if you have any more trouble, just give us a call, OK?
Woman: OK.

The husband is notified of the disposition of his case and seems grateful:

Carl: I kind of want to put it on you this way: I talked to her and kind of convinced her that arresting you wouldn't be a good thing, and believe me, she has grounds to lock you up, pal! If you're going to beef with your wife, do it in your house. And do it without ripping her clothes off! If I were you, I'd stay the hell away from her for awhile. Let her cool off, because she's really upset. Well, I'm going to leave that up to you, but I'll tell you right now, if I get another call . . .
Jim: If you come back you take me to jail.
Carl: You're going—there's no doubt about it if I come back! OK?

This concludes the incident, as well as Hewitt's running analysis of it. The remainder of the tape consists of our group's inquiry into the officer's strategy, and the reasons for it. The following excerpt illustrates this process:

Group Member: Prior to the husband's arriving at the scene where you were with the woman, Carl, the woman insisted about six or seven times that she wanted the man arrested, and you seemed to be deliberately avoiding this question, or any response to this question. Why?
Carl: Well, at this point, I hadn't yet confronted the other party involved in this altercation, and I hadn't really established enough facts to know whether an arrest was going to have to be affected. Until I could establish this fact, I did try to avoid it, in an attempt to bring out more details of what happened.
Group Member: Right at the end, when you were talking to the husband, you told him five different times in five different ways that you didn't want to come back—that he wasn't to hit his wife anymore. Why did you go into this so often?
Carl: I was trying very hard to get the point across to the man that I was very serious in what I was saying. Many times an officer will use this on calls, and I have also, as an out—as a parting statement. But I really was serious at this point, and I wanted to impress this fact upon the individual to the point that he felt the import of what I was trying to say. Although it was rather redundant, at that time I felt it was necessary to get the point across to him.

This tape, and others like it, are a violence-reduction tool because they permit sequential review of situations. If the problem is solved without violence, the strategy can be teased out in steps for possible application elsewhere. If the incident degenerates, the analysis of taped material can reveal how and where it did. The group can then propose alternative courses of action, and trace out their consequences. The result is an inventory of police-civilian games, and of how these are won or lost.

VIOLENCE AS AN OPTION

The objectives of the police civilian "game" cannot be understood, when separated from the rules that govern it. Thus, a topic which proved of constant interest to our group was the relationship between violence and "good" police work. How much conflict results from a real need to move into explosive situations? How much of it results from ill-conceived interference in situations calling for no action? In other words, what would constitute commendably aggressive, as opposed to unprofessionally over-aggressive police work?

The group tackled this question with research. They constructed a critical incident questionnaire, based on situations actually experienced by themselves. They pretested this instrument, reconstructed it through item analysis, and re-administered it to a sample of officers including recruits, command personnel, and the Chief himself.

One set of their findings was that different groups gave different responses to different items. To cite an example, there were items which produced arrests only among recruits. The following is one of these:

> A telephone complaint received of a family disturbance: the complainant refuses to identify himself. The officer responds, and encounters a black man, approximately 30 years old.

The report states:

> Officer approaches scene and hears sound of argument. Officer knocks. Argument stops. Door opened by subject wearing T-shirt. Officer asks if police needed. Subject says, 'No, pig!' and slams door in officer's face.

What happened next? For the older officer nothing much. Some would leave at once, and others would seek information first. But a largish number of recruits (eight out of 22) felt that they would seek to arrest. What accounts for this difference? The crux of the problem is the perception of critical information, such as the availability (or non-availability) of complainants. Regardless of the merits of the issue, here is a topic which recruit training has seemingly missed.

On a different level, the questionnaire yielded diagnostic information. In reviewing patterns of responses, we found that some officers demonstrated chronic indecisiveness, which left them pensively lingering in the wrong places. Other officers showed an affinity for mobilizing help, and thus produced organizational "over-kill". Others manifested a "bull in the china shop" syndrome, and charged indelicately into every crisis. A fourth group showed a propensity to retaliate verbally, thus escalating conflict.

A third approach to the questionnaire focussed on communications within the police department. Several of our incidents resulted in arrests, although command personnel indicated they would not take action. In at least one instance, the issue was an interpretation of law, easily subject to clarification.

These sort of findings illustrate how action research conducted by subject-matter experts can increase the sophistication of staff, open new areas of investigation, and suggest reforms.

ORGANIZATIONAL CHANGE FROM WITHIN

Several of our group projects were directed at organizational change. We conducted surveys of departmental activities—communication and training—that could affect the chances of violence. We made recommendations, and members of the group were delegated to work out the details of new programs.

One example of such activity was a survey of the selection of training officers—men who "break-in" recruits when they reach the street. The importance of this area rests on the premise, as valid among police as in universities, that peer influence can neutralize the impact of classroom instruction. The novice is susceptible to the views of "experienced" tutors because initiation experiences tend to be overwhelming in their complexity, and require interpretation. A mis-assigned trainer can, thus, leave his charge with career-long habits that spell problems for himself and others.

In considering the problem, our group became concerned about the pairing of trainers and trainees, and about monitoring of the process. They made recommendations suggesting a new position (training officer coordinator) and streamlined procedures.

FROM PROFESSIONAL POLICE TO POLICE PROFESSIONALS

I have illustrated the range of our group's activities. As noted, we collected data: we have brought about review and reform. Our efforts have evoked interest around the country where they have been described by the officers themselves, at state and regional meetings.

But I would suggest that these impressive pay-offs are far less important than that of converting members of our group into professionals who can help mold their profession. These seven men can now conceptualize their own work, and share insights with their colleagues. They can conduct training, and thus directly improve the quality of police contacts. More important, subsequent generations (the men—trained by the men who are trained by our men) can play similar roles. This trend, once initiated, is designed to be self-perpetuating. It creates a vehicle whereby the police institution, and other institutions, can renew themselves and improve themselves from within.

THE PSYCHOLOGY OF PARTICIPATION, REVISITED

Three decades ago, Gordon Allport enjoined social scientists to consider "the psychology of participation." Allport cited laboratory findings, and summarized pioneer work in industry. He pointed out that effective group membership (large and small) presupposes the sharing of goals; that it presumes that each member plays a meaningful role in the achievement of democracy.

On the current scene, participation is an endemic and obsessive theme. It preoccupies adolescents and concerns black militants, welfare clients, women, and institutional inmates; it permeates the ideology of radicals and conservatives; it is a vague but appealing slogan for everyone—including social scientists.

Yet, among social scientists, Allport's injunction remains unheeded. We have no systematic inquiry into "the psychology of participation," and no body of thought or knowledge. No one has defined "participation," classified it, sorted its components, or traced its implications. We have not studied the impact of participatory membership on individuals and institutions. We assume participation "works," but we can furnish no blueprints or instructions.

Because the gap exists, the practitioner must fill it. Change-oriented projects must show results—and failures—in detail. They must trace the landmarks of progress and plot its pitfalls. They must self-consciously inventory the anatomy of change. Such is the enterprise in which our Oakland police officers are currently engaged.

ABOUT THE AUTHOR: *Hans Toch is professor of psychology, School of Criminal Justice, State University of New York, Albany. He received his Ph.D. in psychology in 1955 from Princeton University.*

A study of conflicts between the police and probation departments with several approaches to conflict resolution.

Conflict Resolution in Criminal Justice

**VINCENT O'LEARY
DONALD J. NEWMAN**

In recent years, there has been a growing emphasis on treating police, courts, and corrections as part of a unified system of criminal justice. While this total system concept has important values, it can oversimplify a complex structure of persons and agencies in interaction with one another. And in the process of that interaction, conflicts arise. Although conflicts can serve positive ends, many of those in criminal justice tend to defeat the achievement of goals of the total system and of its parts.

In order to better understand such conflicts, a conference was held at the School of Criminal Justice at Albany in which probation and police officials were asked to identify types of conflict existing between their agencies. The four types studied were: (1) conflict based on dissensus reflecting differences in values among groups within a system; (2) conflict arising from status and esteem differentials between individuals; (3) operational conflict which is centered in the differences which occur when interrelated agencies seek to serve their own organizational requirements; and (4) perceptual conflict, the result of distortions which prevent a clear image of the duties, functions, and purposes of others in the system from being transmitted effectively.

A variety of resolution techniques are suggested which are specific to kinds of conflict. Alternative methods of a conflict resolution which might be pursued in criminal justice are discussed.

Reprinted, with permission of the National Council on Crime and Delinquency, from *Journal of Research in Crime and Delinquency*, July 1970, pp. 99-119.

The idea that criminal justice agencies, from police through prosecutors and courts, to prisons and parole boards can best be dealt with collectively as a unitary system of criminal justice, has gained prominence in recent years. The work of the President's Crime Commission,[1] the studies of the American Bar Foundation,[2] and the emerging focus on system analysis[3] have all converged to heighten interest in perceiving the criminal justice apparatus as a single system. This conception has some strong merits. After all, the diverse agencies do share broad allegiance to objectives of crime control and prevention. The efforts of one agency have consequences for others; the activities of the police, for example, have very direct influence on court calendars and eventually affect prison populations. Persons processed through the system as they move from the status of suspect, to defendant, to convicted offender, to inmate, and finally to parolee, with (hopefully) eventual discharge from sentence, forge a link among the agencies. This system concept is of great importance for current research and planning. Inter-agency studies are clearly insufficient to provide a basis for understanding and evaluating total efforts of crime control, and parochial planning cannot possibly achieve any desired changes in overall criminal justice administration.

While the total system concept has important values, it also poses important conceptual and operational problems. Treating criminal justice agencies as a complex organization held together by the network of decisions that flow among them, oversimplifies what is actually a very complex structure. It glosses over some very difficult relationships among agencies and professions and even tends to treat the criminal process in simplistic terms. It is almost too easy to equate the criminal justice system with complex organizations like corporations, hospitals, or armies that have received traditional analysis by social scientists. The fact is, the criminal justice system is not an organization, certainly not in any conventional sense. It has many sources of authority and power relationships, and its decision network does not flow along as a single process, or follow a linear chain of command, but is

---

[1] The President's Commission on Law Enforcement and the Administration of Justice, *The Challenge of Crime in a Free Society*, Washington, D.C.: U.S. Government Printing Office, 1967; note especially pages 8 and 9.

[2] See W. Lafave, *Arrest: The Decision to Take a Suspect into Custody*, Boston: Little, Brown and Co., 1965; D. Newman, *Conviction: The Determination of Guilt or Innocence Without Trial*, Boston: Little, Brown and Co., 1966; L. Tiffany, D. McIntyre, and D. Rotenberg, *Detection of Crime: Stopping and Questioning, Search and Seizure, Encouragement and Entrapment*, Boston: Little, Brown and Co., 1967.

[3] See A. Blumstein, "Systems Analysis and the Criminal Justice System," *The Annals*, 374:92-100, November, 1967.

literally composed of many subprocesses for dealing with different types of offenses and different types of offenders.

The intricacy of this system has been dealt with in greater detail elsewhere;[4] it is only necessary to point out here that the structure of the criminal justice system is actually a loose federation of offices and agencies—police, prosecutors, prisons, probation agents, parole boards, trial and appellate courts, satellite services such as welfare agencies, and consultant professions like psychology and psychiatry. Though the various agencies of the system work together, their formal relationship is amorphous, largely because they are structurally independent. There is, for example, no line-and-staff relationship between police and prosecutors, or between these and courts and correctional personnel. Some agencies are locally based and funded, others are statewide (or national) with, in turn, their own budgets and distinct career requirements. Likewise, while all criminal justice agencies may share some very broad objectives, like the diminution or prevention of crime, each agency has its own specific purposes, job tasks, and standards for performance evaluation as well as unique skills and methods of operations. Therefore, while at one level it is possible to say that both police and probation are part of the same system of criminal justice, and are both working toward common ends, at another level it is not only possible, but important to view them as discrete agencies with immediate objectives and techniques distinct from one another, and in some cases, perhaps, contradictory in purpose or method.

Agency Conflict in Criminal Justice Administration

Because criminal justice agencies are separated from one another by difference in tradition, staffing patterns, budget, status, and sometimes even by distance, there is bound to be some degree of tension and conflict among them, no matter how functionally interdependent they are in overall operation. Once the system concept is applied to the criminal justice apparatus, whether for purposes of research, planning, or allocation of resources, conflicts which are intrinsic are certain to surface. The police can no longer be satisfied with measuring their success simply by arrest data, nor can correctional administrators develop programs and professional standards for staff in splendid isolation from the activities of police, prosecutors, courts, and other agencies and offices in, or alternative to, criminal processing. In short, the total system concept is more than a theoretical construct; it has

---

[4]See F. J. Remington, D. J. Newman, E. L. Kimball, Marygold Melli, and H. Goldstein, *Criminal Justice Administration*, Indianapolis: Bobbs-Merrill, 1969, Chap. 1, pp. 3-47.

operational significance in that each agency in the system (and each person in any agency) must view its role and functions as part of a whole.

This does not mean that each agency is the whole, or that all agencies must share the same objectives or use the same techniques or methods. Nor must each be so attuned to the needs and purposes of others that differences blur and purposes coalesce. This would be impossible and, perhaps, undesirable. The police, after all, have certain mandates and have developed certain specific devices for achieving them, which, in turn, are different from the mandates and techniques of the prosecutor, trial court, probation officer, prison warden, parole board, and field agent. While all are part of the same system and often deal with many of the same persons, they are indeed specialized agencies with different demands and loyalties. To ignore differences, or to denigrate multiple objectives, is as serious as to ignore the interrelationships of agencies and decision networks in the total crime control effort. The problem, therefore, is to deal with a complex multi-agency system for administering criminal justice, recognizing and perhaps operationally reconciling legitimate differences, while at the same time, reducing conflicts and controversies that are unnecessary and dysfunctional.

Problems of conflict inherent in criminal justice are not unique. A considerable body of literature has developed, particularly in recent years, about this phenomenon at the interpersonal, group, and organizational level. Although the substantive basis of conflict varies from system to system, the same processes have been identified and studied in many settings.[5] And a variety of strategies to cope with them have been suggested.[6]

From these studies of conflict, a number of things have been learned about this characteristic of man and his organizations. On one hand, conflict can mean destruction, a loss of resources, and failure to achieve personal or organizational goals. On the other, it can lead to increased personal motivation and organizational productivity. It can have integrating as well as destructive results on individuals and systems. It can even have a creative outcome, leading to the development

---

[5] See especially R. Kahn and Elise Boulding, *Power and Conflict in Organizations,* New York: Basic Books, Inc., 1964; K. E. Boulding, *Conflict and Defense, A General Theory,* New York: Harper and Row, 1962; and L. Coser, *The Functions of Social Conflict,* New York: The Free Press, 1964.

[6] For example, see R. E. Walton, "Legal Justice, Power Bargaining, and Social Science Intervention: Mechanisms for Settling Disputes," *Institute for Research in the Behavioral, Economic and Management Sciences,* Institute Paper No. 194, March, 1968; and R. R. Blake and Jane Mouton, H. Shepard, "Strategies for Improving Headquarters-Field Relations," *Managing Intergroup Conflict in Industry,* Houston, Texas: Gulf Publishing Co., 1964, pp. 114-121.

of new forms of cooperative interaction between individuals and systems.[7]

The point is that conflict is not necessarily bad, and indeed, our system of government builds conflict into its processes by providing for separate sources of authority in the executive, judicial and legislative branches. Lipset argues that the very existence of a stable democracy requires the manifestation of conflict:

> Cleavage—where it is legitimate—contributes to the integration of societies and organizations consensus on the norms of tolerance which a society or organization accepts has often developed only as a result of basic conflict and requires the continuance of conflict to sustain it.[8]

From this perspective, conflict is seen as necessary to growth and constructive transactions among people and among organizations. Thus, the goal should not be to try to eliminate all conflict within the criminal justice system, but that which is clearly and importantly dysfunctional.[9] A more modest, and more feasible goal is to devise means of managing conflict to permit the system to operate effectively, while suffering a minimum of destructive consequences and suppression.[10]

Analysis of Police-Probation Conflicts

In order to analyze the nature and extent of conflicts in and between criminal justice agencies, it is necessary to determine whether such conflicts and controversies as occur emanate from the same or from a number of different sources. It seems likely that some conflict may occur because of differences in functions and objectives of specific agencies. In essence, the roots of this conflict are operational—that is, it originates because of disagreements about the purposes of law enforcement, sentencing, or community treatment, and can be directly traced to either the methods or the purposes of specific agencies at points where their activities touch. For example, in achieving their enforcement goals, the police may well see a need for means of identifying probationers and parolees, perhaps subjecting them to more

---

[7]M. Deutsch, "Conflicts: Productive and Destructive," *Journal of Social Issues*, 25(1):7-41, 1969.

[8]S. M. Lipset, *Political Man, the Social Bases of Politics*, Garden City, New York: Anchor Books, 1963, p. 1.

[9]Elise Boulding, "Further Reflections on Conflict Management," *Power and Conflict in Organizations*, R. Kahn and Elise Boulding (eds.), New York: Basic Books, Inc., 1964, pp. 14-50.

[10]H. A. Shepard, "Responses to Situations of Competition and Conflict," *Power and Conflict in Organizations*, R. Kahn and Elise Boulding, (eds.), New York: Basic Books, Inc., 1964, pp. 127-135.

intense surveillance, and even desire them to be more readily accessible to interrogation or search than suspects not under sentence. At the same time, probation and parole field agents may see such police objectives and techniques as counter-productive to their mandate to help offenders adjust in the community. This level of conflict, primarily operational and functional, relates to the work tasks and objectives of relatively discrete, autonomous criminal justice agencies.

On the other hand, conflict may emanate from sources not directly related to agency objectives and tasks. For example, there may be certain identifiable ideological variations (i.e., differences in beliefs and values) between persons who enter and are trained to function in different criminal justice agencies. Some of these differences may be pre-existing, that is, the value-structure of the person may influence the type of criminal justice task he chooses, (or which is open to him) and is therefore less a function of job tasks than of recruitment. A case could be made, for example, that it is likely that different types of persons with identifiably different value orientations are attracted to police work than to probation and parole work. Certainly it would be startling if all persons who are operative in the criminal justice system—policemen, prosecutors, defense counsel, judges, probation officers, prison wardens, psychologists, parole board members, and parole field agents—would show exactly the same distribution of beliefs and values about matters relevant to criminal justice administration on a common attitude or value questionnaire. Unless recruits are studied, however, it is very difficult to determine whether any differences in values and beliefs precede job choice, or whether they are developed as a result of differential educational and training indoctrination that occurs across the criminal justice system. Operationally, it probably makes little difference whether such value differences precede entry into the criminal justice system, or flow from differential indoctrination. If indeed such ideological differences do exist in measurable degree, they may form the basis of conflict related to, yet importantly different from, that arising from differential agency roles.

Although frequently publicly disclaimed, the fact is that the various criminal justice agencies are not co-equals in the criminal justice system in terms of policy-making power, rewards and perogatives, or general status and prestige. The plain fact is that a trial court judge has a higher community prestige, greater monetary rewards, and, at least formally, a broader power base than a police officer. The same type of comparison holds true for numerous other combinations of functionaries in criminal justice. Whatever the source of status differentials, that is, whether they are a reflection of different requirements and relative scarcity in the market place, or social class differences in recruiting, or whether they rest on a more generalized ideal of public worth, it is quite possible that differences in status, real or perceived as real, may form yet another basis of conflict within the criminal justice system.

If intrasystem conflict does emanate from different sources and occur on different levels, then it becomes important to identify these sources and levels, if for no other reason than to develop meaningful strategies to reduce dysfunctional conflict. Techniques and devices designed to ameliorate functional conflict may be totally inappropriate to meet conflict emanating from perceived status differences or conflict, which is ideologically intrinsic. To this end (and without attempting to answer all questions of sources of conflict or strategies for change), a week-long experiment involving 31 police officials and probation officials constituting teams from eight major eastern cities was undertaken at the School of Criminal Justice at the State University of New York at Albany.[11]

The major purpose of the meeting was to attempt to identify the types of conflict which existed at the interface of two segments of the criminal justice system—in this case, police and probation agencies. The goal was to increase understanding of the nature of conflicts at this point in the system, and to possibly identify strategies to better cope with them. Presumably, the techniques used, as well as the resolution strategies suggested, would have applicability to other points of conflict within the spectrum of criminal justice—police versus courts, prison versus parole, or prosecutor versus police.

The participants were mature public officials of high rank within their agencies. All were over 40 years of age, with considerable experience in the criminal justice field. All were fairly well-educated; none had less than some college experience. (See Table I.) Probation executives were slightly older and had attained a higher level of education. On the other hand, police officials tended to have been employed longer by their present agencies than did the probation officials. Almost all of the police had been with their current employer more than 15 years while a significant number of the probation officials more recently joined their present organization. This is less a commentary on differences in individuals and more on the differences in practice between two fields. Lateral transfer occurs much more frequently between agencies in the probation field than between police departments. It is a rare instance when a police official rises to a high

---

[11]The conference was co-sponsored by the National Council on Crime and Delinquency, the International Association of Chiefs of Police, the New York Department of Correction and Division of Local Police.

level, which all of these participants had attained, without a substantial length of service in an agency.

A distinctive feature of the program was the use of data from specially constructed questionnaires, some of which were completed by the participants before they arrived, and some during the course of the program. These questionnaires were designed to describe some of the characteristics of the conflict existing between probation and police agencies. Results were fed back to participants at various points during the meeting and their reactions solicited. Four general classifications of conflict—dissensus, status-esteem discrepancy, differential operational tasks and interests, and perceptual distortion—were

Table I
Characteristics of Participants

AGE			
Years	Probation	Police	Total
41-50	5	10	15
51-60	7	5 12	
61-65	4	—	4

LENGTH OF SERVICE WITH PRESENT AGENCY			
Years	Probation	Police	Total
1-5	1	1	2
6-10	5	1	6
11-15	5	—	5
Over 15	5	13	18

HIGHEST LEVEL OF EDUCATION COMPLETED			
Grade	Probation	Police	Total
Some College	—	9	9
B.A. Degree	—	1	1
Some Graduate	5	2	7
Graduate Degree	11	3	14

ADMINISTRATIVE LEVEL			
Position	Probation	Police	Total
Chief or Director	5	1	6
Deputy Chief or Director	8	8	16
Bureau Chief	2	4	6
Inspector or Supervisor	1	2	3

selected for analysis.[12] These are not mutually exclusive; on the contrary, they are highly interrelated. Perhaps they can best be thought of as different levels of discord—varying views of essentially the same phenomenon—rather than as distinct categories.

Although the number of participants was small, the differences of opinion between the two groups were very consistent. These differences appear especially important in view of the participant's relatively high level of education and rank. It is quite probable that the disagreements between police and probation officials found here would be further accentuated among personnel at lower levels of their organizational hierarchies. The data yield clues for further research and suggest methods of conflict resolution which seem to have a reasonable chance of being effective.

Conflict Based on Dissensus

The first type of conflict examined was that which arises out of differences in the values among members or groups of members within a system.[13] This type of conflict is basically ideological and rooted in differences in beliefs and norms. It arises from the interaction of individuals or groups, each of whom are highly motivated to keep the core of their own set of values intact. Dissensual conflict may be based on either questions of what is right or wrong, or over differences in methods of achieving goals.

Probation and police officials are part of a system which requires their fairly frequent interaction. In a situation like this, if differences of important values exist which can be tied into the system, the probabilities are high that disputes will occur between members of each group whenever issues affecting both are at stake. Often the issue appears simple to reconcile until the covert underpinnings of the conflict are understood.[14] It is not uncommon, for example, for the head of a probation agency who is recruited from another region and thought to represent sharply variant political and cultural values, to have problems with a police department over routine operational issues while a "native" administrator can follow precisely the same course with little or no conflict.

---

[12]These classifications were suggested primarily by the work of Richard Walton of Harvard University who generously made available a substantial body of material to the authors.

[13]For a discussion of this type of conflict in an inter-personal framework, see D. Summers, "Conflict, Compromise, and Belief Change in a Decision-Making Task," *Journal of Conflict Resolution,*" 12(2):215-221, June, 1968.

[14]See K. Boulding, "The Individual as a Party to Conflict," *Conflict and Defense*, New York: Harper and Bros., 1962, pp. 80-104.

The kinds of values over which dissensus may exist are almost unlimited. For our purposes, we attempted to sample opinions of police and probation officials around issues which would likely affect the character of their interaction, and yet would transcend essentially parochial concerns. One such scale was constructed to test tolerance of deviant behavior.[15] To avoid answers which were too closely locked into occupational activities, questions were used in this scale which did not include operational issues likely to be encountered by police or probation officials in the course of their work. The questions were directed at more personal attitudes. Results are shown in Table II. Overall, the probation officers displayed a positive response to these items with a total score of +8.41; the police responded negatively with a total score of −2.69.[16] The amount of disagreement varied by specific questions, but in all cases the probation officials' responses were consistently in the direction of greater toleration than were the police's. It is quite clear that there existed between the two groups a generalized difference in view about deviants.

These conflicting attitudes may be a reflection of individual personality differences in the distinctive kinds of persons attracted to the two occupational groups. Or it might be argued that these differences are simply reflections of values imbedded in police and probation cultures which are imparted to respective members of the two professions.[17] The distinctions have, at best, only marginal usefulness to one faced with the practical task of designing resolution strategies for the kinds of conflict represented here.

Efforts directed toward changing traits within individuals which are derived extrinsically to the setting in which conflict is manifested can be undertaken only with great cost and with doubtful consequences. Perhaps, the only way by which such sources of conflict can be dealt with efficiently is through profound changes in recruitment techniques and policies. One such approach involves the extensive use of psychological tests and interviews of candidates by clinically trained

---

[15] Several sets of questions were used to probe this and each of the other areas of conflict. For the purposes of this article, only one set will be presented to illustrate each area. The Tolerance of Deviance scale was developed by Edward Ryan of the School of Criminal Justice.

[16] Since only 31 persons were involved in the conference and it is impossible to establish the representativeness of the group, tests of statistical significance were calculated simply to indicate differences which seem worthy of further study. Unless otherwise indicated, the differences in totals shown in each table are significant at least at the .10 level.

[17] To contrast these points of view, see M. Sandford, "Individual Conflict and Organizational Interaction," *Power and Conflict in Organizations, op. cit., supra* note 5, pp. 94-104; and R. Faris, "Interaction Levels and Intergroup Relations," M. Sherif, *Intergroup Relations and Leadership,* New York: Wiley and Sons, 1962, pp. 24-45.

Table II
Tolerance Toward Deviance

	MEAN SCORES				
	POLICE		PROBATION		
QUESTIONS	Actual Answer	Adjusted Score	Actual Answer	Adjusted Score	Difference from Police
1. A high school principal should have the right to send home boys with long hair.	+.69*	(−.69)**	−.93	(+.93)**	+1.62
2. A homosexual couple should not be allowed to cohabit in your community.	+.77	(−.77)	−1.00	(+1.00)	+1.77
3. Prostitution should be legalized and, if controlled, should be allowed to operate openly in a restricted area.	−1.38	(−1.38)	+.06	(+.06)	+1.44
4. A former child molester who has served his time should be allowed to join my local bowling club.	+.39	(+.39)	+1.00	(+1.00)	+.61
5. If your son starts to imitate hippies, you should insist that he clean up and get a haircut.	+.84	(−.84)	−.13	(+.13)	+.97
6. Welfare recipients should not be able to receive subsidized rents for housing in middle class areas.	−.54	(+.54)	−1.18	(+1.18)	+.64
7. The legal rights of a conscientious objector should be decreased.	−.15	(+.15)	−1.68	(+1.68)	+1.53
8. Student demonstrators should be subject to more discipline.	+2.23	(−2.23)	+1.37	(−1.37)	+.86
9. Penalties for smoking marijuana should be increased.	−.61	(+.61)	−1.68	(+1.68)	+1.07
10. If an ex-convict moved next door to me, I would move.	−1.53	+1.53	−2.12	(+2.12)	+.59
TOTAL		−2.69		+8.41	+11.10

Scores can range from +3 to −3.

The positive or negative signs in columns one and three were reversed for the adjusted score whenever a question was asked in a negative form. Thus, the more positive the adjusted score, the higher the degree of tolerance.

personnel. Thus far, however, results from these efforts are quite inconclusive.[18] For the resolution of conflict between members of a system—the focus of these efforts—it seems most sensible to assume that the major determinants of relevant behavior, and the likely locus of successful interventions, reside in the network of contemporary relationships in and around the organizations under study. This does not mean that values and beliefs are held any less intensively; it simply suggests that they may be dealt with more effectively from that frame of reference.

Conflict Based on Status Differences

A second important kind of conflict identified by researchers is that which arises from differences in personal esteem and perceived status among members of a system.[19] One way of describing status is as the relative social ranking of an individual—probation officers are accorded one level of social importance and acceptance by the community; police officers another. Esteem can be defined as the individual's own ranking of his position. Conflict can arise when there are distinct differences between one's personal estimate of his worth (esteem) and that which is reflected by others (status). Such differences can cause resentment and competition with those in the same system. Under such conditions, the individual will likely strive to redress the differences in competing values which are forced on him.

In our study, police and probation officials were asked to compare their jobs in terms of the esteem with which they viewed them and their estimate of the status others accorded them.[20] The results are included in Tables III and IV. In Table III, the data show the esteem, as measured by the questions asked, with which each group holds itself as compared to the other. On the whole, probation officers see their job as more difficult, slightly more professional and more acceptable as an occupation for their sons than a policeman's job. The policeman, although he sees the probation officer's job as somewhat more difficult than his, would be slightly prouder if his son became a policeman rather than a probation officer and disagrees that the probation officer is more professional than he. On the whole, the police see their job as about equal in worth to that of the probation officer.

Table IV shows how each group perceives the definitions by others of the worth of their occupation as compared to the opposite group.

---

[18]Pres. Com. on Law Enforcement . . . *op. cit.*, p. 110.

[19]See R. Kahn, and D. Wolfe, "Role Conflicts in Organizations," *Power and Conflict in Organizations, op. cit. supra* note 5, pp. 115-126.

[20]Questions in these particular scales were adapted from M. Banton, *The Policeman in the Community,* New York: Basic Books, Inc., 1964.

The changes from Table III are rather dramatic. Although the probation officers see the status accorded them, as compared to police, fairly well in line with their own estimate, the situation with the police is quite different. On every item they see their job being held in much lower regard than that of the probation officer. Thus, while both groups view their own career choice in high esteem, the police feel that the prestige accorded their profession—their status is markedly slower than that accorded probation agents.

Table III
Relative Esteem for Own Job as Compared to Other

| | MEAN SCORES ||
QUESTIONS	Police Value of Own Job Compared to Probation	Probation Value of Own Job Compared to Police
1. I would be proud if my son became a (policeman) (probation officer).	+.46*	+1.00
2. The average (policeman) (probation officer) is capable of performing the duties of a (probation officer) (policeman).	−.30	+.75
3. A (probation officer) is more of a "professional" than is a (police officer.)	+.53	+.06
4. Most of the duties of a (police officer) (probation officer) can be learned by anyone of average intelligence in a six month period.	−.69	+.62
TOTAL RELATIVE ESTEEM DIFFERENCE	0**	+2.43**

*A positive score indicates the degree to which the group accords itself a higher value than the opposite group; a negative score indicates less value. A zero indicates that the group sees itself as equal to the other group. Scores could range from −6 to +6.

**Differences between totals not statistically significant at .10 level.

The strain inherent in such discrepancies between perceived esteem and status are fairly obvious. In the day-to-day transactions between probation and police officials, to the extent these findings can be generalized, there is likely to be a constant source of conflict arising from these differences. Anger, most often expressed covertly, and a pervasive sense of unfairness are almost certainly likely to color the relationships between representatives of the two systems. The resolution of conflict arising from this source requires a set of techniques quite different from those called for in dealing with dissensual conflict.

Table IV
Perceived Status of Own Job as Compared to Other

QUESTIONS	Police Perception of Status Accorded Their Job by Others Compared to Probation	Probation Perception of Status Accorded Their Job by Others Compared to Police
1. Most people think (police officers) (probation officers) work at the job they do because they were not good enough to get another job.	−1.61*	+.75
2. A (police officer) (probation officer) would be most likely accepted by the local country club.	−.84	+.31
3. A court is not likely to accept the expertise of the (police officer) (probation officer).	−.46	+.75
4. Most people in my community would be proud to have their sons become (police officers) (probation officers).	−.92	+.31
TOTAL RELATIVE STATUS DIFFERENCE	−3.83	+2.12

*A positive score indicates the degree to which the group perceives others according their profession a higher value as compared to the opposite group; a negative score indicates the perceived degree of negative value accorded by others as compared to the opposite group. Scores can range from +6 to −6.

Conflict Based on Differences in Operational Tasks and Interests

A third perspective on conflict between probation and police agencies can be obtained by studying the different functions served by each as they share responsibility for handling offenders and seek to serve their own organizational requirements in the process. In order to measure these issues, a series of paragraph length statements about practical police and probation situations were presented to the two groups. They were asked to express their views as to the most desirable outcome.

Table V shows a summary of the problems presented and the average response to them by probation and police officials. There are marked discrepancies between the two groups, particularly around questions two, three, seven, nine, and ten. In question two, probation officers indicate their strong feeling that the probation department is a treatment agency and should not make arrests at any time, whereas the police think that probation officers are, in part at least, law enforcement officials and should make arrests for probation violations. In question three, probation officers strongly oppose giving the police a blanket list of the names of probationers, while the police only slightly oppose such an action. In question seven, the police somewhat agree while probation officers disagree with the suggestion that the police department be given the right to make recommendations directly to the court on whether individuals should be granted probation or not. In question nine, the police disagree, and the probation officers somewhat agree, with a probation officer's refusal to turn over his file for police use. In question ten, the police would tend to refuse probation to a youngster because of its possible effect on others, whereas the probation officers would grant it.

Dissensus or discrepant role expectations may explain some of these disagreements but a significant portion of this conflict seems to be rooted more in the day-to-day demands on a policeman or probation officer as such. The frame of reference is organizational rather than individual.[21] Probation and police officials have responsibility for executing tasks which at certain points intersect. Questions arise as to whom will expend what degree of energy in carrying out those tasks. The organizational imperative is to minimize expenditures either in servicing the needs of other systems, or in readjusting internal mechanisms to accomplish joint tasks more effectively. Conflicts arise as two organizations require similar but scarce resources.

Game theory models have been employed quite effectively to analyze this type of conflict.[22] Building on such analysis, some writers suggest that it is possible to escape the bounds of a win-lose orientation in which one system must gain at the expense of the other. Conditions can

---
[21]See K. Boulding, *op. cit.*, pp. 145-165.

[22]See A. Rapaport, "Critiques of Game Theory," *Behavioral Science*, 4:49-66, 1959.

Table V
Operational Situations

QUESTION SUMMARY	Police Score	Probation Score	Difference
1. Police request revocation of probationer for rule violation when new crime can't be proved.	2.72*	4.06*	1.34
2. Police contend probation department should be required to arrest probation violators.	2.20	4.33	2.13
3. Probation department refuses police department request for a list of names of persons on probation.	3.45	1.40	2.05
4. Probation department refuses police request to hold probationer in custody pending investigation.	2.63	2.00	.63
5. Police department wants information, which youth counselors may gather, shared with them.	1.99	3.41	1.42
6. Police department requests 16 year old youth be held in detention.	2.81	3.26	.45
7. Police department believes it should be given right to make recommendations to judge.	2.72	4.53	1.81
8. Probation department will not allow probationers to act as informer for police.	3.90	3.60	.30
9. Probation department refuses police request for access to a probationer's case file.	4.45	2.60	1.85
10. Police department argues that a man with serious prior record should not receive probation.	3.18	5.00	1.82
TOTAL			13.80

*The lower the score, which has an upper limit of 6, the greater the agreement with the actions described in the statement. In the questionnaire each statement was actually about two paragraphs in length.

be described in which cooperation can provide a basis for the distribution of resources to maximize joint gain and, indeed, at times to provide mutual help.[23]

The attainment of those necessary conditions is the key task.

Conflict Based on Distorted Perception

A fourth approach to the study of conflict is centered in the perceptual distortions which prevent a clear image of the duties, functions, and purposes of one agency or profession from reaching another in conflict with it. Distortions may arise from the lack of interaction between persons or organizations; more frequently they stem from the defective quality of the interaction which does occur. The important point is that, whatever their basis, they have the potential of becoming in themselves sources for creating and enlarging conflict.

It was possible to scale several aspects of perceptual distortion in the interactions between police and probation officials at the experimental conference. Table VI is an example of one such effort. It shows the amount of conflict which police and probation officials independently estimated existed between the two groups. These data were obtained by asking each participant, in advance of the conference, to predict how an average policeman and an average probation officer would respond to the ten operational problems. The estimated differences were then compared with the actual differences between the groups. Both groups overestimated the amount of conflict which actually existed between them. Further analysis of these and other data shows the greater inaccuracy among probation officials was caused by a consistent overestimation of negative police attitudes. The assertion by some probation officials that the police participants were unique, and that their attitudes did not reflect typical police attitude, was vigorously denied by the police group. The police participants, to support their argument, pointed out they had to predict each other's responses in advance, and most participants had no idea who would be represented at the conference and, in fact, representatives from various cities had generally never met before.

The differences in perception which exist can arise from misunderstandings about value systems or there may be dysfunctions in the mechanisms which provide information to members of each system about the other. In either case, the probability is substantial that members of these two groups would inappropriately respond to each other by assuming conflicts which were much less than actually existed.

---

[23]M. Deutsch, "Cooperation and Trust: Some Theoretical Notes," M. R. Jones, (ed.), *Nebraska Symposium on Motivation 1962,* Lincoln: University of Nebraska Press, 1962, pp. 275-318.

This is a particularly costly kind of conflict which must be reduced to deal efficiently with those conflicts which are more reality based.

Possible Approaches to Conflict Resolution

There now exists a number of techniques and approaches to conflict resolution established as effective under various conditions involving interpersonal, intergroup, or interorganizational conflict which, with appropriate modifications, could be employed to reduce dysfunctional conflict in and between criminal justice agencies. Some techniques, however, although possibly efficacious in certain situations—arbitration in labor management disputes, for example—may be either too elaborate to be feasible or too formal and formidable to be necessary, to lessen stresses between police and probation agencies.[24] From available evidence, the scope and intensity of conflict between these agencies would infrequently call for the heavy artillery of outside negotiation and arbitration, nor does it seem necessary to use

Table VI
Perceived Conflict Between Groups

QUESTION	MEAN SCORES		
	Actual Differences in Responses	Police Estimation of Differences	Probation Estimation of Differences
1	1.4*	2.1	2.5
2	.1	2.2	1.6
3	1.9	2.4	3.2
4	1.7	2.4	3.7
5	.5	2.1	3.3
6	.2	2.3	2.9
7	1.6	2.5	3.1
8	.4	2.4	2.8
9	2.1	1.9	3.3
10	2.7	2.5	3.2
TOTAL DIFFERENCES	12.6	22.8	29.6

*Scores can range from zero, indicating no differences in responses, to a maximum score of 5.

---

[24]See D. Katz, "Approaches to Managing Conflict," R. Kahn and Elise Boulding (eds.), *Power and Conflict in Organizations,* New York: Basic Books, Inc., 1964, pp. 105-114; and H. A. Shepard, "Responses to Situations of Competition and Conflict," R. Kahn and Elise Boulding, (eds.), *Power and Conflict in Organizations,* New York: Basic Books, Inc., 1964, pp. 127-135.

softer, subtler, but no less elaborate approaches to changing unconscious motivations of agency personnel.[25] Within such extremes there are a number of techniques, and variations of them, that would seem potentially appropriate to counteract one or more dimensions of police-probation conflict. Since such conflict as exists is apparently multidimensional, it is doubtful that any single approach will be sufficient to cope equally with functional, dissensus, status, and perceptual differences. Further, no technique or series of techniques will banish conflict on any level; at most, irrational and otherwise dysfunctional differences may be lessened. Other differences, real, operationally significant, and perhaps healthy and necessary, will remain. Only one thing is certain—members of the two professions must be brought together and must interact in situations other than in routine operations for any resolution to occur. This may seem a history of recruitment, training, the growth of agency methods of operation, and professional identity in all of criminal justice has been separate and isolated, one from the other. It is common for police to discuss their problems among themselves, for prosecutors to meet together, for judges to collectively attend sentencing institutes, and for correctional personnel to interact only with colleagues. It is rare, rather than common, for probation and police officers to meet other than in the line of duty. Distance and separateness in education, training, and even in social situations, crystallizes and intensifies whatever bases of misunderstanding and conflict are intrinsic between the agencies.

A series of conflict reduction techniques were employed and subsequently evaluated by the staff and participants at the Albany conference for their applicability in similar sessions. Those evaluations, and research findings in other settings, indicate the following to be among the more promising measures.

1. Confrontation and Discussion

Because of the operate-in-isolation characteristic of criminal justice agencies, a simple bringing together of representatives from different agencies may have greater payoff than the same approach in close-knit, unitary line-and-staff organizations. While the motivation of such meetings, perhaps, would be most meaningful if focussed on interrelated operational problems (police access to probation records; probation agent protection of clients from police harassment), the possible reduction of conflict may not be limited to better awareness of the

---

[25] For a discussion of unconscious motivations and conflicts, see Merritt R. Sanford, "Individual Conflict and Organizational Interaction," R. Kahn and Elise Boulding (eds.), *Power and Conflict in Organizations,* New York: Basic Books, Inc., 1964, pp. 94-104.

others' operational problems, goals, and techniques. The mere fact of interaction and the sharing of everyday concerns in abstraction from the pressures of a single case may also serve to dispel stereotypes of each other as persons, as well as representatives of agencies. At the Albany conference, for example, it was more common than not for police officers and probation personnel from the same city to be strangers to each other. Names were familiar in many cases, but there was little association of personalities prior to the conference. The discussion of differences in a neutral setting is a valuable tool in reducing interagency conflict, particularly that arising from perceptual distortion of differences in interests.[26] Certainly it should be a first step.

2. Allegiance to Superordinate Goals

The structure of the criminal justice system with its distinct agencies and professions, provides a climate in which single agency purposes and objectives tend to dominate enforcement efforts. It is rare for any agency, or person, in an operational position to offer *primary* allegiance to the purposes of the entire criminal justice system. Crimes cleared by arrest may satisfy the police, convictions, the prosecutor and court and a low rate of recidivism, correctional authorities. Yet in broad perspective, all these efforts are directed to some common ends—the reduction of crime in the society, for example—and, under the right circumstances, discrete agencies can be made to see their relationships to each other and their common allegiance to certain long-range goals. Some of these goals may be quite abstract and high-sounding—like crime reduction or prevention. Others may be more pragmatic, though less noble, such as achieving a smooth, trouble-free, efficient, and effective flow of cases. No agency enjoys trouble, political heat, or failure, either short-run or long-term. Whether admirable or mundane, there are common hopes and purposes that discrete agencies can agree upon and in this sense, can be led to see their working together as cooperative rather than competitive. There is some evidence that when groups experiencing conflict can interact towards superordinate goals, not only do the effects of dissensual conflict become reduced, but unfavorable stereotypes are markedly lessened.[27]

---

[26]See R. Beckhard, "The Confrontation Meeting," *Harvard Business Review*, 45(2):149-153, 1967.

[27]M. Sherif and Carolyn W. Sherif, "Intergroup Relations," *An Outline of Social Psychology*, New York: Harper and Bros., 1956, pp. 280-332; M. Sherif, "Superordinate Goals in the Reduction of Intergroup Conflict," *American Journal of Sociology*, 43:349-356, 1958, and M. Sherif and C. W. Sherif, *Outline of Social Psychology*, revised, New York: Harper and Bros., 1956; but see J. A. Robinson, "Further Problems of Research on International Relations," M. Sherif, (ed.), *Intergroup Relations and Leadership*, New York: Wiley and Sons, Inc., 1962, pp. 205-208.

3. Reverse Role Playing

Role-reversal is a common technique for conflict resolution, showing its most promise under conditions where conflict is not based on strongly divergent moral and personal values.[28] While care—indeed expertise—is required in setting-up conditions where role reversal can be best employed, it does seem to have a strong potential for use in resolving some forms of criminal justice interagency conflict. The advantage of having a policeman confront and solve the kinds of problems common to probation officers, and vice-versa, is not only the exchange of operational perspectives, but may serve to reduce self-defensiveness, increased perceived similarity between roles, and strengthen awareness of the positive features of the other's viewpoint and the dubious aspects of one's own position.[29] Structured role reversal can be useful in decreasing operational conflict and that based on distorted perceptions.

4. Game Theory Techniques

While confrontation and discussion, the sharing of goals, and role reversal may each in turn ameliorate some of the bases of interagency conflict, it may also prove valuable to demonstrate the importance of cooperation and the cost of dysfunctional competition to achieve resolution of some forms of conflict, cognitive as well as operational. Various applications of game theory techniques, some simple and others fairly elaborate, have been used in experimental settings with some success in resolving conflict.[30] Whatever particular game theory approach may be borrowed or developed to deal with criminal justice concerns, the basic objective of minimizing a win-lose orientation and providing demonstrable payoff for sharing and cooperation, must be the aim. One advantage of the game theory approach is that it often is, or can be, contentually neutral. That is, demonstrations of its effectiveness can be made without reference to real, operational conflicts between agencies, so that its results are generalizable beyond specific concerns. At the same time, it can be applied, or the lessons learned from neutral games can be applied, to real life police-probation or other interagency problems. The combination of learning from neutral games and from shared behavior games may be able, in the first instance, to lessen dissensus and in the second to carry over to reduce

---

[28] Barbara F. Muney and M. Deutsch, "The Effects of Role-Reversal During the Discussion of Opposing Viewpoints," *Journal of Conflict Resolution*, 12(3):345-356, September, 1968.

[29] *Ibid.*

[30] D. A. Summers, "Conflict, Compromise, and Belief Change in a Decision-Making Task," *Journal of Conflict Resolution*, 12(2):215-221, June, 1968; and V. Aubert, "Competition Resolution," *Journal of Conflict Resolution*, 7(1):24-42, March, 1963.

functional conflict. For this to occur, it is necessary, however, to demonstrate payoff not only in neutral simulation terms, but also realistic payoffs in terms of shared agency objectives.

5. Intergroup Conflict

In many settings it has proven useful to conceptualize many of these issues as essentially a problem of intergroup conflict in which persons believe in the propriety of their own group activity and believe that they must win or lose in a contest with other groups. This approach to the problem seems to hold considerable promise for application to criminal justice and should be explored vigorously. There is a tendency too often to think of persons who take opposite positions as deviant, and to ascribe to their behavior negative personal motives.[31] Police and probation officials need to understand the powerful group based sources of conflict which operates between the two, and the problems they face because of it.[32] Stress on solving immediate crisis has too often left basic disputes unresolved, and they have simply continued to rage.

A number of specific techniques for intergroup conflict resolution have been suggested.[33] Data are available on a wide array of factors such as the behavior of delegates and leaders,[34] the utility of feedback,[35] and leadership roles.[36] Intergroup laboratory exercises can be useful in dealing with some of these problems. Research findings indicate that there will be a residual of conflict around old problems after such interventions, but once the basis and effects of intergroup conflict are understood, new problems can be faced more effectively.

Additional Approaches to Conflict Resolution

Conflicts originating from ideological differences between persons or professions, or resulting from status differentials, not only as perceived but as real, are probably the most difficult to ameliorate. As a

---

[31] M. Sherif, "Intergroup Relations and Leadership," *Intergroup Relations and Leadership,* New York: Wiley and Sons, Inc., 1962, pp. 3-21.

[32] R. R. Blake, *Managing Intergroup Conflict in Industry,* Houston, Texas: Gulf Publishing Company, 1964, pp. 1-17.

[33] R. R. Blake, "The Intergroup Dynamics of Win-Lose Conflict and Problem-Solving Collaboration in Union Management Relations," M. Sherif, (ed.), *Intergroup Relations and Leadership,* New York: Wiley and Sons, Inc., 1962, pp. 94-140.

[34] Margaret Herman, "Negotiation in Leader and Delegate Groups," *Journal of Conflict Resolution,* 12(3):332-344, September, 1968.

[35] H. Hornstein, "The Effects of Process Analysis and Ties to his Group upon the Negotiator's Attitudes Toward the Outcomes of Negotiations," *Journal of Applied Behavioral Science* 2(4):449-463, 1966.

[36] R. Stogdell, "Intragroup-Intergroup Theory and Research," M. Sherif, (ed.), *Intergroup Relations and Leadership,* New York: Wiley and Sons, Inc., 1962, pp. 48-65.

spin-off from other approaches—discussion, reverse-role, or gaming—there may indeed occur, over time, alterations in value sets. Certainly if distorted perceptions of the others' roles and purposes can be corrected, value differences, while possibly still existing in measurable degree, may come to play a less important part in blocking resolution of operational conflicts. Likewise, distorted perceptions of status differences could well vanish, but, of course, resolution of real differences in prestige—measured by salary, or title or any of the other social indicators—is beyond the immediate control of police and probation officers or of any other criminal justice functionaries. Yet, if other dysfunctional aspects of conflict can be reduced, if stereotypes can be broken, and if job tasks can be viewed and followed through with less jealousy and misunderstanding, it may be that a sense of internal relationships can eventually effect external ascriptions of status. If one consequence of conflict resolution is a better sense of colleagueship and common destiny, then it becomes increasingly difficult to accept and perpetuate such status differences as do exist. It is possible that a more generalized measure of prestige can be directed to the criminal justice system as a whole, if indeed it becomes viewed as a system, rather than, as now, ascribed in different measures to distinct parts of it.

A tactic which has been suggested in other settings to foster collaboration is to expand mutual task responsibilities.[37] In every community, the police are charged with the responsibilities of investigation and arrest, and usually are constrained officially from undertaking correctional activities. Probation officers are supposed to rehabilitate and not to be concerned with general community protection. To reduce job specialization, some experimentation with job enlargement might be undertaken. Police, for example, might be given explicit and officially sanctioned correctional tasks such as helping in job placement or intervening in the community to see that opportunities such as recreational facilities are available to offenders.

Task expansion activities could involve organizational changes as well. Building on Likert's notion of the "link pin," various types of interdepartmental planning and operating units can be visualized.[38] Few such formally structured liaisons now exist in which the agents of segments of the system assume a criminal justice focus instead of their traditional narrow concerns. An important part of resolution strategies aimed at role conflicts must involve making the larger system more salient.

---

[37]R. Walton, *Interdepartmental Conflict and its Management: A General Model and Review*, Lafayette, Indiana: Krannert Graduate School of Industrial Administration, Purdue University, March, 1968.

[38]R. Likert, *New Patterns in Management*, New York: McGraw-Hill, 1961.

In this regard, it would be conceivable for various agencies and offices within the criminal justice system to work collectively and plan together about matters of common concern ranging from proposing new legislation, to collective bargaining for salaries and job security, to such matters as the planning for, allocation to, and mutual employment of community resources. Indeed, offices in federal crime control agencies are currently insisting on overall system planning, interagency requests, and total state, regional or metropolitan programs, in their function of allocating funds for criminal justice matters. As long as this is so, interagency conflicts must be at least muted so that cooperative planning and funding can take place.

It may well be that the various devices used in conflict resolution between labor-management, student-administration, teachers-school boards, and in similar common conflict situations, will be of some value in criminal justice agencies. Such techniques are many and varied, including third party intervention,[39] negotiation,[40] and even some forms of conflict adjudication.[41] While these, at present, are dim and distant, models of their use exist in the arsenal of conflict resolution devices and may eventually prove desirable and helpful to the criminal justice system.

This extrapolates well beyond the probation-police experiment described here. What was learned from this conference was the value of confrontation and shared work-tasks between criminal justice agencies. If dysfunctional conflict resolution is a worthwhile goal in criminal justice administration, it is apparent that it cannot be achieved to any great extent by one agency or profession gathering its members in meetings, discussions, and conferences which exclude others in the system. The most fruitful item in any blueprint for the future mandates shared concerns and experiences. A system of criminal justice cannot exist and properly function if it is treated solely as a linkage of discrete parts. Not only must there be a bringing together, there must be regular, reliable, and informative feed-back to all participants not only of information about the others, but about themselves, before, during, and after confrontation. Participation, one with another,

---

[39]See R. E. Walton, "Interpersonal Confrontation and Basic Third Party Functions: A Case Study," *Journal of Applied Behavioral Science*, 4(3):327-350, 1967; and R. E. Walton, "Third Party Roles in Interdepartmental Conflict," *Industrial Relations*, 7:29-43, October 1967.

[40]Margaret G. Hermann and N. Kogan, "Negotiation in Leader and Delegate Groups," *Journal of Conflict Resolution*, 12(3):332-344, September, 1968, and S. Siegel and L. E. Fouraker, *Bargaining and Group Decision Making*, New York: McGraw-Hill, 1960.

[41]W. G. Scott, *The Management of Conflict: Appeal Systems in Organization*, Homewood, Ill.: Richard D. Irwin, Inc., 1965.

feedback, response, and follow-up are essential ingredients in any conflict resolution program.

The need for further experimentation and research is obvious and, as is traditional in all such ventures, strongly advocated. It may be eventually possible to have conflict resolution sessions involving more than two agencies or professions. Police, judges, wardens or prosecutors, probation officers, police and clinical treatment personnel may at some future time find such conferences meaningful and helpful. In any event, pressures from funding sources, as well as the realistic needs of operational agencies, would seem to make interagency conflict resolution of high priority among criminal justice concerns.

ABOUT THE AUTHORS: *Vincent O'Leary is professor of criminal justice at the State University of New York (Albany). He received his M.A. in Sociology in 1954 from the University of Washington.*

Donald J. Newman is professor of criminal justice at the State University of New York (Albany). He received his Ph.D. in sociology in 1954 from the University of Wisconsin.

RESOURCES FOR FURTHER READING

USEFUL PERIODICALS FOR THE CRIMINAL JUSTICE PRACTITIONER: AN ANNOTATED LIST

ADMINISTRATIVE SCIENCE QUARTERLY
  Graduate School of Business & Public Administration, Cornell University, Ithaca, New York 14850.
  Its aim is to promote understanding of administration in all types of organizations—business, governmental, educational, hospital, and military—and in various cultural contexts.

AMERICAN JOURNAL OF CORRECTION
  Bruce Publishing Company, 2642 University Avenue, St. Paul, Minnesota 55114.
  Covers continuing developments in American Correctional Association and affiliated organizations and committees. Contains articles on names in the neurological news, new products of use to custodial and administrative personnel, conferences and institute schedules, and current book reviews.

AMERICAN OPINION
  Robert Welch, Inc., Belmont, Massachusetts 02178.
  Political philosophy and affairs edited for conservatives and anti-Communists. Features articles on national and international affairs. Research is emphasized over speculation and opinion. Special reports from correspondents abroad. Reviews on books about political affairs.

CALIFORNIA MANAGEMENT REVIEW
  University of California, Berkeley, California 94720.
  Presents articles on various problems dealing with management and labor relations. Contains illustrations and charts.

COMPUTERS AND AUTOMATION

Berkeley Enterprises, Inc., 815 Washington St., Newtonville, Massachusetts 02160.

Computers and data processors: the design, applications, and implications of data processing systems; articles, news, forum, reference information, papers, computer census.

CRIME AND DELINQUENCY

National Council on Crime and Delinquency, NCCD Center, Paramus, New Jersey 07652.

Covers all aspects of the criminal justice system, particularly juvenile, family, criminal courts, law enforcement, and correctional institutes. Types of material used: book reviews, editorials, features.

CRIMINAL JUSTICE NEWSLETTER

National Council on Crime and Delinquency, Continental Plaza, 411 Hackensack Avenue, Hackensack, New Jersey 07601.

A biweekly report on significant developments in criminology for leaders in criminal justice administration.

DATAMATION

F. D. Thompson Publications, 35 Mason Street, Greenwich, Connecticut 06830.

Covers the information-processing field, including general purpose digital computers, analog, special purpose, and process control machines. For manufacturers, users and consultants, and engineering personnel.

ENFORCEMENT JOURNAL, THE OFFICIAL POLICE REVIEW

National Police Officers Association of America, Inc., Police Hall of Fame Building, Venice, Florida 33595.

Feature articles on law enforcement: court decisions, new tactics, narcotics, awards and citations, new products, police training, and insurance programs; and book reviews.

FEDERAL PROBATION
Supreme Court Building, Washington, D.C. 20544.

A journal of correctional philosophy and practice; contains book reviews, charts, and abstracts.

HARVARD BUSINESS REVIEW
Harvard Business School, Soldiers Field, Boston, Massachusetts 02163.

For thoughtful businessmen. Presents scholarly articles on business and finance.

ISSUES IN CRIMINOLOGY
101 Haviland Hall, University of California, Berkeley, California 94720.

Presents information on the latest issues facing the criminologist, e.g., legislation, police science, and techniques.

JOURNAL OF APPLIED BEHAVIORAL SCIENCE
NTL Institute for Applied Behavioral Sciences. Associated with the National Education Association, 1201 Sixteenth Street, N.W., Washington, D. C. 20036.

Research in the behavioral sciences to aid those engaged in guiding planned change in individuals, groups, organizations, communities, and national and world affairs.

JOURNAL OF CRIMINAL JUSTICE NEWSLETTER
Institute of Judicial Administration, 33 Washington Square West, New York, New York 10011.

Alerts attorneys and public officials to current activities of law enforcement planning, legislatures, the courts, police, and statistics. Each issue features a special report which gives pros and cons of an issue.

JOURNAL OF CRIMINAL LAW, CRIMINOLOGY AND POLICE SCIENCE

(Now published as *Journal of Police Science and Administration*) 428 East Preston Street, Baltimore, Maryland 21202.

A scientific journal primarily concerned with technical and legal abstracts. Of use to professionals in the field of crime detection and prevention.

JOURNAL OF POLICE SCIENCE AND ADMINISTRATION

International Association of Chiefs of Police, Inc., 11 Firstfield Road, Gaithersburg, Maryland 20760.

A scholarly journal concerned with technical and general criminal justice issues. Of use to all professionals in the field of criminal justice.

JURIMETRICS JOURNAL

American Bar Association Special Committee on Electronic Data Retrieval, 1155 East 60th Street, Chicago, Illinois 60637.

Covers uses of modern logic in law; uses of modern methods of information retrieval in law; uses of quantitative methods for the analysis of legal decision making; and the relationship between (a) developments in science and technology and (b) law.

JUSTICE

Justice Publishers, Inc., 922 National Press Building, Washington, D.C. 20004.

A monthly publication devoted to law enforcement. Articles pertain to prosecution, corrections, public safety, and industrial security.

LAW AND ORDER MAGAZINE

The Coop Organization, Inc., 37 West 38th Street, New York, New York 10018.

"How to" management and operations information for municipal police. Subjects covered: communications, education, public relations, photography, collective violence, traffic control, police science, clothing, vehicles, weapons, youth, and drugs.

THE NATION
   The Nation Company, 333 Sixth Avenue, New York, New York 10018.
   A journal of politics, economics, education, foreign policy, law, labor and other social issues, literature, and the arts.

NATIONAL REVIEW
   150 E. 35th Street, New York, New York 10016.
   Political, literary, and social topics; arts and manners; poetry; puzzles, etc. From a conservative standpoint.

NATIONAL SHERIFF
   The National Sheriff's Association, Suite 209, 1250 Connecticut Avenue, Washington, D.C. 20036.
   Contains news and features pertaining to law enforcement. Dedicated to the continual professionalization of law enforcement in general and of the office of sheriff in particular.

NATION'S BUSINESS
   Chamber of Commerce of the United States, 1615 H Street, N.W., Washington, D.C. 20005.
   A monthly publication that discusses current business trends, social and political issues, and financial news.

THE POLICE CHIEF
   International Association of Chiefs of Police, Inc., 11 Firstfield Road, Gaithersburg, Maryland 20760.
   Professional magazine of law enforcement agencies of local, state, and federal governments. Articles are helpful to practitioner and student.

PROGRESSIVE LAW ENFORCEMENT
   Pace Setter Promotions, P. O. Box 13548, Houston, Texas 77019.
   A bimonthly publication designed to inform law enforcement officials of new products and their application.

PSYCHOLOGY TODAY

Ziff-Davis Publishing, 1 Park Avenue, New York, New York 10016.

Theoretical and experimental, social and clinical research from psychology, sociology, and anthropology, written by social science professionals for the educated layman.

PUBLIC ADMINISTRATION REVIEW

American Society for Public Administration, 1225 Connecticut Avenue, N.W., Washington, D.C. 20036.

Pertinent articles and book reviews on public administration.

PUBLIC MANAGEMENT

International City Managers, 1140 Connecticut Avenue, N.W., Washington, D.C. 20036.

Developments in management and operations in the local government field, especially city government, police, fire, public works, urban renewal, and other local government services.

TRAINING & DEVELOPMENT JOURNAL

American Society for Training & Development, P. O. Box 5307, Madison, Wisconsin 53705.

Employee training and development. Originally established as "The Journal of Industrial Training." In addition to membership, publication is received by those in industry responsible for personnel training.

A BRIEF BIBLIOGRAPHY

Adams, T. F. *Training Officers' Handbook.* Springfield, Ill.: Charles C Thomas, 1964.

Alexander, R. P. Selection and education of the judiciary—Some unfinished tasks. *Pennsylvania Bar Association Quarterly,* October 1968, *40,* 57.

Beckhard, R. The confrontation meeting. *Harvard Business Review,* March-April 1967, pp. 149-155.

Bennis, W. G. A new role for the behavioral sciences: Effecting organizational change. *Administrative Science Quarterly,* September 1963, *8*(2), 125-166.

Bennis, W. G. *Changing organizations.* New York: McGraw-Hill, 1966.

Bennis, W. G. *Organization development: Its nature, origin and prospects.* Reading, Mass.: Addison-Wesley, 1969.

Bennis, W. G. A funny thing happened on the way to the future. *American Psychologist,* July 1970, *15*(7), 595-608.

Berkley, G. E. *The administrative revolution: Notes on the passing of organization man.* Englewood Cliffs, N.J.: Prentice-Hall, 1971.

Blake, R. R., & Mouton, J. S. *Building a dynamic corporation through grid organization development.* Houston, Tex.: Gulf Publishing, 1968.

Blake, R. R., & Mouton, J. S. A behavioral science design for the development of society. *The Journal of Applied Behavioral Science,* 1971, *7*(2), 146-163.

Blansfield, M. G. Depth analysis of organizational life. *California Management Review,* Winter 1962, *5*(2), 29-42.

Brewer, D. D. *In-service training for probation, parole and correctional personnel.* Athens: University of Georgia Press, February, 1968. (Monograph)

Brightman, R. W. *Computer assisted instruction program for police training.* Washington, D.C.: Law Enforcement Assistance Administration, 1971.

Bristow, A. P., & Gabard, E. C. *Decision making in police administration.* Springfield, Ill.: Charles C Thomas, 1961.

Burns, T., & Stalker, G. M. *Management of innovation.* London: Pergamon Press, 1961.

Caiden, G. *The dynamics of public administration: Guidelines to current transformations in theory and practice.* New York: Holt, Rinehart and Winston, 1971.

California Human Relations Agency, Department of the Youth Authority. "Training for Tomorrow: A Design for Creating and Facilitating a Comprehensive Program of Manpower Development Services for California Corrections." In *Final Report: California Correctional Training Project, Phase II.* Sacramento, Ca.: Author, March 1970.

Carpenter, G. B. *Law enforcement training materials directory.* Glenn Dale, Md.: Capitol Press, 1969.

Colbert, J., & Hohn, M. *Guide to manpower training.* Morningside Heights, N.Y.: Behavioral Publishers, 1971.

Crockett, T. S., & Stinchcomb, J. D. *Guidelines for law enforcement education programs in community and junior colleges.* Washington, D.C.: American Association of Junior Colleges, 1968. (Monograph)

Drabek, T. E. *Laboratory simulation of a police communications system under stress.* Columbus: Ohio State University Press, 1968.

Ferguson, R. F. *Creativity in law enforcement: The Covina field experiment.* San Diego, Ca.: Institute of Public and Urban Affairs, San Diego State College, May 1970. (Monograph)

Fleishman, E. A., Harris, E. F., & Burtt, H. E. *Leadership and supervision in industry: Evaluation of a supervisory training program.* Columbus: Ohio State University Press, 1955.

Frank, B. Planning in-service training programs. In *Proceedings of the 97th Annual Congress of Correction* (August 1967). Washington, D.C.: American Correctional Association, 1968, pp. 190-194.

Freeman, S. A systems approach to law enforcement training. *The Police Chief,* August 1968, pp. 61-69.

French, W. Organization development objectives, assumptions and strategies. *California Management Review,* Winter 1969, *12*(2), 23-34.

French, W., & Bell, C. *Organization development: Behavioral science interventions for organization improvement.* Englewood Cliffs, N.J.: Prentice-Hall, 1973.

Gagne, R. M. *The conditions of learning.* New York: Holt, Rinehart and Winston, 1967.

Gammage, A. *Police training in the United States.* Springfield, Ill.: Charles C Thomas, 1963.

Geilerman, S. W. *Management by motivation.* New York: American Management Association, 1968.

Geis, G., & Tenney, C. W., Jr. Evaluating a training institute for juvenile court judges. *Community mental health,* 1968. *4*(6), 461-468.

Germann, A. C. *Police executive development.* Springfield, Ill.: Charles C Thomas, 1962.

Golembiewski, R. *Organizing men and power: Patterns of behavior and line-staff models.* Chicago, Ill.: Rand McNally, 1967.

Greiner, L. E. Patterns of organization change. *Harvard Business Review,* May-June 1967, *65,* 119-130.

Gutman, D. An experiment in judicial education. *Judicature,* April 1969, pp. 366-369.

Hacon, R. J. *Conflict and human relations training.* London: Pergamon Press, 1965.

Haney, W. V. *Communication and organizational behavior* (Rev. ed.). Homewood, Ill.: Irwin, 1967.

Hersey, P., & Blanchard, K. Life cycle theory of leadership. *Training and Development Journal,* May 1969, pp. 26-34.

Hughes, C. L. *Goal setting: Key to individual and organizational effectiveness.* New York: American Management Association, 1965.

Inbar, M. & Stoll, C. *Simulation and gaming in social science.* New York: The Free Press, 1971.

International Association of Chiefs of Police. *Law enforcement education directory, 1970.* Washington, D.C.: Author, 1970.

Jacobs, P. I., Maier, M. H., & Stolurow, L. W. *Guide to evaluating self-instructional programs.* New York: Holt, Rinehart and Winston, 1966.

Johnson, E. H. In-serving training: A key to correctional progress. *Criminologica,* November 1966, *4,* 16-26.

Joint Commission on Correctional Manpower and Training. *Targets for in-service training.* Washington, D.C.: Author, 1967.

Joint Commission of Correctional Manpower and Training. *A time to act: Final report.* Washington, D.C.: Author, 1969.

Jones, J. E., & Pfeiffer, J. W. (Eds.). *The 1973 annual handbook for group facilitators.* La Jolla, Ca.: University Associates, 1973.

Jones, J. E., & Pfeiffer, J. W. (Eds.). *The 1975 annual handbook for group facilitators.* La Jolla, Ca.: University Associates, 1975.

Lawrie, J. W. Leadership and magical thinking. *Personnel Journal,* September 1970, pp. 26-32.

Lejins, P. *Introducing a law enforcement curriculum at a state university.* Washington, D.C.: U.S. Government Printing Office, 1970.

Marien, M. (Ed.) *The hot list Delphi: An exploratory survey of essential reading for the future.* Syracuse, N.Y.: Syracuse University Research Corporation, 1972.

McAshan, H. H. *Writing behavioral objectives: A new approach.* New York: Harper & Row, 1970.

McGehee, W., & Thayer, P. W. *Training in business and industry.* New York: John Wiley, 1961.

McGregor, D. *The human side of enterprise.* New York: McGraw-Hill, 1960.

McGregor, D. *The professional manager.* New York: McGraw-Hill, 1967.

McManus, G. P., et al. *Police training and performance study.* Washington, D.C.: Law Enforcement Assistance Administration, 1970.

Miller, D. C. Using behavioral science to solve organization problems. *Personnel Administration,* January-February 1968, *31,* 21-29.

Myers, M. S. Every employee a manager. *California Management Review,* Spring 1968, *10,* 9-20.

National Advisory Commission on Criminal Justice Standards and Goals. *Community crime prevention.* Washington, D.C.: U.S. Government Printing Office, 1973. (a)

National Advisory Commission on Criminal Justice Standards and Goals. *Corrections.* Washington, D.C.: U.S. Government Printing Office, 1973. (b)

National Advisory Commission on Criminal Justice Standards and Goals. *Courts.* Washington, D.C.: U.S. Government Printing Office, 1973. (c)

National Advisory Commission on Criminal Justice Standards and Goals. *Criminal Justice System.* Washington, D.C.: U.S. Government Printing Office, 1973. (d)

National Advisory Commission on Criminal Justice Standards and Goals. *A national strategy to reduce crime.* Washington, D.C.: U.S. Government Printing Office, 1973. (e)

National Advisory Commission on Criminal Justice Standards and Goals. *Police.* Washington, D.C.: U.S. Government Printing Office, 1973. (f)

National Commission on Productivity. *Opportunities for improving productivity in police services.* Washington, D.C.: Author, 1973.

N.I.L.E.C.J. *Computer assisted instruction program for police training.* Washington, D.C.: U.S. Government Printing Office, 1971.

O'Neill, M. E., & Lance, J. E. Education vs. training: A distinction. *Journal of California Law Enforcement.* April 1970, *4* (4), 201-203.

Pell, A. R. *Police Leadership.* Springfield, Ill.: Charles C Thomas, 1967.

Pfeiffer, J. W., & Jones, J. E. (Eds.). *The 1972 annual handbook for group facilitators.* La Jolla, Ca.: University Associates, 1972.

Pfeiffer, J. W., & Jones, J. E. (Eds.). *The 1974 annual handbook for group facilitators.* La Jolla, Ca.: University Associates, 1974.

Pfeiffer, J. W., & Jones, J. E. (Eds.). *A handbook of structured experiences for human relations training* (Vols. I, II, III, and IV). La Jolla, Ca.: University Associates, 1969 & 1974; 1970 & 1974; 1971 & 1974; 1973.

Pfiffner, J. M., & Sherwood, F. *Administrative Organization.* Englewood Cliffs, N.J.: Prentice-Hall, 1960.

Piven, H., & Alcabes, A. *Education, Training, and Manpower in Corrections and Law Enforcement* (Source Book I: Education in Colleges and Universities 1965-1966, 1966-1967; Source Book II: In-Service Training, 1965 and 1966; Source Book III: Manpower, Workloads, and Salaries, 1965 and 1966; and Source Book IV: Advocated Innovations in Education and Training). Washington, D.C.: U.S. Department of Health, Education, and Welfare, 1968.

President's Commission on Law Enforcement and Administration of Justice. *Task force report: Corrections.* Washington, D.C.: U.S. Government Printing Office, 1967.

Project STAR (Systems and Training Analysis of Requirements). *Systems and training analysis of requirements for criminal justice system participants, part I: Technical and management proposal.* Marina Del Rey, Ca.: American Justice Institute, May 20, 1970.

Project STAR. *Survey of role perceptions for operational criminal justice personnel: Data summary.* Marina Del Rey, Ca.: American Justice Institute, April 21, 1971.

Project STAR. *Survey of role perceptions for operational criminal justice personnel: Preliminary research design.* Marina Del Rey, Ca.: American Justice Institute, November 3, 1971.

Project STAR. *Survey of role perceptions for operational criminal justice personnel: Preliminary questionnaire.* Marina Del Rey, Ca.: American Justice Institute, November 24, 1971.

Project STAR. *Survey of role perceptions for operational criminal justice personnel: Pretest questionnaire.* Marina Del Rey, Ca.: American Justice Institute, December 15, 1971.

Project STAR. *Survey of role perceptions for operational criminal justice personnel: Questionnaire.* Marina Del Rey, Ca.: American Justice Institute, February 1, 1972. (a)

Project STAR. *Survey of role perceptions for operational criminal justice personnel: Survey administrators' manual.* Marina Del Rey, Ca.: American Justice Institute, February 1, 1972. (b)

Project STAR. *Future roles of criminal justice personnel: Position papers.* Marina Del Rey, Ca.: American Justice Institute, March 2, 1972.

Project STAR. *Public opinion of criminal justice in California: A survey conducted by Field Research Corporation.* Marina Del Rey, Ca.: American Justice Institute, April 15, 1972.

Project STAR. *Method for police role performance analysis.* Marina Del Rey, Ca.: American Justice Institute, June 5, 1972.

Project STAR. *Method for corrections role performance analysis.* Marina Del Rey, Ca.: American Justice Institute, August 18, 1972.

Project STAR. *Method for role performance analysis of prosecuting and defense attorneys.* Marina Del Rey, Ca.: American Justice Institute, November 6, 1972.

Project STAR. *Criminal justice roles, tasks, and performance objectives.* Marina Del Rey, Ca.: American Justice Institute, May 31, 1973.

Rosove, P. E. *The impact of social trends on crime and criminal justice.* Project STAR. Marina Del Rey, Ca.: American Justice Institute, March 23, 1972.

Rubin, T., & Smith, J. F. The future of the juvenile court: Implications for correctional manpower and training. *Juvenile Court Journal,* Fall 1968, *19*(3), 21-36.

Ryan, A. T. Educational management by systems techniques in correctional institutions. *Educational Technology,* February 1972, *12*(2), 18-26.

Stenzel, A. K., & Feeny, H. M. *Volunteer training and development: A manual for community groups.* New York: Seabury Press, 1968.

Sterling, James W. *Changes in role concept of police officers.* Washington, D.C.: International Association of Chiefs of Police, 1968.

Stogdill, R. M. (Ed.). *The process of model-building in the behavioral sciences.* Columbus: Ohio State University Press, 1971.

Tannenbaum, R., & Davis, S. A. *Values, man and organizations,* Reprint 202, Los Angeles: University of California at Los Angeles, 1969.

Tannenbaum, R., & Schmidt, W. H. How to choose a leadership pattern. *Harvard Business Review,* 1969, pp. 95-101.

Whisenand, P. *Police supervision: Theory and practice.* Englewood Cliffs, N.J.: Prentice-Hall, 1971.

Whisenand, P., & Ferguson, F. *The managing of police organizations.* Englewood Cliffs, N.J.: Prentice-Hall, 1973.

APPENDIX I

NATIONAL ADVISORY COMMISSION REPORTS ON STANDARDS AND GOALS FOR CRIMINAL JUSTICE

The National Advisory Commission on Criminal Justice Standards and Goals produced six reports in 1973 relating to the criminal justice system. One report, *A National Strategy to Reduce Crime*, contained a narrative description of the major proposals made by the Commission; the standards and recommendations of the Commission appeared in five companion reports—*Criminal Justice System, Community Crime Prevention, Police, Courts*, and *Corrections*. These reports are summarized here for the reader's convenience; however, the reports themselves should be consulted for the precise rationale and description of the standards and recommendations. They are available from the United States Government Printing Office, Washington, D.C., 20402.

REPORT: CRIMINAL JUSTICE SYSTEM

REPORT REFERENCE AND SYNOPSIS

Standards:
1.1 Assure that criminal justice planning is crime-oriented.
1.2 Improve the linkage between criminal justice planning and budgeting.
1.3 Set minimum statewide standards for recipients of criminal justice grants and subgrants.
1.4 Develop criminal justice planning capabilities.
1.5 Encourage the participation of operating agencies and the public in the criminal justice planning process.

Recommendation:
1.1 Urge the Federal government to apply these standards in its own planning.

Standards:
3.1 Coordinate the development of criminal justice information systems and make maximum use of collected data.

3.2 Establish a State criminal justice information system that provides certain services.
3.3 Provide localities with information systems that support the needs of local criminal justice agencies.
3.4 Provide every component of the criminal justice system with an information system that supports interagency needs.

Standards:
4.1 Define the proper function of a police information system.
4.2 Utilize information to improve the department's crime analysis capability.
4.3 Develop a police manpower resource allocation and control system.
4.4 Specify maximum allowable delay for information delivery.
4.5 Insure that all police agencies participate in the Uniform Crime Report program.
4.6 Expand collection of crime data.
4.7 Insure quality control of crime data.
4.8 Establish a geocoding system for crime analysis.

Standards:
5.1 Provide background data and case history for criminal justice decision making.
5.2 Provide information on caseflow to permit efficient calendar management.
5.3 Provide capability to determine monthly criminal justice caseflow and workloads.
5.4 Provide data to support charge determination and case handling.
5.5 Create capability for continued research and evaluation.
5.6 Record action taken in regard to one individual and one distinct offense and record the number of criminal events.

Standards:
6.1 Define the needs of a corrections information system.
6.2 Apply uniform definitions to all like correctional data.
6.3 Design a corrections data base that is flexible enough to allow for expansion.
6.4 Collect certain data about the offender.
6.5 Account for offender population and movement.
6.6 Describe the corrections experience of the offender.
6.7 Evaluate the performance of the corrections system.

Standards:
7.1 Provide for compatible design of offender-based transaction statistics and computerized criminal history systems.
7.2 Develop single data collection procedures for offender-based transaction statistics and computerized criminal history data by criminal justice agencies.

7.3 Develop data bases simultaneously for offender-based transaction statistics and computerized criminal history systems.
7.4 Restrict dissemination of criminal justice information.
7.5 Insure completeness and accuracy of offender data.
7.6 Safeguard systems containing criminal offender data.
7.7 Establish computer interfaces for criminal justice information systems.
7.8 Insure availability of criminal justice information systems.

Standards:
8.1 Insure the privacy and security of criminal justice information systems.
8.2 Define the scope of criminal justice information systems files.
8.3 Limit access and dissemination of criminal justice information.
8.4 Guarantee the right of the individual to review information in criminal justice information systems relating to him.
8.5 Adopt a system of classifying criminal justice system data.
8.6 Protect criminal justice information from environmental hazards.
8.7 Implement a personnel clearance system.
8.8 Establish criteria for the use of criminal justice information for research.

Standards:
9.1 Insure standardized terminology following the National Crime Information Center example.
9.2 Establish specific program language requirements for criminal justice information systems.
9.3 Assure adequate teleprocessing capability.

Standards:
10.1 Take legislative actions to support the development of criminal justice information systems.
10.2 Establish criminal justice user groups.
10.3 Establish a plan for development of criminal justice information and statistics systems at State and local levels.
10.4 Consolidate services to provide criminal justice information support where it is not otherwise economically feasible.
10.5 Require conformity with all standards of this report as a condition for grant approval.

Standards:
11.1 Monitor the criminal justice information system analysis, design, development, and initial steps leading to implementation.
11.2 Monitor the implementation of the system to determine the cost and performance of the system and its component parts.
11.3 Conduct evaluations to determine the effectiveness of information system components.

Standards:
12.1 Develop, implement, and evaluate criminal justice education and training programs.
12.2 Establish criminal justice system curricula.

270 Criminal Justice Group Training

Standards:
13.1 Revise criminal codes in States where codes have not been revised in the past decade.
13.2 Complete revision of criminal codes.
13.3 Simplify the penalty structure in criminal codes.
13.4 Revise corrections laws.
13.5 Create a drafting body to carry out criminal code revision.
13.6 Revise criminal procedure laws.
13.7 Support drafted criminal law legislation with interpretative commentaries.
13.8 Assure smooth transition to the new law through education.
13.9 Continue law revision efforts through a permanent commission.

REPORT: COMMUNITY CRIME PREVENTION

REPORT REFERENCE AND SYNOPSIS

Recommendations:
2.1 Distribute public service on the basis of need.
2.2 Dispense government services through neighborhood centers.
2.3 Enact public right-to-know laws.
2.4 Broadcast local government meetings and hearings.
2.5 Conduct public hearings on local issues.
2.6 Establish neighborhood governments.
2.7 Create a central office of complaint and information.
2.8 Broadcast local Action Line programs.

Standards:
3.1 Coordinate youth services through youth services bureaus.
3.2 Operate youth services bureaus independent of the justice system.
3.3 Divert offenders into youth services bureaus.
3.4 Provide direct and referral services to youths.
3.5 Hire professional, paraprofessional, and volunteer staff.
3.6 Plan youth program evaluation and research.
3.7 Appropriate funds for youth services bureaus.
3.8 Legislate establishment and funding of youth services bureaus.

Recommendations:
4.1 Adopt multimodality drug treatment systems.
4.2 Create crisis intervention and drug emergency centers.
4.3 Establish methadone maintenance programs.
4.4 Establish narcotic antagonist treatment programs.
4.5 Create drug-free therapeutic community facilities.
4.6 Organize residential drug treatment programs.
4.7 Encourage broader flexibility in varying treatment approaches.
4.8 Enable defendants to refer themselves voluntarily to drug treatment programs.

4.9   Establish training programs for drug treatment personnel.
4.10 Plan comprehensive, community-wide drug prevention.
4.11 Coordinate drug programs through a State agency.
4.12 Coordinate Federal, State, and local drug programs.

Recommendations:
5.1   Expand job opportunities for disadvantaged youth.
5.2   Broaden after-school and summer employment programs.
5.3   Establish pretrial intervention programs.
5.4   Expand job opportunities for offenders and ex-offenders.
5.5   Remove ex-offender employment barriers.
5.6   Create public employment programs for ex-offenders.
5.7   Expand job opportunities for former drug abusers.
5.8   Target employment, income, and credit efforts in poverty areas.
5.9   Require employers' compliance with antidiscrimination laws.
5.10 Increase support of minority businesses.
5.11 Alleviate housing and transportation discrimination.

Recommendations:
6.1   Adopt teacher training programs for parents.
6.2   Exemplify justice and democracy in school operations.
6.3   Guarantee literacy to elementary school students.
6.4   Provide special language services for bicultural students.
6.5   Develop career preparation programs in schools.
6.6   Provide effective supportive services in schools.
6.7   Offer alternative education programs for deviant students.
6.8   Open schools for community activities.
6.9   Adopt merit training and promotion policies for teachers.

Recommendation:
7.1   Develop recreation programs for delinquency prevention.

Recommendations:
8.1   Enlist religious community participation in crime prevention.
8.2   Encourage religious institutions to educate their constituencies about the crime problem.
8.3   Enlist religious institution support of crime prevention.
8.4   Open church facilities for community programs.
8.5   Promote religious group participation in the justice system.

Recommendations:
9.1   Design buildings that incorporate security measures.
9.2   Include security requirements in building codes.
9.3   Improve street lighting in high crime areas.
9.4   Adopt shoplifting prevention techniques in retail establishments.
9.5   Legislate car theft prevention programs.
9.6   Involve citizens in law enforcement.

Standards:
10.1 Adopt an Ethics Code for public officials and employees.
10.2 Create an Ethics Board to enforce the Ethics Code.
10.3 Disclose public officials' financial and professional interests.
10.4 Include conflicts of interest in the State criminal code.

Standards:
11.1 Disclose candidates' receipts and expenditures.
11.2 Limit political campaign spending.
11.3 Prohibit campaign contributions from government-connected businessmen.
11.4 Prohibit campaign gifts from unions, trade groups, corporations.

Standard:
12.1 Establish a State procurement agency.

Standards:
13.1 Develop equitable criteria for zoning, licensing, and tax assessment.
13.2 Formulate specific criteria for government decision making.
13.3 Publicize zoning, licensing, and tax assessment actions.

Standards:
14.1 Set capability and integrity standards for local procedures.
14.2 Create a State office to attack corruption and organized crime.

REPORT: POLICE

REPORT REFERENCE AND SYNOPSIS

Standards:
   1.1 Formulate policies governing police functions, objectives, and priorities.
   1.2 Publicize and respect the limits of police activity.
   1.3 Formalize police use of discretion.
   1.4 Improve communication and relations with the public.
   1.5 Enhance police officers' understanding of their role and of the culture of their community.
   1.6 Publicize police policies and practices.
   1.7 Promote relations with the media.

Standards:
   2.1 Develop workable agency goals and objectives.
   2.2 Establish written policies to help employees attain agency goals and objectives.
   2.3 Establish a formal police inspection system.

Standards:
   3.1 Establish geographic team policing.
   3.2 Involve the public in neighborhood crime prevention efforts.

Standards:
4.1 Coordinate planning and crime control efforts with other components of the criminal justice system.
4.2 Develop cooperative procedures with courts and corrections agencies.
4.3 Formalize diversion procedures to insure equitable treatment.
4.4 Utilize alternatives to arrest and pretrial detention.
4.5 Develop court follow-up practices for selected cases.

Recommendations:
4.1 Divert drug addicts and alcoholics to treatment centers.
4.2 Allow telephoned petitions for search warrants.
4.3 Enact State legislation prohibiting private surveillance and authorizing court-supervised electronic surveillance.

Standards:
5.1 Establish a police service that meets the needs of the community.
5.2 Consolidate police agencies for greater effectiveness and efficiency.
5.3 Implement administrative and operational planning methods.
5.4 Assign responsibility for agency and jurisdictional planning.
5.5 Participate in any community planning that can affect crime.
5.6 Assign responsibility for fiscal management of the agency.
5.7 Develop fiscal management procedures.
5.8 Derive maximum benefit from government funding.

Recommendations:
5.1 Formalize relationships between public and private police agencies.
5.2 Form a National Institute of Law Enforcement and a Criminal Justice Advisory Committee.
5.3 Develop standardized measures of agency performance.

Standards:
6.1 Determine the applicability of team policing.
6.2 Plan, train for, and publicize implementation of team policing.

Standards:
7.1 Plan for coordinating activities of relevant agencies during mass disorders and natural disasters.
7.2 Delegate to the police chief executive responsibility for resources in unusual occurrences.
7.3 Develop an interim control system for use during unusual occurrences.
7.4 Develop a procedure for mass processing of arrestees.
7.5 Legislate an efficient, constitutionally sound crisis procedure.
7.6 Implement training programs for unusual occurrence control procedures.

Standards:
8.1 Define the role of patrol officers.
8.2 Upgrade the status and salary of patrol officers.
8.3 Develop a responsive patrol deployment system.

Standards:
9.1 Authorize only essential assignment specialization.
9.2 Specify selection criteria for specialist personnel.
9.3 Review agency specializations annually.
9.4 Provide State specialists to local agencies.
9.5 Formulate policies governing delinquents and youth offenders.
9.6 Control traffic violations through preventive patrol and enforcement.
9.7 Train patrol officers to conduct preliminary investigations.
9.8 Create a mobile unit for special crime problems.
9.9 Establish policy and capability for vice operations.
9.10 Develop agency narcotics and drugs investigative capability.
9.11 Develop a statewide intelligence network that has privacy safeguards.

Standards:
10.1 Employ civilian personnel in supportive positions.
10.2 Employ reserve officers.

Standards:
11.1 Establish working relationships with outside professionals.
11.2 Acquire legal assistance when necessary.
11.3 Create a State police management consultation service.

Standards:
12.1 Train technicians to gather physical evidence.
12.2 Consolidate criminal laboratories to serve local, regional, and State needs.
12.3 Establish a secure and efficient filing system for evidential items.
12.4 Guarantee adequate jail services and management.

Recommendation:
12.1 Establish crime laboratory certification standards.

Standards:
13.1 Actively recruit applicants.
13.2 Recruit college-educated personnel.
13.3 Insure nondiscriminatory recruitment practices.
13.4 Implement minimum police officer selection standards.
13.5 Formalize a nondiscriminatory applicant screening process.
13.6 Encourage the employment of women.

Recommendations:
13.1 Develop job-related applicant tests.
13.2 Develop an applicant scoring system.

Standards:
14.1 Maintain salaries competitive with private business.
14.2 Establish a merit-based position classification system.

Standards:
15.1 Upgrade entry-level educational requirements.
15.2 Implement police officer educational incentives.
15.3 Affiliate training programs with academic institutions.

Recommendation:
15.1 Outline police curriculum requirements.

Standards:
16.1 Establish State minimum training standards.
16.2 Develop effective training programs.
16.3 Provide training prior to work assignment.
16.4 Provide interpersonal communications training.
16.5 Establish routine in-service training programs.
16.6 Develop training quality control measures.
16.7 Develop police training academies and criminal justice training centers.

Standards:
17.1 Offer self-development programs for qualified personnel.
17.2 Implement formal personnel development programs.
17.3 Review personnel periodically for advancements.
17.4 Authorize police chief executive control of promotions.
17.5 Establish a personnel information system.

Standards:
18.1 Maintain effective employee regulations.
18.2 Formalize policies regulating police employee organizations.
18.3 Allow a collective negotiation process.
18.4 Prohibit work stoppages by policemen.

Standards:
19.1 Formulate internal discipline procedures.
19.2 Implement misconduct complaint procedures.
19.3 Create a specialized internal discipline investigative unit.
19.4 Insure swift and fair investigation of misconduct.
19.5 Authorize police chief executive adjudication of complaints.
19.6 Implement positive programs to prevent misconduct.

Recommendation:
19.1 Study methods of reducing police corruption.

Standards:
20.1 Require physical and psychological examinations of applicants.
20.2 Establish continuing physical fitness standards.
20.3 Establish an employee services unit.
20.4 Offer a complete health insurance program.

Recommendation:
20.1 Compensate duty-connected injury, death, and disease.

Standards:
21.1 Specify apparel and equipment standards.
21.2 Require standard firearms, ammunition, and auxiliary equipment.
21.3 Provide all uniforms and equipment.

Standards:
22.1 Evaluate transportation equipment annually.
22.2 Acquire and maintain necessary transportation equipment.
22.3 Conduct a fleet safety program.

Recommendations:
22.1 Evaluate transportation equipment annually.
22.2 Acquire and maintain necessary transportation equipment.
22.3 Conduct a fleet safety program.

Recommendation:
22.1 Test transportation equipment nationally.

Standards:
23.1 Develop a rapid and accurate telephone system.
23.2 Insure rapid and accurate police communication.
23.3 Insure an efficient radio communications system.

Recommendations:
23.1 Conduct research on a digital communications system.
23.2 Set national communications equipment standards.
23.3 Evaluate radio frequency requirements.

Standards:
24.1 Standardize reports of criminal activity.
24.2 Establish an accurate, rapid-access record system.
24.3 Standardize local information systems.
24.4 Coordinate Federal, State, and local information systems.

REPORT: COURTS

REPORT REFERENCE AND SYNOPSIS

Standards:
1.1 Screen certain accused persons out of the criminal justice system.
1.2 Formulate written guidelines for screening decisions.

Standards:
2.1 Utilize, as appropriate, diversion into non-criminal justice programs before trial.
2.2 Develop guidelines for diversion decisions.

Standards:
3.1 Prohibit plea negotiation in all courts by not later than 1978.
3.2 Document in the court records the basis for a negotiated guilty plea and the reason for its acceptance.
3.3 Formulate written policies governing plea negotiations.
3.4 Establish a time limit after which plea negotiations may no longer be conducted.
3.5 Provide service of counsel before plea negotiations.
3.6 Assure proper conduct by prosecutors in obtaining guilty pleas.
3.7 Review all guilty pleas and negotiations.
3.8 Assure that a plea of guilty is not considered when determining sentence.

Standards:
4.1 Assure that the period from arrest to trial does not exceed 60 days in felonies and 30 days in misdemeanors.
4.2 Maximize use of citation or summons in lieu of arrest.
4.3 Eliminate preliminary hearings in misdemeanor proceedings.
4.4 Adopt policies governing use and function of grand juries.
4.5 Present arrested persons before a judicial officer within 6 hours after arrest.
4.6 Eliminate private bail bond agencies; utilize a wide range of pretrial release programs, including release on recognizance.
4.7 Adopt provisions to apprehend rapidly and deal severely with persons who violate release conditions.
4.8 Hold preliminary hearings within 2 weeks after arrest; eliminate formal arraignment.
4.9 Broaden pretrial discovery by both prosecution and defense.
4.10 File all motions within 15 days after preliminary hearing or indictment; hear motions within 5 days.
4.11 Establish criteria for assigning cases to the trial docket.
4.12 Limit granting of continuances.
4.13 Assure that only judges examine jurors; limit the number of peremptory challenges.
4.14 Adopt policies limiting number of jurors to fewer than 12 but more than six in all but the most serious cases.
4.15 Restrict evidence, testimony, and argument to that which is relevant to the issue of innocence or guilt; utilize full trial days.

Recommendations:
4.1 Study the exclusionary rule and formulate alternatives.
4.2 Study the use of videotaped trials in criminal cases; establish pilot projects.

Standard:
5.1 Adopt a policy stipulating that all sentencing is performed by the trial judge.

Standards:
6.1 Provide the opportunity to every convicted person for one full and fair review.
6.2 Provide a full-time professional staff of lawyers in the reviewing court.
6.3 Assure that review procedures are flexible and tailored to each case.
6.4 Establish time limits for review proceedings.
6.5 Specify exceptional circumstances that warrant additional review.
6.6 Assure that reviewing courts do not readjudicate claims already adjudicated on the merits by a court of competent jurisdiction.
6.7 Assure that determinations of fact by either a trial or reviewing court are conclusive absent a constitutional violation undermining the fact finding process.
6.8 Assure that claims are not adjudicated in further reviews which were not asserted at trial or which were disclaimed at trial by the defendant.
6.9 Assure that a reviewing court always states the reasons for its decision; limit publication to significant cases.

Recommendations:
6.1 Develop means of producing trial transcripts speedily.
6.2 Study cases of delay in review proceedings.
6.3 Study reports and recommendations of the Advisory Council for Appellate Justice.

Standards:
7.1 Select judges on the basis of merit qualifications.
7.2 Establish mandatory retirement for all judges at age 65.
7.3 Base salaries and benefits of State judges on the Federal model.
7.4 Subject judges to discipline or removal for cause by a judicial conduct commission.
7.5 Create and maintain a comprehensive program of continuing judicial education.

Standards:
8.1 Assure that State courts are unified courts of record, financed by the State, administered on a statewide basis, and presided over by full-time judges admitted to the practice of law.
8.2 Dispose administratively of all traffic cases except certain serious offenses.

Standards:
9.1 Establish policies for the administration of the State's courts.
9.2 Vest in a presiding judge ultimate local administrative judicial authority in each trial jurisdiction.
9.3 Assure that local and regional trial courts have a full-time court administrator.
9.4 Assure that ultimate responsibility for the management and flow of cases rests with the judges of the trial court.

- 9.5 Establish coordinating councils to survey court administration practices in the State.
- 9.6 Establish a forum for interchange between court personnel and the community.

Standards:
- 10.1 Provide adequate physical facilities for court processing of criminal defendants.
- 10.2 Provide information concerning court processes to the public and to participants in the criminal justice system.
- 10.3 Coordinate responsibility among the court, news media, the public, and the bar for providing information to the public about the courts.
- 10.4 Assure that court personnel are representative of the community served by the court.
- 10.5 Assure that judges and court personnel participate in criminal justice planning activities.
- 10.6 Call witnesses only when necessary; make use of telephone alert.
- 10.7 Assure that witness compensation is realistic and equitable.

Standards:
- 11.1 Utilize computer services consistent with the needs and caseloads of the courts.
- 11.2 Employ automated legal research services on an experimental basis.

Recommendation:
- 11.1 Instruct law students in use of legal research systems.

Standards:
- 12.1 Assure that prosecutors are full-time skilled professionals, authorized to serve a minimum term of 4 years, and compensated adequately.
- 12.2 Select and retain assistant prosecutors on the basis of legal ability; assure that they serve full-time and are compensated adequately.
- 12.3 Provide prosecutors with supporting staff and facilities comparable to that of similar size private law firms.
- 12.4 Establish a State-level entity to provide support to local prosecutors.
- 12.5 Utilize education programs to assure the highest professional competence.
- 12.6 Establish file control and statistical systems in prosecutors' offices.
- 12.7 Assure that each prosecutor develops written office policies and practices.
- 12.8 Assure that prosecutors have an active role in crime investigation, with adequate investigative staff and subpoena powers.
- 12.9 Assure that prosecutors maintain relationships with other criminal justice agencies.

Standards:
- 13.1 Make available public representation to eligible defendants at all stages in all criminal proceedings.

13.2 Assure that any individual provided public representation pay any portion of the cost he can assume without undue hardship.
13.3 Enable all applicants for defender services to apply directly to the public defender or appointing authority for representation.
13.4 Make counsel available to corrections inmates, indigent parolees, and indigent probationers on matters relevant to their status.
13.5 Establish a full-time public defender organization and assigned counsel system involving the private bar in every jurisdiction.
13.6 Assure that defender services are consistent with local needs and financed by the State.
13.7 Assure that public defenders are full time and adequately compensated.
13.8 Assure that public defenders are nominated by a selection board and appointed by the Governor.
13.9 Keep free from political pressures the duties of public defenders.
13.10 Base upon merit, hiring, retention, and promotion policies for public defender staff attorneys.
13.11 Assure that salaries for public defender staff attorneys are comparable to those of associate attorneys in local private law firms.
13.12 Assure that the caseload of a public defender office is not excessive.
13.13 Assure that the public defender is sensitive to the problems of his client community.
13.14 Provide public defender offices with adequate supportive services and personnel.
13.15 Vest responsibility in the public defender for maintaining a panel of private attorneys for defense work.
13.16 Provide systematic and comprehensive training to public defenders and assigned counsel.

Standards:
14.1 Place jurisdiction of the sort presently vested in juvenile courts over juveniles in a family court.
14.2 Create a special intake unit of the family court.
14.3 Process certain juvenile delinquency cases as adult criminal prosecutions.
14.4 Provide adjudicative hearings in delinquency cases separate from disposition hearings.
14.5 Make disposition hearings in delinquency cases separate from adjudicative hearings.

Standards:
15.1 Assure that every plan for the administration of justice in a mass disorder contains a court processing section.
15.2 Assure that the court plan is concerned with both judicial policy and court management.
15.3 Assure that a prosecutorial plan is developed by the local prosecutor(s).
15.4 Assure that the plan for providing defense services during a mass disorder is developed by the local public defender(s).

REPORT: CORRECTIONS

REPORT REFERENCE AND SYNOPSIS

Standards:
2.1 Guarantee offenders' access to courts.
2.2 Guarantee offenders' access to legal assistance.
2.3 Guarantee offenders' access to legal materials.
2.4 Protect offenders from personal abuse.
2.5 Guarantee healthful surroundings for inmates.
2.6 Guarantee adequate medical care for inmates.
2.7 Regulate institutional search and seizure.
2.8 Assure nondiscriminatory treatment of offenders.
2.9 Guarantee rehabilitation programs for offenders.
2.10 Legislate safeguards for retention and restoration of rights.
2.11 Establish rules of inmate conduct.
2.12 Establish uniform disciplinary procedures.
2.13 Adopt procedures for change of inmate status.
2.14 Establish offenders' grievance.
2.15 Guarantee free expression and association to offenders.
2.16 Guarantee offenders' freedom of religious beliefs and practices.
2.17 Guarantee offenders' communication with the public.
2.18 Establish redress procedures for violations of offenders' rights.

Standard:
3.1 Implement formal diversion programs.

Standards:
4.1 Develop a comprehensive pretrial process improvement plan.
4.2 Engage in comprehensive planning before building detention facilities.
4.3 Formulate procedures for use of summons, citation, and arrest warrants.
4.4 Develop alternatives to pretrial detention.
4.5 Develop procedures for pretrial release and detention.
4.6 Legislate authority over pretrial detainees.
4.7 Develop pretrial procedures governing allegedly incompetent defendants.
4.8 Protect the rights of pretrial detainees.
4.9 Establish rehabilitation programs for pretrial detainees.
4.10 Develop procedures to expedite trials.

Standards:
5.1 Establish judicial sentencing of defendants.
5.2 Establish sentencing practices for nondangerous offenders.
5.3 Establish sentencing practices for serious offenders.
5.4 Establish sentencing procedures governing probation.
5.5 Establish criteria for fines.

5.6 Adopt policies governing multiple sentences.
5.7 Disallow mitigation of sentence based on guilty plea.
5.8 Allow credit against sentence for time served.
5.9 Authorize continuing court jurisdiction over sentenced offenders.
5.10 Require judicial visits to correctional facilities.
5.11 Conduct sentencing councils, institutes, and reviews.
5.12 Conduct statewide sentencing institutes.
5.13 Create sentencing councils for judges.
5.14 Require content-specified presentence reports.
5.15 Restrict preadjudication disclosure of presentence reports.
5.16 Disclose presentence reports to defense and prosecution.
5.17 Guarantee defendants' rights at sentencing hearings.
5.18 Develop procedural guidelines for sentencing hearings.
5.19 Impose sentence according to sentencing hearing evidence.

Standards:
6.1 Develop a comprehensive classification system.
6.2 Establish classification policies for correctional institutions.
6.3 Establish community classification teams.

Standards:
7.1 Develop a range of community-based alternatives to institutionalization.
7.2 Insure correctional cooperation with community agencies.
7.3 Seek public involvement in corrections.
7.4 Establish procedures for gradual release of inmates.

Standards:
8.1 Authorize police to divert juveniles.
8.2 Establish a juvenile court intake unit.
8.3 Apply total system planning concepts to juvenile detention centers.
8.4 Evaluate juvenile intake and detention personnel policies.

Standards:
9.1 Undertake total system planning for community corrections.
9.2 Incorporate local correctional functions within the State system.
9.3 Formulate State standards for local facilities.
9.4 Establish pretrial intake services.
9.5 Upgrade pretrial admission services and processes.
9.6 Upgrade the qualifications of local correctional personnel.
9.7 Protect the health and welfare of adults in community facilities.
9.8 Provide programs for adults in jails.
9.9 Develop release programs for convicted adults.
9.10 Evaluate the physical environment of jails.

Standards:
10.1 Place probation under executive branch jurisdiction.
10.2 Establish a probation service delivery service.

10.3 Provide misdemeanant probation services.
10.4 Develop a State probation manpower unit.
10.5 Establish release on recognizance procedures and staff.

Standards:
11.1 Seek alternatives to new State institutions.
11.2 Modify State institutions to serve inmate needs.
11.3 Modify the social environment of institutions.
11.4 Individualize institutional programs.
11.5 Devise programs for special offender types.
11.6 Provide constructive programs for women offenders.
11.7 Develop a full range of institutional religious programs.
11.8 Provide recreation programs for inmates.
11.9 Offer individual and group counseling for inmates.
11.10 Operate labor and industrial programs that aid in re-entry.

Standards:
12.1 Establish independent State parole boards.
12.2 Specify qualifications of parole board members.
12.3 Specify procedure and requirements for granting parole.
12.4 Specify parole revocation procedures and alternatives.
12.5 Coordinate institutional and field services and functions.
12.6 Develop community services for parolees.
12.7 Individualize parole conditions.
12.8 Develop parole manpower and training programs.

Standards:
13.1 Professionalize correctional management.
13.2 Develop a correctional planning process.
13.3 Train management in offender and employee relations.
13.4 Prohibit but prepare for work stoppages and job actions.

Standards:
14.1 Discontinue unwarranted personnel restrictions.
14.2 Recruit and employ minority group individuals.
14.3 Recruit and employ women.
14.4 Recruit and employ ex-offenders.
14.5 Recruit and use volunteers.
14.6 Revise personnel practices to retain staff.
14.7 Adopt a participatory management program.
14.8 Plan for manpower redistribution to community programs.
14.9 Establish a State program for justice system education.
14.10 Implement correctional internship and work-study programs.
14.11 Create staff development programs.

Standards:
15.1 Maintain a State correctional information system.
15.2 Provide staff for systems analysis and statistical research.

15.3 Design an information system to supply service needs.
15.4 Develop a data base with criminal justice system interface.
15.5 Measure recidivism and program performance.

Standards:
16.1 Enact a correctional code.
16.2 Enact regulation of administrative procedures.
16.3 Legislate definition and implementation of offender rights.
16.4 Legislate the unification of corrections.
16.5 Define personnel standards by law.
16.6 Ratify interstate correctional agreements.
16.7 Define crime categories and maximum sentences.
16.8 Legislate criteria for court sentencing alternatives.
16.9 Restrict court delinquency jurisdiction and detention.
16.10 Require presentence investigations by law.
16.11 Formulate criteria and procedures for probation decisions.
16.12 Legislate commitment, classification, and transfer procedures.
16.13 Lift unreasonable restrictions on prison labor and industry.
16.14 Legislate authorization for community-based correctional programs.
16.15 Clarify parole procedures and eligibility requirements.
16.16 Establish pardon power and procedure.
16.17 Repeal laws restricting offender rights.

APPENDIX II

GOAL SETTING AND GUIDELINES FOR EVALUATION

All organizations exist for a specific purpose; to achieve this purpose, goals and objectives must be established. Without this sense of direction, confusion exists. Goal-directed organizations are more efficient than those who are completely unplanned and unorganized. The alternative to being goal directed is to drift, to float, and to achieve in a random manner.

A goal is an object or end that an individual, group, or organization strives to achieve. Objectives are the specific, but limited, steps used in reaching the goal. For example:

> GOAL: To improve the processing time of offenders in the criminal justice system.

This goal states what the system would like to accomplish in processing offenders. However, it provides no objectives—steps in achieving the goal. These steps must be identifiable, measurable, and have a time frame. They may be of primary or secondary importance. Using the previously stated goal, the objectives might be:

> *Primary Importance:* To reduce the criminal justice processing time of offenders by ten days within the next year.
>
> *Secondary Importance:* To save an estimated $70,000 by reducing the criminal justice processing time within the next year.

Objectives form the basis of an evaluation model. Another important component of the model is the development of the program and its specific elements. The program must be in specifics in order to provide an understanding and a base for evaluation. For example, a police manager might state that he has a

---

The majority of this material is adapted by permission of the author from a paper by Dr. Robert Carter, University of Southern California. See "Citation Release: An Evaluation Activity," p. 74.

school officer resource program, but he may have revealed very little about the program. To fully understand the program, details are needed:

>Who and what agencies are involved?
>How and when did they get involved?
>What is their level of involvement?

Not all program components can be readily identified; some remain hidden and surface only when the program is in operation. However, most components are sufficiently defined so that they provide a basis for evaluation.

When objective and program are merged into a model, the impetus for evaluation is clear, as shown in Figure 1. Programs are evaluated against or in terms of objectives.

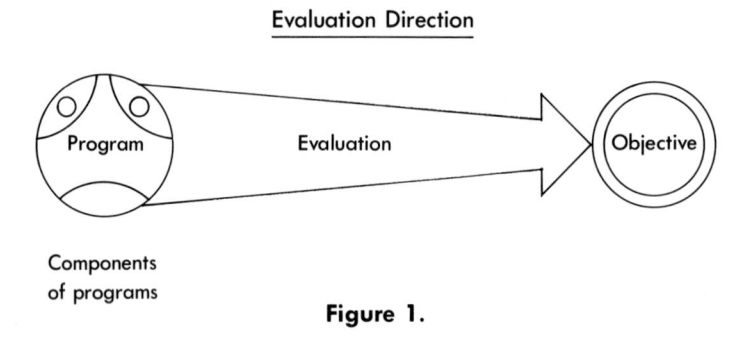

Figure 1.

Evaluation cannot be achieved in a vacuum nor exclusively on the basis of programs and objectives. There is a need to determine *criteria* on how well programs and objectives merge—the third element of evaluation. These criteria must be precise and identifiable and must serve as an indicator of how well the objectives fit the program. *Criteria* are composed of the following:

>Costs
>Time frame
>Manpower required
>Agency capability
>Political feasibility
>Ease of operation
>Social feasibility.

The fourth component is evaluation methodology. Evaluation methodology is the technique of evaluation. It answers four important questions:

1. *Who* will do the evaluation: the agency, the consultant, the group, etc.?
2. *When* will the evaluation take place: at the beginning, throughout, or at the end of the project?
3. *Where* will the evaluation take place: school campus, office?
4. *How* will the evaluation take place: questionnaires, computer analysis, etc.?

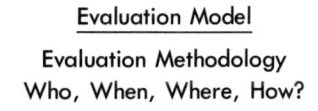

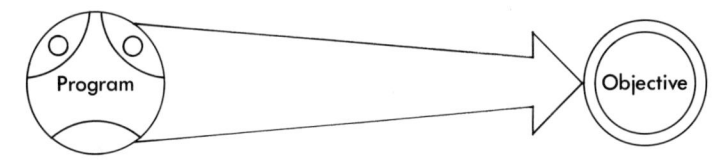

Evaluation Model

Evaluation Methodology
Who, When, Where, How?

Time, Costs, Political Feasibility, Etc.
Criteria

Figure 2.

The evaluation model deals with evaluating a single program by a set of criteria utilizing a specific methodology. As presented, the model does not assume existence of alternatives. If alternative programs exist, and this is common, the alternative program that is most appropriate needs to be determined. In making a comparison, for example, between program A and B, it is absolutely vital to recognize that an accurate and meaningful evaluation is impossible when using different criteria, evaluation methodologies, or objectives. Program A and B cannot be evaluated, one against the other, if objectives are changed or if different sets of criteria or evaluation methodologies are used.

Of the four evaluation components, objectives, programs, criteria, and evaluation methodologies, only the program may be varied; everything else must remain constant. The model for comparing two or more programs is seen in Figure 3.

Methodology
Who, When, Where, and How?

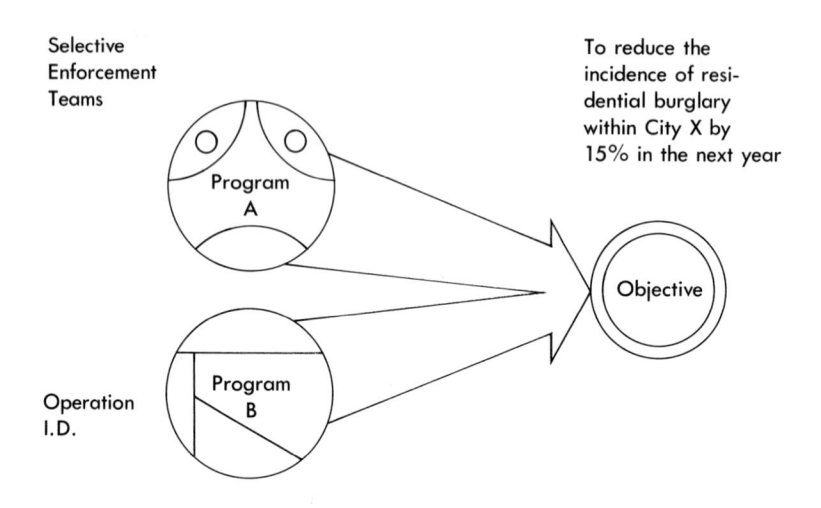

Selective Enforcement Teams

Program A

Operation I.D.

Program B

To reduce the incidence of residential burglary within City X by 15% in the next year

Objective

Time, Costs, Political Feasibility, Etc.
Criteria

Figure 3.

When alternative programs, using common criteria and the same evaluation methodology, are evaluated against the same objectives, a determination as to which program is the better of the alternatives is achieved through the utilization of two factors: (1) which program best meets the objectives, and (2) how each program measures up against the criteria.

Figure 4 indicates the program that best meets the criteria enabling one to select the most suitable program for implementation.

	Costs	Time Frame	Manpower Required	Agency Capability	Political Feasibility	Ease of Operation	Social Feasibility	Total	
Program "A"	5	5	4	4	5	5	5	33	
Program "B"	5	5	2	5	2	4	1	24	
Etc.									

1-5 Scale: 5 = Exceedingly high in meeting criteria
1 = Relatively low in meeting criteria

Figure 4.

Each criteria must be examined in light of the alternatives, and priorities from high to low must be established for each criteria. From Figure 4 it can be seen that the first priority is cost, the second priority is time frame, and the third priority is manpower required, etc. It can then be asked:

1. How do the programs compare as to cost?
2. How do they compare as to time frame for completion?
3. How do they compare relative to manpower required?

If both programs cost the same and all other criteria are equal, but "A" is more easily put into operation than "B," then "A" is the appropriate choice.

In summation, evaluation has been examined in terms of a model with four essential components. Evaluation begins with objectives, and continues through programs, criteria, and evaluation methodologies. In practical application these components may be combined in an evaluation plan. Each component is independent of one another and at some point must be isolated and examined separately. Goals give the direction needed to establish objectives and to evaluate the effectiveness of accomplishing the desired goal.